Managing Human Resource Development An Indian Perspective

DR. KRISHNA MOHAN MATHUR

GYAN PUBLISHING HOUSE

New Delhi-110002

Managing Human Resource Development
An Indian Perspective

ISBN : 9788121207430

Published in 2001 in India by
Gyan Publishing House
5, Ansari Road, Darya Ganj,
New Delhi - 110002

Phones : **011-47034999, 9811692060**

E-mail : **books@gyanbooks.com**

visit our web site At http://www.gyanbooks.com

Laser Typeset at : Manas Typesetter, Delhi

Printed at : Mehra Offsett Press

Dedication

Most respectfully dedicated with gratitude to

my parents—

Father **Late Shri Prem Narain Mathur**

and

Mother Late Smt. Vigyan (Gyan Vati) Mathur

who gave me guidance, support, initial education, Dharmic Sanskars and always served as sources of light and strength

Contents

Preface

Human resource development is a dynamic process, which continues evolving out new knowledge and practices, necessitated by the exigencies of the situational challenges, fuelled by human idealism, supported by a growing knowledge base about human systems and chiselled by pioneering practitioners. HRD has become very important not only in administration but also for the corporate world. Globalisation and technological changes have opened up many new opportunities and all national economics are undergoing rapid and often wrenching transformations. In such a scenario human resource development becomes very important as new opportunities are emerging. We are also witnessing a power shift. Unfortunately, the general public and even many senior managers do not understand the complex challenges of human resources development today. Human resource development is one of the most dynamic fields within the management arena and there are immense potentials of human development. Managing the human resource development examines the managerial side of HRD—how to organise, implement and evaluate HRD and presents an Indian perspective of various HRD challenges. Human Resource Development is expected to enhance the abilities, skills, techniques and value system of individuals to meet their needs within the organisational system of which individuals are vital assets. HRD plays crucial roles in preparing and developing people to meet the challenges of external and internal changes. HRD helps in building and nurturing a culture of excellence and organisational learning. In the present era of globalisation and liberalisation, Human Resource Develpment plays an important role in organisational initiatives which help reduce worker's compensation costs and raise morale. HRD is a strategic and coherent approach to the management of the organisation's most valued assests—the people and ultimately the achievement of the corporate objectives is to gain competitive advantage, has finally dawned upon the Indian CEOs with a global vision. The computer revolution with internet linking facility, adult education and life-long learner, increasing internationalisation of business, the transformation of the work force the knowledge workers, the replacement of training courses, workshops and seminars with curriculae, libraries and online internet learning, have brought paradigm shift in modern society. During various workshops, and seminars organised by the author, the need for a comprehensive book on HRD had been voiced again and again. The present book is a humble effort by the author to give various perceptions and perspectives on HRD and its management in corporate world and in service sector of the government. The present book in basically an Indian perspective meant for all practising managers and management trainees of India preparing for Master of Business Administration or Master of Business Economics of various Indian Universities. It is expected to be useful for Indian managers in adding value to their performance in the organisation. Today we need more books by Indian authors who can give case histories of Indian business organisations and truly depict the cultural and socio-economic millieus and existing value system of India. The present book attempts to present an Indian perspective of managing human resource development.

The present book has ten chapters and attempts to provide a managerial perception of human resource development. The first chapter covers various aspects of managing HRD. Various management processes of planning, organising, staffing, directing, coordinating, monitoring, motivating and leading in the context of HRD have been highlighted in the first chapter. The second chapter covers the ethical and spiritual dimensions of HRD. Today many management experts and business leaders are speaking of "expanding consciousness" in organisation, manifesting in processes like valuing interconnectedness, stewardship of resources, creating joyful work places, working from compassion and actively showing concern for the global ecology. It is now being realised that people need to grow materially, personally, professionally, ethically and spiritually as part of their own evolution. Today there is a growing emphasis on ethical behaviour and managerial ethics. Third chapter provides a macro-approach to HRD and analyses the present Indian education policy. The fourth chapter discusses HRD in administration in the context of liberalisation and globalisation. The fifth chapter discusses the rationale and various principles of HRD for workers. Employee participation in trade unions and their role in HRD self-development for workers and thrust areas for employee development have been highlighted. The sixth chapter deals with human resource training and analyses the systems' concept of training. It deals with types of training programmes, training environment, training methodology and techniques and various emerging challenges to training. Chapter seven deals with counselling and mentoring as HRD techniques. Mentoring and counselling are two very useful HRD strategies for development of various faculties of the corporate personnel. An interesting case study given at the end of this chapter raises useful issues for discussions during workshops and training programmes. Chapter eight analyses the various perceptions and techniques of evaluation of various HRD and problems in evaluation of HRD have been highlighted in this chapter. Chapter nine deals with various challenges faced in implementation of HRD. It discusses why implementation gaps occur and how implementation of HRD is the most challenging problem in the present day context. Tenth chapter deals with HRD challenges for the Indian Police. Appendix A is a Revised Version of the paper presented by the author at a national seminar at Udaipur on Management Education.

Global assignments to HRD professional for gaining cross-cultural experience have resulted in a mass exodus of Indian HRD professionals to markets abroad. Essentially, the book draws upon my exciting and in the Indian context, rare experience of teaching HRD not only to administrators, managers and senior police officers but also to post-graduate students at various universities as a visiting faculty. The material owes much to various workshops and seminars held in India which were attended by practising managers and management educator. At the end of each chapter I have provided a long list of books which have been referred to by me in the preparation of various topics. "Let noble thoughts comes to us from every side," says Rig-Veda. It is in a spirit of learning that I acknowledge my gratitude to various authors whose books have served as sources of learning to me and whose references have been made at suitable places to reinforce my views. Viewed from the macro-perspective, India today faces the greatest challenges of HRD when India's population has crossed the figure of one hundred crore on 11th May 2000. India is a land of contradictions, where the problems of braindrain and high illiteracy exist side by side. Management of human resource development needs both national and corporate perspectives. To provide education, nutrition, health, equity, security, growth, vocational training, quality of life, productivity skills and sustainable wholesome development to one hundred crore population of India are the most difficult challenges before the nation. Managing human resource development demands a broader perspective, human development at individuals level, group level and organisational level. Role of HRD in organisation HRD mechanism, HRD processes and HRD outcomes have been highlighted in the present work. In the new economic order, the art of HRD has to be mastered by the managers. The art of HRD begins with selection and induction techniques to skill analysis, creating learning opportunities, motivational gambits, management of people, resources and performance and ends with development and rewarding of employees for post-retirement employment. The present book gives the readers an Indian perspective of managing human resource development.

The book has taken almost five years in its completion. As Director (Inspector General of Police) Internal Security Academy, CRPF, Mount Abu, I had the priviledge of association and interaction with a large number of management experts and professors and I have been benefitted immensely. I want to give thanks to Prof. Azhar Kazmi, Dean, Aligarh Muslim University,

Prof. M.N. Khandelwal, Dean, M.D.S. University, Ajmer and Prof. B.P. Bhatnagar, now Vice Chancellor, Rajasthan Vidyapeeth, Udaipur and Dr. R. N. Singh, Former Vice-Chancellor of Udaipur and Rajasthan University, Jaipur. Dr. Om Prakash, former Vice-Chancellor has been my mentor and source of inspiration. My thanks are due to all of them for their encouragement, support and patronage. I have been greatly influenced by the writings of Prof. S. K. Chakraborty of Calcutta who has done pioneering work in developing vedantic insights into management science. I have found his ideas very inspiring and stimulating. I am unable to fathom his profound influence over my thinking and writings. During last four decades, I have been associated with human resource development in my various capacities. One of the objectives of writings this book is to share my views, thoughts, perceptions, and perspectives on HRD with the upcoming managers who may cut down time to learn from experience. As Henry Ford said, "By the time a man is ready to graduate from the university of experience, he is too old to work." Nothing can really rival what we can learn from experience of others because trial and error by oneself is certainly a new experience and overlong way of learning things. Management trainees doing MBA/MBE with specialisation in HRD often find difficulty in comprehending the subject due to non-availability of a book containing basic concepts and theories at one place. Need for a comprehensive textbook on HRD has again and again been voiced by the various trainees. This volume is a small sincere effort in that direction. The book is expected to help not only management trainees but also the average pressured and harried manager. The book has been organised in a way that the reader can get an overall perspective of the philosophical and conceptual issues involved in HRD and a panoramic view of HRD practices in a dynamic and growth oriented corporate world. The present book is meant for a wider audience. However, no claims are being made for the originality or comprehensiveness of the book although a modest attempt has been made to cover various perspectives of HRD in the present volume. Conventional acknowledgements are really inadequate to express how much this book owes to all those whose inspired me in various ways and who gave me various types of supports. I am also thankful to the student of MBA and MBE of MDS University, Ajmer; Aligarh Muslim University, Aligarh; Rajasthan Vidyapeeth, Udaipur and officer trainees at Internal Security Academy, Mount Abu who gave me an opportunity to interact with them and crystallize my various concepts and ideas. I am thankful to the librarians and the staff of various universities and Internal Security Academy, Mt. Abu who have given me facilities for referring books and journals without any reservations. My very special thanks are due to Sh. Ravi Sharma of Uniservice Computer Consultant, Ajmer and his dedicated staff who have meticulously deciphered the manuscript and brought out typed script for the use of the publisher. My thanks are due to Sh. B.P. Garg, CEO and Sh. Amit Garg, Director, Publications, Gyan Publishing House, Daryaganj, New Delhi who brought out the book in a record time with excellent get up and printing. Critical comments and feedback will be most welcome from readers, and suggestions for improvement will be gratefully acknowledged and considered for incorporation in the next revised edition.

I feel beholden to Swami Iswarananda Giri Ji Maharaj of Sant Sarover, Mount Abu for his kind blessings and constant spiritual inspiration to me. My wife Prabha and members of my family Shikha, Niraj, Samvit, Pragya, Prakhar, Prabhav and Shiv Shubhang gave me the moral and psychological support and encouraged me by sparing from all domestic liabilities and commitments for devoting full attention to complete the work. My overriding debt continues to be to my wife Prabha who provided me with the time, support and inspiration to prepare this book. It is truly our book. My son Shiv Shubhang has carried out the first editing of the book and has offered many useful suggestions in various chapters and gave me editorial help. This book is a humble offering to Almighty Lord Shiva whose grace and blessings remained the divine force behind my academic endeavours. Actually I am only an instrument for carry out His designated task and deserve no credit at all.

Dr. Krishna Mohan Mathur

1

Managing Human Resource Development

Human beings are both the spectators and actors in the great drama of existence. Man is his own greatest mystery. He does not understand himself completely. He comprehends but little of his organic processes and even less of his unique capacity to perceive the world about him; last of all does he understand his noblest and most mysterious faculty, the ability to transcend himself and perceive himself in the act of perception[1] Sir Julian Huxley, eminent biologist and humanist, in his lecture on "Ten Evolutionary Vision" delivered at the closing session of the 1959 Chicago University symposium on "Evolution After Darwin" says; "In the light of our present knowledge, man's most comprehensive aim is seen not as mere survival, not as numerical increase, not as increased complexity of organisations or increased control over his environment but as greater fulfilment —the fuller realization of mere possibilities by the human species collectively and more of its component members individually".[2] In the *Bhagwat Gita* and various Upanishads, Indian seers expounded *Adhyatma Vidya* as the science of human possibilities. When you look at the sparkling eyes of a new-born little baby, hardly seven pounds in weight, with very tender human organism, you cannot normally see the enormous energy and capabilities dormant somewhere within its depth, you do not know that one day he or she can become a great scientist, a great olympic gold medal winner, a great statesman, a great saint or a great social reformer. All these possibilities are hidden in that little baby. In today's world, there has been a lot of development of various physical and social sciences but the science of the man has not developed satisfactorily. While many modern scientists feel that unless the science of man advances in step with the sciences of nature, man will become increasingly weakened, and the success of his physical sciences will become his defeats. India's greatest contribution has been in the field of the science of man, the science of man in depth to distinguish it from modern subjects like physiology, anatomy and behavioral science. In Sanskrit, the science of man has been said as *Adhyatma Vidya.* In the *Chandogya Upanishad* there is an utterance—*TAT TVAM ASI* "That Thou Art" Enormous energies, says *Vedanta,* are dormant in every one of us, in every being in the world like the infinite quantum energy field. Conceiving the ultimate reality within the universe and man as infinite quantum energy of pure consciousness, "*CHIT SAKTI* "and designated as "*Para-Prakarti* ", Supreme Nature, as *Adya-Sakti,* Primordidal Energy and as *Devi,* the Divine Mother. The *Devi-Mahatmyam* sings her hymns of praise.[3] Just as we have wind power, sea-wave-power, thermal and hydel power, nuclear power, with every human being there are many different types and levels of powers which have not so far been properly studied by the western science. Indian seers and saints have seen and realised that infinite potential behind the finite human organic individuality. Swami Vivakanand in February, 1897 in his address on "The Missions of the Vedanta "uttered the following Vedantic truth. "Arise, Awake, Awake from this hypnotism of weakness. None is really weak; the soul is infinite, omnipotent and omniscient. Teach yourself, teach every one, his real nature, call upon the sleeping soul and see how it awakes. Power will come, glory will come, goodness will come, purity will come and everything that is excellent with come, when this sleeping soul is roused to self-conscious activity."[4] We generally talk of physical and intellectual growth of the individual but do not talk about spiritual growth of man. *Vedanta* teaches us not merely about human muscular dimension, his neural dimension, intellectual dimension but also the spiritual dimension. *Svetasvatara Upanishad* says, "Men may (through their technical skill) roll up all space like a piece of leather; still there will be no end of sorrow for them without realizing the luminous one (within)".[5] Besides physical and intellectual growth, man must seek growth in a new dimension, namely the spiritual dimension of man. Beyond the merely physical and intellectual, there is the infinite and divine nature of man referred to in the *Tat Tvam Asi MahaMantra*. When that spiritual and ethical dimension becomes slightly manifest in character and conduct of a human being, a new energy of high quality and quantity becomes available to every human being. All humanistic impulses, all capacity for ethical response, for love, for dedication, for service and even the capacity for teamwork, are only the by-products of man's growth in the spiritual dimension.[6] Management of human resources should ideally aim at developing the spiritual dimension of each human being, besides developing his physical, intellectual and professional dimension. Swami Vivekanand once said, "Man's development lies in rising above both external nature and internal nature." Human resources development should be used for giving individual practical theory of ethico- moral conduct and sharpen his spiritual quest for self-realisation. Positive virtues of truthfulness, sincerity, honesty, obedience, humility, purity, endurance and consideration for others have to be developed in human beings for spiritual growth of the individuals. The true growth and flowering of human personality lies in the joy of "giving" and the triple combination of *Satyam, Shivam-Sundaram* (Truth, Goodness- Beauty). Ethics and values must remain the centre of our concern for human resource development. Human Resource Development is concerned with holistic development of human beings.

Management is work with its own skills, tools and technique. Management is the life-giving, acting, dynamic organ for performing certain given tasks and responsibilities. The essence of management does not know but doing, its test is result and its only authority is performance. Those persons, who have the responsibility for onerous task of management of human resource development; need to conceptualize HRD properly. "Development is really a building strategy, a growth strategy—investing money in people for the future." says Frank T. Morgan. Human resource development is a total integrated system which develops the competencies, values, skills and knowledge at individual, dyadic, group and organisational level as a continuous and planned process with the ultimate object of making qualitative and quantitative contribution to the professional well-being and pride of the employees as well as achieving social and organisational goals. HRD is needed to develop a proper climate in the organisations and must identify its philosophy, objectives, policies and action plans keeping in view the internal and external environmental factors affecting the total HRD system. The ultimate objective of HRD is to ensure that every aspect of organisation, employment, motivation and management of people in integrated with the strategic mission of the organisation and contributes to the successful achievement of that mission. Human Resource means "a body of persons held together, by belief, in communication, origin, speech, culture, political union or a body of persons linked by common knowledge or working in an organisation. "Globalisation demands global skills and competencies. HRD has been integrated and has to ensure all round development of the employees and nurturing of a HRD climate. Now that we are into the 21st century, one has to move from transactional management to transformational management. Managers have to visualise their roles as leading the workers, getting work done through dynamic, enthusiastic, charismatic leadership, making work a joy and worker, members of an extended family. Development is partly a participatory process where people have to decide their own need for development. The critical constituent within an organisation is the human resource globalisation of the economy which is demanding quality of product with quality of life through total quality management approach. HRD has to play the role of a "change-agent" and HRD executives have to imbibe personal qualities such as judgement, drive and determination, vision, objectivity balance, breadth of prospective commitment, individuality and integrity, self discipline and empathy.[7] HRD interventions have to step beyond techniques and keep emphasising the spirit behind the technique by creating employee's involvement. There are many human predicaments in HRD because development measures envisage decentralisation of administrative structures, restraint on unchecked consumerism, optimal exploration of human resources and effective people's participation. Human resource development must cover all employees of the organisation and must take special care of the workers and low-paid employees.

Managing Human Resource Development

Management implies "getting things done through the efforts of the other people". In the present context, it is the process by which managers create, direct, maintain and operate through systematic human efforts to attain desired goals and objectives. HRD can have both National perspectives and Corporate perspective.

Managing HRD is a stupendous task, which include planning for HRD, organising and staffing the HRD department and facilitates, directing HRD interventions and controlling HRD through regular monitoring and evaluation on a continuous basis. Management of human resource development in public and private enterprise is very big business indeed. Management of human resource development is affected by demographic, political, economic and social trends; and challenges for HRD are today unparalleled in history. It is practically impossible to define and describe the full dimension of management of human resource development in government, business and industry today. Matrix showing management of HRD is given as fig. 1 Management of HRD will be discussed in later part of this chapter.

Fig. 1 Matrix Showing / Human Resource Development Management

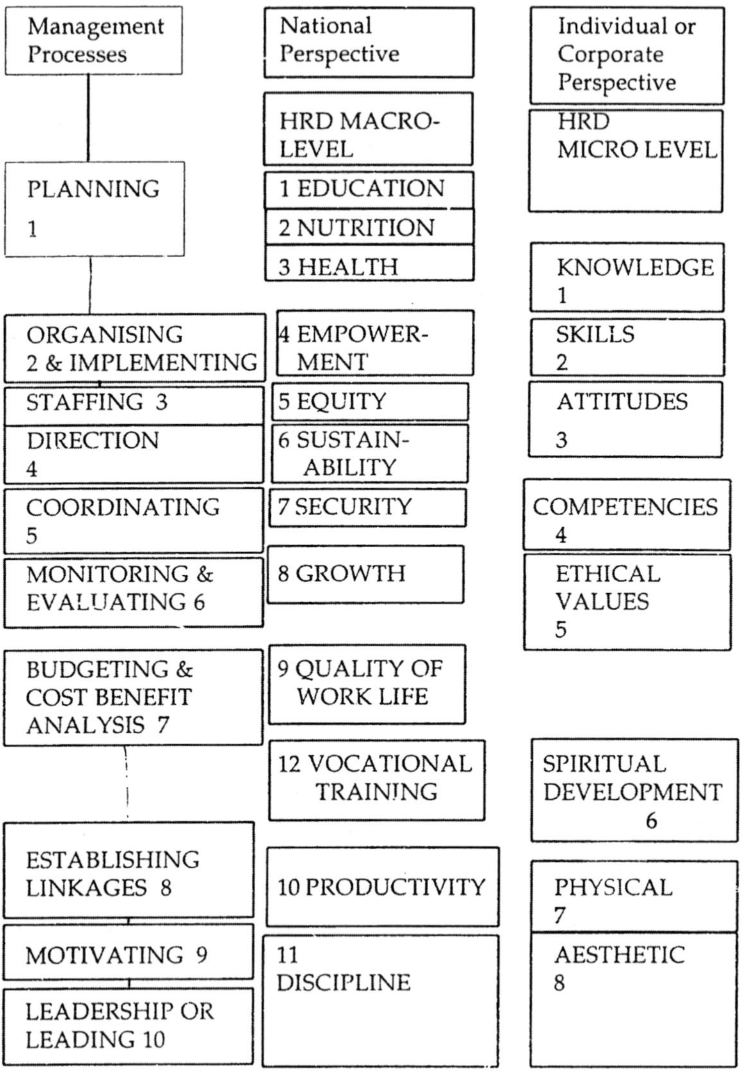

HRD - A VEDANTIC APPROACH - Need for Ethical, Spiritual and Social Development

Human Development and Human Resource Development

AS MACRO-LEVEL CONCEPT

Human development is concerned about the development of all members of the society and important dimensions of human development are:

1. Empowerment—participation of people.
2. Equity—equal opportunities and fairness.
3. Productivity—remunerative employment.
4. Security of livelihood.
5. Sustainability—access to opportunities over long period of time.
6. Growth and advancement.
7. Education and Training.
8. Nutrition.
9. Health.
10. Discipline and social morality.
11. Quality of work—life.

According to United Nations Development Programme publications titled " Human Development Report 1995" the basic objectives of human development are to ensure three essential components:

1. Equality of opportunities for all people in society;
2. Sustainability of such opportunities from one generation to the next; and
3. Empowerment of people so that they participate in and benefit from development process.[8] Short-term advances in human development are possible but they will not be sustainable without further growth. Life expectancy, health, educational attainments, political participation, human security, housing, nutrition and adequate subsistence living are some of the demensions

of human development. Empowerment, cooperation, equity, sustainability and security are now considered as basic dimensions of human development.[9] Development does not start with goods; it starts with people, with education, organisation and discipline, without these three, resources remain latent, untapped potential."[10] Human Development is a total integrated concept, not confined only to education or vocational training, but development of individual and collective groups in matters of health, education, nutrition, shelter and all round well - being with an assurance of a quality of work life. The optimisation of human resources calls for a conducive managerial climate based on human relation. Recognising human dignity, competence and potential on one hand, and accepting compatibility of individual and group goals to the organisational objectives, on the other, human relations facilitate integration of people into a work situation that motivates them to work together productivity, cooperatively and with economic, psychological and social satisfactions."[11] Human resource development is concerned with human beings who are resources for an organisation—may be a business, industry or service sector. Human development refers to the macro level development of the people of a country or region or even international community. HRD should aim at fuller and total all round development of human personality and its various dimensions such as:

1. Physical—health, vigour, strength, stamina;
2. Intellectual—knowledge for its own sake;
3. Moral and ethical aspects;
4. Aesthetic—appreciation of beauty of form, sound and thought;
5. Professional and skill development;
6. Religious and spiritual—psychological and transcendental relating to self (*Atman*).

Concept of Human Resources Development, Climate Variables and HRD Outcomes

The difference in the level of economic development of the countries is largely a reflection of the differences in the quality of their human factor. The key element in this preposition is that of values, attitude, general orientation and quality of people of a country which determine its economic development.[12] HRD activities in different spheres play a vital role in developing employees aptitudes, potentials, strategies and skills required for individual and organisational growth. In the present day changing environment, HRD holds the key to develop valuable human resources with the objective of:

(a) Developing personnel into being more resourceful, energetic and creative;

(b) Developing team spirits in organisation and encouraging the people to grow and change to be consistent with the changing values and demands;

(c) Enabling individuals to solve complex problems more competently, effectively and creatively with innovations;

(d) Developing a greater degree to commitment and attachment to the organisations;

(e) Developing an environment where HRD values can flourish;

(f) Creating an urge in people to achieve excellence in their specialised fields and professions.

The importance of HRD as a catalytic agent of growth change and organisational development has been increasingly recognised. Human Resource Development, from the organisational point of view, is a well-planned, systematic, dynamic process in which all employees of the organisation are adequately and periodically helped and motivated to acquire and develop technical, managerial and behavioral knowledge, skills, competencies and mould the values, beliefs, attitude and aptitude necessary to effectively perform present and future

Dr. T.V. Rao in 1986 has suggested a comprehensive HRD concept, which is given in Fig. 2 below:

Fig. 2 A Schematic Presentation of Linkages between HRD Instruments, Processes, Outcome and Organizational Effectiveness (Rao 1986)

HRD Mechanisms or Instruments	*HRD Processes and Climate Variables*	*HRD Outcome Variable*	*Organisational Effectiveness Dimensions*
1. HRD Department 2. Performance appraisal 3. Review discussions feedback 4, Counselling sessions 5. Role analysis exercises 6. Potential development exercises 7. Training 8. Communication policies 9. Job- rotation 10. OD - exercies 11. Rewards 12. Job-enrichment 13. Programmes 14. Other mechanisms	1. Role clarity 2. Planning of development by every employee 3. Awareness of competencies required for job 4. Pro-active orientation 5. More trust 6. Collaboration and team work 7. Authenticity 8. Openness 9. Risk taking 10. Value generation 11. Clarification of norms 12. Increased communication 13. More objective rewards 14. Generation of objective data on employees etc. Personnel policies, top management style and commitment, investments on HRD, previous, culture, line managers	1. More competent people 2. Better development roles 3. Higher work commitment and job involvement 4. More problem solving 5. Better utilization of human resources 6. Higher job satisfaction and work motivation 7. Better generation of internal resources 8. Better organizational health 9. More team work, synergy and respect for each other.	1. Higher productivity 2. Growth and diversification 3. Cost reducation 4. More profits 5. Better image Other Factors Environments, technology, resource availability, history nature of business etc.

roles by realising the highest human potentials with a view to contribute positively to the organisational, group, individual and social goals. Since the core of human resource development is the self, the final test of the effectiveness of the HRD efforts is the changes including improved self-understanding and self-confidence, higher motivation (taking initiative, perseverance, meaningful relationships etc.) impact making and belief that one can shape most of one's destiny.[13] The functions of HRD are considered necessary for the development of human resources with a view:

(1) to ensure the optimum use of available human resources at all levels so that they deliver the best possible output/services/results.

(2) to meet the dynamic needs of individual development in terms of skills, attitudes, aptitudes, knowledge and professional expertise.

(3) to meet the challenges put forward by changes in technology, job-systems and working methods, technical developments etc. and to prepare the manpower accordingly to meet challenges of globalisation.

(4) to meet the needs and requirements of a developing economy having challenges of poverty, unemployment and low output.

(5) to ensure employee's high morale, full capacity utilisation resulting in higher productivity etc.

(6) to meet the dynamic needs or organisational development and requirements of social order.

Essentially HRD is a process of developing competencies of individual employees, dyadic groups (superior and employee), team, inter-teams and the total organisation to achieve and maximize the convergence of organisational goals and personal needs of the employees.[14] HRD is not only the responsibility of the top management but also of line managers. HRD sub-systems should not be thought of in isolation, but a more holistic and integrated approach is always needed. HRD is a pro-active approach to human beings and not a coping stance-strategy for development of human resources. It suggests ways and means to remove the surpluses and it shortages, suggest ways of building and effective utilization of trained human resource to an optimum scale. According to Prof. Harbion " The essential components of such a strategy are the following:

1. The building of appropriate incentives,
2. Effective training of employed manpower, and
3. The rational development of formal education.[15]

In ancient India, human development and learning was conducted by highly developed seers and *Rishis* in their own *ashrams*. The word *ashram* stands for a serene and calm, sacred and simple locale in the wooded surrounding where individuals were trained and developed by their teachers (*Gurus*). Valmiki *ashrams*, Vashist *ashram*, Sandipan *ashram*, were centres of great learning and human transformation. There was a balance between *Dharma*, *Arth*, *Kama* and *Moksha* as four goals of human life but *ashrams* also gave great importance to the spiritual, and transcendental dimensions and, the uniqueness of such *ashrams* was " secular—ethical, economic symbiosis". These *ashrams* were centres of great learning and human resource development.[15a]

Human resource generally refers to the total knowledge, skills, creative abilities, talents and aptitudes of an organisation's work force as well as the values and attitudes of an individual involved. It is the sum total of inherent attributes, acquired knowledge and skills represented by the talents and aptitudes of the employed persons. The Human Resource Development is concerned with the improvement of the above said attributes of an individual as well as a group of individuals. It is the process of increasing the knowledge, the skills and the capacities of all the people in an undertaking and a society.[16] Alfred Marshall emphasised the importance of education as a national investment. In his view "the most valuable of all capital is that investment in human beings.[17] Theodore W. Schmaltz in his noble lecture (1979) said, " The decisive factors of production in improving the welfare of people are not space energy and crop-land, the decisive factor is the improvement in population quality."[18] G.O.I. Seventh Five Year Plan (1985-90) in its mid-term appraisal has observed; "The development of human resources is both a means and an end-education, cultural expression and improved health are desirable in themselves. But they are also an essential base for social and economic development." Though Schultz has been promoting this thesis since early sixties, the empirical studies by Abramovitz (1956), Solow (1957) and Kendruck (1961) had also highlighted the need for human resource development.Nowadays there is " the creed of investment in human capital," it is the Schultzian lesson which is being recited.[19] Human Resource Development is essentially a humanistic concept based on respect for dignity of the man and on a belief in the limitless potential of human beings. Dr. Leonard Nadler in the United States in 1969 defined HRD as:

1. A series of organised activities.
2. Conducted within a specified time, and designed to produce behavioral change.

He used the term HRD to refer to three activities, namely, Training, Education and Development. In Nadler's framework, training is focussed on the present job, education on the future job and development is concerned with producing learning experiences to the employees so that they may be ready to move in new directions that organisational change may require. Nadler's concept of HRD is one-sided in as much as it looks at people from the organisations's point of view. India's concept of HRD, developed by Pareek and Rao, is concerned with a free creature, his urge for self fulfillment and his growth potential as a human being. The mythological story of Ram devotee Hanuman who thought that he cannot leap across the sea to Lanka, got the leap to Lanka when others reminded him of his potential and when a favourable environment was created. The Pareek-Rao concept of HRD emphasizes on HRD climate and culture. "One of the things we have been struggling to get across is how we make HRD an effort by companies to value human beings, to openness.[20] In India while corporate HRD has been subject of intensive study for the last two decades, the macro-HRD issues have received very little attention even in the academic circles. M. B. Athreya has done commendable thinking in his article "HRD for India Vision 21st Century". More work on macro-issues of HRD needs to be done. The ultimate target of HRD should be to prepare and develop "Enlightened Big men" and " Better men with adequate wisdom of "SELF". Pareek and Rao have clarified the terminology by saying; "The term human resource is sometimes criticised mainly on the ground that is treats people as a "resource" and not as humans beings..... Human resources may be interpreted as resource to be recognised and appreciated and one which has to be treated differently, as a human one and not like other material resources.[21] Rao and Pareek emphasize that the HRD system is not a formula that can be applied with mathematical precision; the size of the organisation, its state of growth, its organisational culture, the state of technology, the existing personnel system and there health, and a number of other internal and external factors would determine how the HRD can be usefully applied to the organisation for developing technical and administrative skills of their employees. Rao and Pareek in their initial thinking applied HRD only to the managerial levels and have mentioned four main difficulties in introducing HRD systems for workers. These are: possible problems with unions, problems of control at this level, low level of education and the system of seniority based promotions in vouge for workers. However, later Pareek and Rao held that "It is necessary to pay attention to all four aspects of the workers affairs; industrial relations, worker welfare, worker development and quality of work life including job-enrichment, job design, work re-organisation. Human resource development is a dynamic process by which the employees of an organisation are helped in a continuous and planned way to acquire and sharpen their competencies to perfom various functions. Competencies can be broadly divided into the following categories:

1. Technical competencies and skills;

2. Managerial competencies—inter personal communication and relationships;
3. Process competencies—conflict resolution, problems of commitment; and cooperation-team building;
4. Helping competencies—feedback to others, providing necessary assistance and cooperation.
5. Coping competencies—morale boosting, taking people out of frustration.

Dr. Mrityunjay B. Athreya had recommended a more Holistic approach at the National Conference of the HRD Network, at Chennai (September,1987). "The ultimate purpose of HRD is to ensure full participation of the individual in job and life.... HRD aims to move executives, superiors and workmen towards fuller participation, so that their potential can be utilised to the benefit of themselves and the organisation. HRD is a total activity for any organisation and there is a strong need for reallocating the resources to people lower down. A comprehensive HRD strategy has to be supported by HRD systems extending right down to the workman. Workers can become useful partners in increasing productivity if they are given proper participation in the management of industry. According to Likert "the leader and other processes (including HRD).in the organisation must be such as to ensure a maximum probability that in all interactions and in all relationships within the organisation each member in the light of his background, values, desires and expectations, will view the experience as supportive and one which builds and maintains his sense of personal worth."[12] Human resources development is not an academic pursuit, nor isolated from the strategy and patterns of economic development. According to Prof Victor Petrov—a Soviet author, one third of India's labour potential in not being used at all. At macro level, HRD should not be confined to short-run narrow sectional interests of country's socioeconomic development in the present day global economy. At macro level, central and state government have to carry out agenda of HRD. Indian state cannot abandon its agenda of economic development for achieving the goals of real social justice and must concentrate on education, health, flood control, environment, railways, roads, defence, irrigation and power. India must develop forth its indigenous capacities and institutions and must believe that " ordinary people possess great strength and wisdom and that when their initiative is given full play, they can accomplish miracles."[12] The solution to provide food, economic and health security to meet the growing demands lies in the adoption of a holistic approach for achieving environment-friendly, sustainable development to protect minimum standards of income, nutrition, health, housing and education to every citizen. HRD is a system's approach to employment management. HRD is a very broad term and should be seen in a broad perspective. The process of HRD in an organisation is initiated right from the day an individual joins an organisation and his induction process is started through a psychological contract. The psychological contract changes and is renewed with time as the needs of the individuals and organisations change. Role definition is an important component of the HRD system.Prof. Udai Pareek has stated that a role is a position a person occupies in an organisation as defined by the expectations from that position by role senders including the role occupant. HRD can help in role matching which may be satisfying both to the organisation and the individual, thereby resulting in minimum human resource wastage and greater productivity.HRD can facilitate manpower planning through potential and performance reviews and necessary counselling to the employees. Training and development are important sub-systems of HRD. In his book "The leadership", a new study by University of Michigan, Professor Noel M. Tichy, it is observed that "distinguished leaders are willing to assume direct responsibility for the development of other leaders. They are teachers who invest a lot of time imparting ideas, values and emotional energy to others by telling stories about their experiences."[23] As Tichy and Cohn put it," A leader who aspires to be a winning teacher organises every meeting, makes every decision and designs every organisational structure with developing others in mind. Successful organisations win because they are run by people who cultivate leaders. Markets, products and technologies come and go but a company that continually produces leaders at all levels, is here to stay because it has people who anticipate and know how to deal with change." Career planning is an important element of HRD. Proper career planning could lead to the fusion of organisations, and individuals, expectations and goals. Human resources can be properly vitalised and improved by proper and fair grant of rewards and teamwork recognition. Appropriate work culture can enhance human resource development in the organisations. An appropriate work culture, which keeps the individual motivated, is a facilitator to HRD. Fair play, justice and absence of anomalies in personnel management can facilitate HRD. HRD should emphasise excellence, ethical values and commitment to the organisation. Ethical and moral discourses can help employees and qualitatively enrich the organisations. Swami Ranganathan says. " Human values transform works into a mission, into a national commitment and this is also what enhances dignity of workers from merely being an employee, into an instrument of human purpose.

Role of HRD in Organisations

HRD acts as a catalyst in several organisational processes necessary for its survival, development and effectiveness. HRD should play an effective role in:

1. Optimising the human resources towards maximum productivity of the highest quality.
2. Enabling employees to grow with the organisation and take pride in the organisation.
3. Helping in the congruence of individual aspirations and organisational expectations.
4. Promoting collaboration and team spirit by establishing a climate of trust, openness, mutuality and interdependence.
5. HRD should play a meaningful role in key activities like manpower planning, career planning, succession planning and development of workers and managers.

6. It should play its roles as developing role, process role, enabling role, and change agent's role.

The goals of HRD systems are to develop:

1. The capabilities of each employee as an individual, in relation to his present role and future expected roles.
2. The dyadic relationships between each employee and his supervisor strengthen superior-subordinate relationship.
3. The team spirit and functioning in every organisational unit (group, department) strengthen team spirit among different teams.
4. Collaboration among different units of the organisation and promote inter-team collaboration.
5. The organisations's overall health and self-renewing capabilities, which in turn increase the enabling capabilities of individual dyads, teams and the entire organisation.[24]
6. And maintain a high motivation level of the employees.
7. Promote climate development and organisational health development.
8. Maintaining harmonious industrial relations and improvement in organisational and technological disciplines.

HRD Network at national conference held at Chennai in 1987 elaborated HRD concept in the following words. "The ultimate aim of HRD is the full participation of the individuals in job and life.... HRD aims to move executives and workmen towards fuller participation, so that their potential can be utilized to the benefit of themselves and the organisations.

HRD Instruments and HRD Dynamics

According to Udai Pareek "Instruments are devices used for collecting data on behavioural aspects to help derive some tentative generalisations. Like other instruments HRD instruments have a referrent (what is to be measured, or diagnosed or a plan of change to be prepared), which consists of units that have some internal consistency and uses and index of some kind to express the results of analysis / diagnosis."[25] Udai Pareek in his latest book "Training Instruments for Human Resource Development" had given 68 instruments out of which there are thirteen instruments on personal and interpersonal orientation, twelve on styles, fifteen on role, and twelve on the organisations. Each instrument has been briefly introduced with relevant instruments for its administration, its reliability validity, norms and correlates. The use of these instruments requires understanding of related theories and interpretation needs sound professional expertise of the instrument administrator. Generally these instruments can be used for selection, research, potential appraisal, individual growth, training and organisational development. However, HRD facilitators may like to develop their own instruments where standardised instruments are not readily available. Dr. T.V. Rao in his book. *The HRD Missionary (1990)* has suggested following instruments to facilitate HRD:

1. Role analysis and development exercises.
2. Performance planning.
3. Performance analysis and review.
4. Performance counselling and interpersonal feedback.
5. Induction training.
6. Training.
7. Job rotations.
8. Potential appraisal and development.
9. Career planning and development.
10. Self-renewal and instruction building exercises.
11. Stress audit and stress management.
12. Organisational development exercises.
13. Personal growth laboratories and worker education programmes.

14. Quality circles.
15. Task forces.
16. Weekly and monthly meetings.
17. Managerial learning networks.
18. Other unconventional development exercises.

The national HRD network conference held in February, 1989 embraced a broader framework. The concept of HRD would broadly include the following:

1. Establishing and maintaining a healthy, productive work culture.
2. Improvement in organisational and technological disciplines.
3. Manpower planning for ensuring optimum utilization of human resources.
4. Improvement in work practices and higher flexibility of work arrangement.
5. Review of organisational structures.
6. Training and development to prepare employees for the new technologies and higher levels of operations.
7. Improving level of motivation in the organisation.
8. Attention to systems, rules, procedures with focus on results.
9. Strengthening of participative and safety systems.
10. Maintaining harmonious industrial relations.

Human Resource Development is an exercise in culture building in creating an awareness of what is ideal and real, what is desirable and feasible, moving from energy to synergy, from competition to cooperation, from concern to cooperation for others, organisations and society, creating a culture of performance, quality and productivity, creating a sense of partnership between people, management and union, scientists and technologists, teachers and students, administrators and citizens. HRD is a means for improving effectiveness in terms of better productivity, reduction of costs, better generations of internal resources, better profits and better customer service. In turn-around situations, organisations have found HRD as an effective means to reorient culture, to improve communication, to change work practices, to improve participation, involvement and commitment. Dynamics of the HRD process can be depicted in the following figure:

Fig. 3 Showing HRD Dynamics.

(A) Change Process	(B) Outcome
— Involvement	— Commitment
— Communication	— Morale
— Building Teams	— Competence
— Manpower Planning	— Better Utilization
— Training and Development	— Teamwork Job
— Organisational Incentives	— Satisfaction
— Industrial Relations	

(C) HRD Process—IPSE

1. I Development of **Identify** of formation
2. P Managing **Power** Effectively
3. S Creating **Synergy** in the organisation so that effective teams and groups can work for organisational goals.
4. E Achieving **Equity** and Justice.

(D) HRD Facilitators:

—Leadership Development
—Org. effectiveness, Better profits, Better Image
—Growth and competitiveness
—Better quality of work life
—Corporate development
—Institution building

The challenges of globalisation, technological innovation, increasing competition and growth through expansion, diversification and acquisition have important implications for human resource development. It is necessary to anticipate trends of change, identify the shape of things to come and to develop a strategic response for developing people to manage the challenge of change.[27] Amartya Sen has deplored the fact that India has so far neglected education, health and the social sector and in the phase of liberalization, neglecting the distributive aspects of food and goods. The competitive edge will come from the corporate ability to make heavy investments in the field of education and vocational training. It is observed that the weakest area in Indian corporate sector is the area of technical training and skill upgradation. HRD is needed in massive dosages and should cut across boundaries of culture, geography and language for providing continuous organisational learning.

Role and Responsibilities of HRD Directors/ Managers

For effective implementation of HRD in the corporate sector, HRD managers/ directors, facilitators or HRD consultants are needed. Dr. T. V. Rao has rightly held that "if implemented properly, integrated HRD systems can contribute significantly to positive cultural changes, increased productivity and excellence in organisations". Dr. Udai Pareek and Dr. T.V. Rao are the HRD pioneers who first developed and integrated HRD system in Larsen and Toubro Ltd., which is among the top ten limited companies in the private sector. According to William R. Tracey, the role, functions, qualifications and credentials of the modern HRD Manager cannot be described and defined in any meaningful way unless they are analyzed in the context of the setting in which the functions must be performed. During the last one decade, HRD has developed many new dimensions and the responsibilities of HRD managers have been enlarged. Political, economic, social, demographic and technological challenges have brought more difficult responsibilities to the HRD managers. HRD managers are broadly responsible for coordinating the efforts of a group of people so that their individual needs and goals are met by engaging in activities that contribute to the attainment of the goals and missions of the organisation that employs them. HRD managers have to focus on the development of the available human resources and broader organisational needs. HRD is responsible for facilitating organisational change and improvement. According to William R. Tracey, "The primary job of the HRD managers is to establish and maintain an environment that will develop people and facilitate cooperative, efficient and effective efforts in the pursuit of organisational goals. The HRD manager accomplishes that job by performing the functions of planning, organizing, staffing, directing and controlling." His responsibilities include writing job, descriptions and applicant specifications, screening and selecting, training and developing, supervising and evaluating, correcting and improving and promoting and terminating HRD supervisors and facilitators. HRD manager is not a job—analyst, a course developer, an instructor, a training programme administrator or an internal consultant but he plays a major role in identifying and solving organisational problems, designing tools and strategies for HRD department and serving as a specialist in organisational renewal and development. HRD managers must forecast the impact of political, economic, social, demographic and technological changes in their organisation in general and on HRD in particular. At macro- level, HRD managers should ensure that their organisations make useful contribution to the achievement of national, social and economic goals. HRD managers must establish close link with all other departments for effective utilization of their products and for better coordination. HRD managers must seek top management commitment to HRD programmes. HRD directors have to manage HRD systems as given in Fig.4.

Planning for HRD System

A plan is a guide for effective action; it is the map to get an organisation from where it is to where it wants to be. As Louis Allen has put it, " A plan is a trap laid to capture the future."[28] Planning for HRD involves assessment of the present status of HRD in the organisation, articulating a philosophy of HRD, predicting the environment of the future, determining goals, anticipating problems, forecasting HRD needs of various employees and the organisation, setting objectives, establishing HRD policies, developing HRD procedures and systems, preparing HRD budgets, and designing a strategy that would overcome barriers to the achievements of desired results. Planning for HRD will include forcasting HRD needs, research and development of HRD strategies and philosophy. Some of

Fig. 4. An Integrated HRD Matrix for Managing HRD.

Figure - A
An Integrated HRD System Matrix

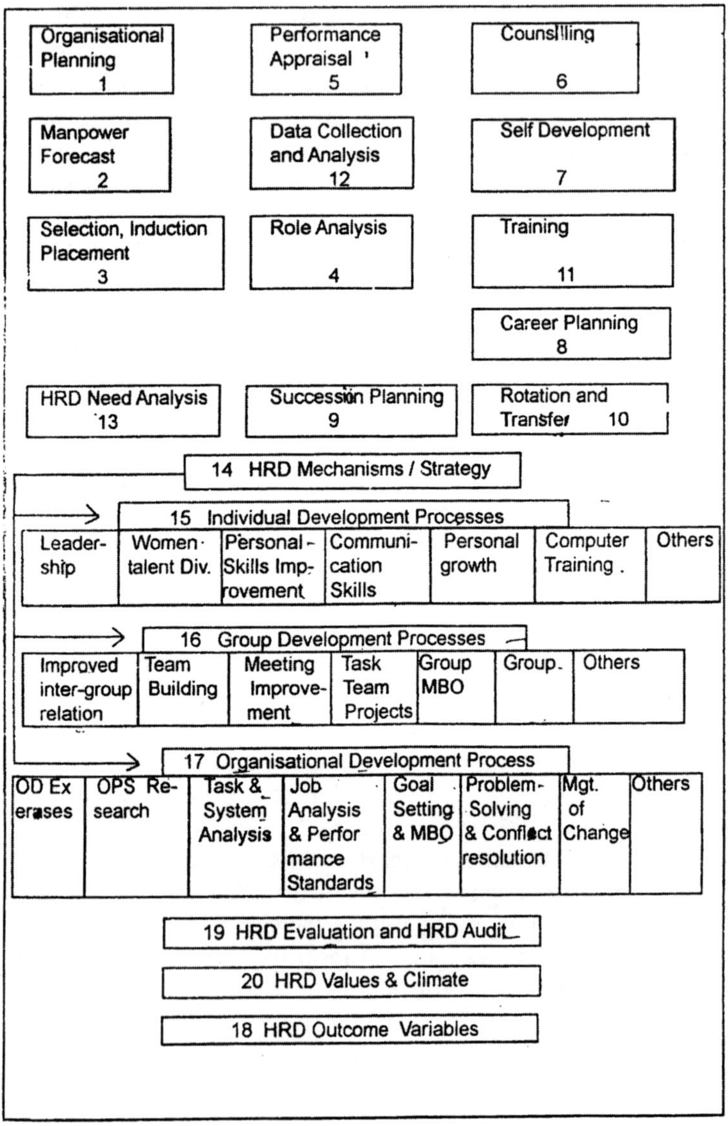

the important steps in HRD must be as under:

1. Develop HRD philosophy and goals.
2. HRD policies and objectives.
3. Identification of HRD needs and HRD forecasts.
4. HRD programmes and interventions.
5. HRD Requirements in terms of manpower, resources and infrastructure.
6. Preparing HRD budgets.
7. HRD research and evaluation programmes.
8. Planning tasks and linkages.
9. Implementation and execution of HRD by working out HRD schedules.
10. Staffing of HRD and generation of professionalism.
11. Limitations of HRD planning and future rescheduling.

Organisation for Human Resource Development

Organisation provides the framework in which a group of HRD professionals and managers can work together to attain the goals and objectives of the activity; organising involves identifying the functions and activities that must be conducted, grouping those activities and assigning each group to a leader with the authority to manage.[29] HRD can be organised in an organisation either with the help of an experienced, competent HRD consultant or by studying other organisations. As a capable organiser, the competent and professional HRD manager carries out the following tasks:

1. Identifies needed HRD activities, functions and interventions;
2. Constructs intelligible HRD department organisational charts;
3. Clarifies relationships between HRD department and other organisational elements;

4. Assigns duties and authority to each functional grouping related to HRD functions and responsibilities;
5. Formulates clear and detailed job-descriptions;
6. Conducts periodical organisational surveys to identify new challenges and HRD needs;
7. Designs HRD structures and manages various HRD activities through managers;
8. Develops and validates various HRD systems and later operates those HRD systems;
9. Seeks support from top level management for HRD and maintains close liaison with them;
10. Periodically carries out research and evaluation of HRD department and their contributions to the organisation;
11. Ensures effective supervision over HRD functionaries and facilitators;
12. Motivates HRD personnel for effective role performance and acts as HRD expert and consultant; and
13. Conducts periodical organisational surveys.

Staffing the HRD Development

Staffing is the joint responsibility of the top level management and HRD chief of the organisation. Staffing is the function, which involves the acquisition, training, orientation, assignment and development of personnel of HRD department and support. Only competent, well-motivated and experienced HRD personnel can ensure that the most carefully planned and conceived HRD activities guarantee the attainment of goals and objectives of the HRD department. Specifically the staffing function includes recruitment, screening, selecting, training, assigning, compensating, developing and promoting personnel who are assigned HRD tasks in the organisation. What is needed is an integrated, progressive programme for recruiting and retaining HRD specialists for the organisation and periodically updating their HRD competencies. HRD staff must have required HRD competencies in terms of HRD professional knowledge. HRD professional skills and personal attitudes and values which can make tham a motivated and dedicated HRD expert.[30] HRD professional knowledge would include HRD philosophy, policies, practices, and system, learning theories, training systems and methods, group dynamics, social science research methods, quality circle and turn-around strategies etc. HRD professional skills include communication skills, persuasive skills, efforts building, conflict management skills, leadership, leadership initiative, creativity etc. Personnel attitudes and values include empathy, openness, pro-activity, sense of fairness, self-discipline, learning orientation etc. It includes defining personnel requirement for HRD jobs to be done, inventoring available human skills, developing and promoting personnel in HRD work.

HRD Department and their Tasks

HRD managers should have adequate links with corporate planning department to get to know periodically the company plans and strategies for future so that HRD efforts are geared up in the right directions. It should also have close interdependencies with the personnel department.

The main objective of the HRD department is to build and nurture a learning environment and development climate in the organisations. According to Dr. T.V. Rao, the HRD departments should have the following tasks.[31]

1. Develop an HRD philosophy for the entire organisation and get the top management committed to it openly and consistently.
2. Keep inspiring the line managers to have a constant desire to learn and develop.
3. Constantly plan and design new methods and systems of developing and strengthening HRD climate.
4. Be aware of the business/social/other goals of the organisation and direct all HRD efforts to achieve these goals.
5. Monitor effectively the implementation of various HRD sub-systems and mechanisms.

6. Work with various associations and inspire them to play a positive role in HRD promotion.
7. Conduct human process research, organisational health surveys and renewal exercises periodically.
8. Influence personnel policies by providing necessary inputs to the personnel department/ top management.

There are many issues related to the structure of the HRD functions, which need to be considered. How should one structure HRD function? Should it be a part of personnel department ? To whom should the HRD chief report? What are the HRD linkages with other departments and organisations? How many HRD staff should an organisation have? Is it necessary to have outside HRD consultants? These questions can be looked into in the context of organisational strength, structural mission, level of human resource department etc. There are many traps and temptations for HRD managers. They may walk into the trap of getting obsessed with observable and easily measurable indications of systems and their implementation. Some of the traps are by virtue of the nature of the HRD functions; some are due to the human nature. HRD managers run the risk of becoming empire builders for themselves or become victims of power-trap.

For the proper development of human resources, an integrated systems approach can have some of the following directions.[32]

1. HRD interventions by internal HRD faculty,
2. HRD interventions by external faculty drawn from HRD professionals,
3. Sponsoring executives to outside HRD programmes,
4. Seminars/workshops on specific topics/problems,
5. Foreign courses in latest technology or advanced management courses,
6. Induction programmes for new entrants,
7. Rotational and on the job training periodically to vari-

ous grades of employees,

8. Training of trainers programmes to create a multiplier effect in the field of human resource development,
9. Participation of executives in national and regional professional meetings/conventions,
10. Circulations of selected reading material on various professionals, technical and management topics on monthly basis,
11. Organised tours/visits to other companies/corporations for interaction and broader understanding,
12. Evaluation and feedback on employees followed by required counselling sessions by HRD professionals,
13. Encouragement of memberships to professional societies/organisations and their active participation with monetary support from the organisation,
14. Evolving an HRD cadre from within the organisation for ensuring continuous HRD activities,
15. Top management support and recognition for acquisition of higher qualifications and achieving praiseworthy performance,
16. Creation of data bank and computerisation of personnel bio-data and profiles,
17. Intensifying O.D. efforts in the areas of sharing the organisational goal setting and other behavioural interventions, and
18. Promotion of various training finances and infrastructural support.

Directing HRD/ Sub-systems/Interventions

As a management function, directing involves guiding and assisting, motivating and activating, stimulating and encouraging, communicating and persuading, building and maintaining morale and work commitment, leading and inspiring and correcting and disciplining wherever needed in a given organisational setting. The main elements of directing are communicating, motivating, appraising and counselling, building and maintaining morale, disciplining and leading. In the specific context of HRD, directing of HRD functions would include the following specific tasks—

1. Triggering pro-active actions for improving HRD systems and interventions.
2. Delegating HRD responsibilities to line managers for improving overall performance.
3. Establishing standards of satisfactory performance and identifying measures of performance.
4. Correcting deficient performance and criticising performance where needed.
5. Overcoming resistance to directions by adopting required strategies (guide resistance into productive effort).
6. Making effective communication by overcoming problems of and barriers to communication.
7. Effective and efficient HRD interventions need invited efforts based on coordinated activities of individuals and groups by developing an atmosphere of trust and confidence.
8. Various HRD sub-systems should be introduced in the organisation in stages so that each system can be properly directed and planned.

Controlling

HRD managers have to exercise effective controls and some of the main activities will be as under:

1. Establishing and applying measurable quality and quantity standards.
2. Measuring performance against standards.
3. Utilizing cost-effective reports system.
4. Performance appraisal of subordinates working in HRD

department.

5. Carrying out periodic HRD audits.
6. Correcting deviations from performance standards.
7. Ensure objective, flexible and economic evaluation of HRD system.

Evaluation of HRD Processes and Sub-systems

The first conference on measuring human resource contribution to business performance took place in London in October, 1995 and in India, in Jan, 1996. Evaluation of HRD has been in vogue in the forms of tests.

Though HRD has evoked tremendous interest from practitioners and academician, evaluating HRD is still controversial. Consultants differ in suggesting evaluative measures. A quality dimension to evaluation has been added by well-known HRD professionals like Udai Pareek, T.V. Rao and M.S.S. Varadhan. Evaluation is described by some as a management philosophy while evaluating HRD is described variously as a part of the personnel function, a programme with distinct objectives and time boundaries, a system and an OD intervention.[33] It has to be clear about "what", "how" and "why" of evaluation. Some authors believe that HRD interventions have been going half circles in the plan-do-check circle. Some thinkers have raised the issue of social sensitivity in evaluation—corruption, downsizing and entrenchments are matters of grave concern. There is a need to undertake specific programmes designed to heighten both social sensitivity and ethical behaviour. The HRD components considered for evaluation should include organisational change, training, empowerment, organisational climate and stress. There are some HRD specialists who point out that there cannot be a standard format to evaluate work which has been done on evaluation of HRD. There is need for more of systematic work on evaluation in the Indian Context. There is no bench mark study on HRD evaluation.

Traces of HRD Movement in Ancient India

The Indian contribution to HRD dates back to our Vedantic

literature and other literary works. The Vedas, Upanishads, the Smritis, the Puranas and other ancient Indian literature constantly talk about human personality, human development, and self-management. The *Gurukul* system can be regarded as the first institutions of HRD in the modern sense. Lord Ram, Laksman, Bharat, Shatrughan got their initial HRD in *Vashist ashram* and Lord Krishna in Sandipan *Rishi ashram* located in *Tapovans*. Indian scriptures believed in holistic bond between man and the universe. Holistic Vedantic living consisted of four goals of human life—Dharma, Arth, Kama and Moksha and divided life into four stages of man's journey—*Brahmacharya* (student ship and self-discipline), *Grhasthya* (householdship), *Vanaprastha* (retirement from active life) and *Sannayasa* (total renuniciation for union with the divine without and within). Indian *Shastras* (scriptures) recommend the marriage of *Dharma Sadhana* with *Karma Sadhana*.[34] *Bhagwat Gita* strongly advocates management of self as the springbroad of all human action and motivation. The *Yoga Sutra* of *Patanjali* suggests eight coordinated steps for self-development—*Yama* (abstinence), *Niyama* (observance), *Asanas* (postures for good health) and *Pranayam* (breath-control). It further recommended *Pratyahara* (withdrawal of senses), *Dharana* (concentration), *Dhyana* (meditation) and *Samadhi* (super-consciousness) as conscious proceses of human development. Chanakya (Kautilya) recommended self-discipline by eschewing anger, lust, greed, vanity, haughtiness and rivalry.

Recent Milestones in HRD in India

Human resource development in recent years gained momentum with the formation of National HRD network on 2nd May, 1985. On 11 September,1990, Academy of HRD was formed and in October, 1990 Prof T.V. Rao took over as Honorary Director of the Academy. In April, 1991 the first diploma programme in HRD was launched. On 3rd August, 1991 Academy of Human Resource Development moved to its own premises of Ahmedabad. On 1st June,1992 Prof. Keith C D' Sooza took over as Executive Director of the Academy of HRD Ahmedabad. On 7th December, 1993 Academy became a registered society under the Societies Registration Act, 1860. On

20th January, 1994 the first convocation of Diploma in HRD was held at Mumbai. In June, 1994 T.V. Rao took over as Director of HRD Academy. On 23rd May, 1994, Doctoral level Fellowship Programme in HRD was started in collaboration with XLRI, Jamshedpur meant for HRD professionals. On 24th August, 1994 HRD Academy signed a memorandum of understanding (MOU) with All India Management Association (AIMA) for joint professional diploma in HRD. From 1st July, 1995, the HRD Academy started functioning at Hyderabad. On 20th August, 1995 Dr. Reddy's Lab Ltd. donated five acres of land to Academy at Miyapur, Hyderabad. On 6th May, 1996, HRD Academy signed a memorandum of understanding with T.A. Pai Institute of Management for joint diploma in HRD. On 4th January, 1996 Industrial and Organisational Assessment Centre was launched. On 30th January, 1996, Academy signed a memorandum of understanding with SYMBIOSIS Centre for Management and Human Resource Development for joint diploma in HRD. On 1st April, 1996 Dr. P. Sethu Madhavan took over as Director in-charge and Prof C. Balaji took over as full time Director in May, 1997. On 23rd May, 1996, Dr. Reddy's Lab Ltd. donated five more acres of land to academy at Miyapur, Hyderabad. On 27th September, Academy signed a memorandum of understanding with International Institute of Professional Studies (IIPS) for joint diploma in HRD. In February, 1989, National HRD Network conference was held at New Delhi where forty-four organisations across the country shared their experiences which have been documented in a book *Towards Organisational Effectiveness through Human Resource Development*. Another book *Alternative Approaches and Strategies of HRD* published two years earlier documented experience of twenty organisations in HRD. These indicate the growing importance being given by the industry in India to HRD as a means of improving productivity, quality and in attaining better competitiveness.

Leadership and Vision for the 21st Century

For managing effective HRD effective leadership is most important. HRD can assist various business groups, corporations, and other service organisations, in identifying, acquiring, deepening and exploiting the necessary core competencies for higher rate of economic growth. HRD can assist various client organisations with a participative process for developing shared vision and strategic plans and in the dynamic process of developing, disseminating and centralising the core values of customer service, quality and efficiency in the global market economy. HRD professionals can help the nation by generating entrepreneurial skills and entrepreneurial creativity, which will achieve India's social, economic and spiritual vision of the 21st century. At local, regional, state and sector levels, HRD body can evolve the following kinds of plans:

(a) Exploiting the economic potential of the area/region/state for additional jobs and self-accelerating economic growth.

(b) Improving the physical environment by social forestry, water management, health, education etc.

(c) Preserving and upgrading cultural heritages such as art forms, pilgrimage and tourist sports.

(d) Build up regional, state and sectoral HRD research and development centres for continuous high quality research. The society envisages the following daunting HRD challenges:

1. Raising India's HDI/Score requires massive, macro HRD in both:— (a) PQL—physical quality of life in terms of access to food, clothing and shelter (b) QL— Quality of life in terms of access to education, health, art and culture.
2. Raising GDI calls for changes in attitudes and care for the female child, her nutrition, literacy, education and economic independence.
3. Enabling millions of women to play a constructive role in building economic growth and social justice system.
4. Social harmony requires attitudinal changes in various groups, communities and sections of society towards others by having goodwill, understanding

and empathy.

5. Developing cultural, aesthetic and spiritual competencies of the people.[35] The most distinguishing feature of leadership is that it deals with the human aspects of organisations and influences behaviour of other personnel to attain the organisational goals. A good HRD leader can motivate the entire HRD department and achieve optimum results in terms of effective HRD functioning. Setting HRD objectives, developing plans, initiating action, evaluating performance and motivating HRD staff are some of the main functions of leadership.

Today internet has become the best tutor in the world. The on live world can make a tremendous difference in helping people to learn. Michael Stevenson, director of education at BBC says: "In the future if you are watching a factual programme, we will be offering in parallel, engaging, interactive online packages that will help you to learn more. You can take the journey as far as tailor made online short courses." Internet has opened a virtual classroom to all although most are in their infancy. The internet is the perfect source of just-in-time knowledge. Having the internet in the house means that the family has an incredibly powerful library, available in the corner waiting to be used.

A Vedantic Approach to HRD

Sankaracharya, commenting on the *Katha Upanishad*, making a reference of infinite spiritual energy resource in man, says that the energy resources within every individual are organised in an ascending scale of subtlety, immensity and inwardness—*suksma, mahantasca, pratyagatma—bhutasca*—Muscular energy in gross, nervous energy in subtler and psychic energy in even more subtle."[36] Men and women are moved by lofty ideals of love and service. Great personalities like Buddha, Jesus, Ramakrishna, Vivekananda and Mahatma Gandhi, who engaged themselves in untiring work entirely disproportionate to their physical and mental food drew their energy from the depth of their personalities called *atma-shakti* (power of *Atman*). The *Kathan Upanishad* proclaims the truth of infinite possibilities in man in the following words. " This infinite *Atman*, being hidden in all beings (like fire in the ashes) does not shine at all, but it can be realised, made manifest, by all who are accustomed to enquire into subtle truths by means of their sharp and subtle reason. The *Atman* is the imprisoned splendour" in all. (Verses III-12). For understanding and comprehending *Atman*, one has to approach the great masters of *Vedanta* who have realized the truth. The *Atman*, the infinite divine self—the *Siva swarup* that is within us is the real self of man.[37] Religion, according to Swami Vivekanand is truly the science of all-round development of human beings which includes physical and intellectual growth as well as spiritual growth. It is , he says, the manifestation of the divinity already in man. This is the science of *Vyakti Vikasa* or *Atma Vikasa* growth and development of individuality, expansion of self-awareness beyond organic limitations. It is in this aspect that human resource development should focus its attention. Vedantic training and managers need to be organised in a systematic way by selecting a proper environment and qualified trainers for getting maximum results.[38] Along with the development of scientific and technical efficiency for successfully dealing with the outer world we must ensure the development of a spiritual efficiency within so that a total human development of man-making and nation-building can take place within our generation. The science of man in depth, this *adhyatma vidya*, holds the key to all healthy human development in our country. There are evidences given by research studies conducted in India that values contribute towards human development. S.K. Chakraborty opines that values such as *Karma, Sanskaras, Gunas, Karmayoga* of *Bhagwad Gita* would promote quality of work-life, ethical managerial behaviour and provide better motivational basis for Indian executives, Chakraborty suggests that purity of mind and self-transcendence (*Moksha*) would enhance quality of decision making in the organisations. India should lead the world as a laboratory on behalf of the mankind to synthesize the mental, physical and professional growth of human beings with their spiritual growth for the good of all mankind. HRD professionals should provide the spiritual vision for the 21st century by spreading the teachings of *adhyatma vidya* (Spiritual Science) and integrate it with physical, mental and professional training. For human resource development, ancient Indian wisdom can provide very useful suggestions and guidelines. Ethics and value system of human resource should be built on the following values based in deep structure of Indian Vedantic Philosophy:

1. The individual must be respected.
2. Cooperation and trust.
3. Jealousy is harmful for human's mental health.
4. *Chitta-Suddhi* or purification of the mind with the noble thoughts of compassion, friendliness, humanity and gratitude.
5. Top quality product resource.
6. Work is worship.
7. Containment of greed.
8. Ethico-moral soundness.
9. Self-discipline and self-restraint.
10. Customer satisfaction.
11. Creativity.
12. The inspiration to give as motivation.
13. Renunciation and detachment from selfish results/ rewards and egoistic demands.[39] In order to develop managers on Vedantic lines, the prevailing excessive cultivation of left-brain, intellect sharpening of human development processes must be moderated by careful attention to right brained, mind -purifying efforts. The theory of meditation on Ishlam and transcendental meditation or mind-relaxing Vedantic exercises can be some of the culture specific processes for the great majority of Indian managers and workers. For human resource development based on Vedantic wisdom, all individuals must be made to integrate human development with values programmes based on the well known

following seven major concepts of Indian thoughts:

1. From Lower Self-Higher Self (*Atman*).
2. Disidentifications and re-identifications of self.
3. The Theory of *Gunas* and dynamics.
4. The Theory of *Karma*.
5. The Giving model of motivations.
6. The Theory and method of *Nishkam Karma*.
7. The Theory of *Sanskars* (or residual Impressions).[40]

Human development on the spiritual plane needs a well-designed programme and qualified trainers to initiate people into Vedantic way of life. In human resource development, the circular relationship between physical health and mental health has to be kept into consideration. Greed, jealousy, envy, egotism, impatience, anger and frustration are some of the impediments to sound mental health and all efforts need to be made to keep individuals free from above impediments and spiritual practices need reinforcement by regular meditation and *satsang* (spiritual congregations) under able teachers and *Gurus*. Family background, *sanskar*, level of spiritual development and association of pious people (*satsang*) are important in initiations of HRD of the spiritual level. There is a need to ensure that managers regularly attend *satsang*. How do we improve upon the effectiveness of the managers to reach the state of excellence? This will largely depend not only upon the four basic skills in management training mentioned by Dr. C.K. Prahalad but on how clean the raw talented or the trained manager continue his "instruments" which enable the all pervasive internal cleanliness for self -development. *Taithreya Upanishad* has referred to them as "five - sheaths "(*Panch Kosha*). The *Taitheriya Upanishad* expounds the concept of SELF through the imaginary multiple overlying sheaths. The outer most is the gross physical sheath or body called *Annamaya Kosha*. The second is the vital sheath called *Pranamaya Kosha*. The third inner layer is mental sheath called *Manomaya Kosha*. The fourth is the sheath of intellect called *Vigyanamaya Kosha*. The fifth inner most sheath is bless cover called *Annadmaya Kosha*. The true *Atman* SELF is beyond all these five sheaths. Body, *Pran*, Mind, Intellect and Ego are the five instruments, which need to be attuned properly for realisation of the true self and enlightenment. For development of the human beings into full personality (*Poornattava*), daily maintenance and HRD technique has been suggested below. The internal instruments, their accretions and methodology to clean up on a daily maintenance schedule can be tabulated as given below and:

Table Showing Vedantic Approach to Daily Maintenance Routine for Human Development

Panch Kosh	*Instru-ment*	*Accretion and Problem Areas*	*Methodo-logy*	*Time-minutes to be spent*
1. Annamaya Kosh	Body	Poor blood circulation	Surya Namashkara and daily Yoga	15 minutes every morning
2. Pranmaya Kosh	Prana	Imblance Inhaling and exhaling	Paranayama	Every morning and evening 5 min. each
3. Manomaya Kosh	Mind	Anxiety	Auto suggestions and meditation	5 to 10 minutes every morning and evening
4. Vigyanamaya Kosh	Intellect	Indecision	Japa and Dharana and satsang	5 to 10 minutes every morning, evening satsang at least weekly for one hour
5. Anandmaya Kosh	Ego	Subjectivity	Dhyana and Transcendental meditation up to samadhi	15 minutes to 45 minutes every morning

The Vedantic concepts and practices cannot be taught in one short-term course, they have to be practiced over long periods with periodical reinforcements by well-planned workshops and training programmes conducted in simple local language. A firm conviction about their utility has to be created. Vedantic training and education for workers and managers needs to be organised in a systematic way by selecting a proper environment and trainers for getting maximum results.[41] Unless there is a paradigm shift in our focus for human resource development as suggested above, we do not see much hope in the traditional western oriented human resource development programmes which completely neglect ethical, moral and spiritual aspect of human-beings. Corporate leaders, manager and professionals have to practice above given methodology as a part of their daily routine. Ancient Indian thinkers and seers recommended above routine in the morning at *Brahma-Mahurt* (early morning first starting at 4 a.m.) and evening at dusk time as part of *sandyavandanam*. These daily recommended practices can help in self development. *Chitta Suddhi* (mental purification) and stress relieving strategy; above recommended practice will ultimately tune up the mental inteliectual and spiritual levels of the managers, enabling them to achieve managerial excellence. In *Bhagwad Geeta*, Chapter XII sloka (stanzas) 13 to 19 enumerate the characteristic features of Man of Perfection and Man of Steady Wisdom. By regularly following the correct mode of conduct and the way of life one can achieve managerial excellence.

Growth can not be achieved overnight, it needs company of holy people (*satsang*), lot of transcendental meditations on a regular basis and self-realisation through *Gyan Yoga*. Swami Vivekananda had in-depth characterised the world as "a moral gymnasium.[42] for human development. Indian ancient wisdom tells us that breath - management is the first step for all spiritual development and health and most certainly for mental good health and human development. Swami Vivekananda believed that "the man who has control over his own mind assuredly will have control over every other mind.... A pure moral man has control of himself and all minds are the same, different parts of one mind."[43] Therefore our efforts for human resource development must pay proper attention to mental and spiritual development and training of control over mind. Probably for HRD practitioners this can be somewhat a tall order in the present day world. Patanjali Yoga Sutra give us complete programme for developing human beings Vedantic knowledge and ethical education can produce in the long run balanced, flexible and effective managers with the power of insight and courage to create and use ethical desirable means to sustain an ambience of liberalism and democratic ethos.[44] Vedantic education can bring human resource development at spiritual, personal, social and organisational levels and can ultimately bring role effectiveness and organisational excellence. From 1983 to 1990, over a hundred in-house programmes have been conducted covering almost 2000 participants from seventeen different organisations under the guidance of Dr. S.K. Chakraborty of IIM, Calcutta. In the field of human resource development, the creative experiments of Swami Vivakananda, Rabindra Nath Tagore and Shri Aurabindo are luminous land-marks. The most meaningful HRD should create an environment where discipline of body and mind and the true values of life are given due priorities, Learning to live the spiritual - ethical way should be induced from childhood through healthy family *sanskaras* and education to ensure full development of human personality in all its different dimensions. India must develop a grand vision for the 21st century and must help human beings to develop economically, socially and spiritually.

REFERENCES

1. Lincoln Barnett, *The Universe and Dr. Einstein* (Mentor Edition —pp. 126-127). Physicist Niels Bohr also held similar views.
2. Sir Julian Huxley—*Evolution After Darwin*—Vol. 1, p. 20.
3. For complete and exhaustive analysis see Swami Ranganathananda, *The Science of Human Energy Resources*—The Indian Institute of Public Administration, New Delhi 1979. pp. 1- 32.
4. *Swami Vivekanand-the Complete Works*—Vol. II, p. 193. R.K. Mission Publication.
5. For further elaboration consult *Svetasvatara Upanishad* VI -20.
6. Swami Ranganathananda, *The Science of Human Energy Resource*—The Indian Institute of Public Administration, New Delhi, 1979, p. 13 This whole para is broadly based on the material collected from the above-referred book for which author in thankful to the Swamiji.
7. For similar views see N.P. Rao—*Human Resource Development and Production Techniques*, APH Publishing Corporation, 5, Ansari Road, New Delhi, 1997, p. 6.

8. Human Development Reoprt, 1995, Published by the United Nations Development Programme, Oxford University Press, Delhi, 1995, p.1.

9. Human Development Report, 1996, Published by United Nations Development Programme, Oxford University Press, New, York, 1996, pp. 55-56.

10. G. Myrdal-*Asian Drama-An Inquiry into the Poverty of Nations*—New York Panthelon, Vol. III, p. 196.

11. Keith Davis, *The Dynamics of Organisational Behaviour,* M.C. Hill, 1967, p. 5.

12. Eli Girzberg", *Men and his Work* Edited by Aale S. Beach - "Managing People at Work" Macmillan Publication Co. Inc, New York, 1980, pp. 3 - 4.

13. J.S. Horn, *Away with all pests*—Modern Reader, New York, 1971.

14. Udai Pareek, *Training Instruments for Human Resource Development*—Tata Mc Graw Hill Publishing Company Private Ltd, New Delhi, 1997, p. 75.

15. Udai Pareek, *The Role of Top Management in HRD in Banks.* Edited by Anil Khandelwal, p. 177.

15[a]. B.K. Sarkar, *The Positive Background of Human Sociology* Vol. XXXII, Book 1 p. 6.

16. F.H. Harbison, "*Human Resource Development Planning in Modernising Economics.* International Labour Review—May, 1962, p. 44.

17. Further details consult Sarkar, B.K., *The Positive Background of Hindu Sociology,* Panini office, Allahabad, 1937. Vol. XXXII, B.K. 1, p. 6. Also S.K. Chakrabarty—*Management by Values— Towards Cultural Congruence,* Oxford University Press, 1991, Delhi Ch. 8.

18. Federick Harbison and Charles Myers, *Education, Manpower and Economic Growth,* Oxford and IBH, New Delhi, 1968, p. 2.

19. Alfred Marshall—*Principles of Economics,* Mac Millan, London, 1964, p. 469.

20. Theodore W. Schultz, Nobel Lecture; the Economics of Being Poor, *Journal of Political Economy,* Vol. 88 (4), August, 1980, p. 639.

21. Sir W. Arthur Lewis, The *Celebrated Development Economist* and W.W Rostow, the *Stages of Growth Theorist,* advocated this type of transformation by developing human resources.

22. T.V. Rao, and DF Pereira, *Recent Experiences in Human Resource Development*, Oxford and IBH, New Delhi, 1986.

23. Pareek and Rao, *Designing and Managing Human Resource Systems* (1982), Oxford and IBH, New Delhi.

24. Rensis Likert, *New Patterns in Management*, McGraw Hill, 1961, p. 103.

25. Noel M. Tichy and Eli Cohen, *The Leadership Engine—How Winning Companies Build Leaders at Every Level*, Harper Business, 367, p. 526.

26. T.Venkateswara Rao, *Integrated Human Resource Development Systems* in Rao & Pereira (Eds) *Recent Experiences in Human Resources*, Oxford & IBH Publishing Co. Pvt. Ltd., New Delhi, 1988, p. 5

27. Udai Pareek, *Training Instruments for Human Resource Development*. Tata McGraw Hill Publishing Company Ltd., New Delhi, 1997, p. 9.

28. Dharni P. Sinha, Human Resource Development—The Indian Challenge—in BL Maheshwari & D.P. Sinha—Management of Change through Human Resource Development—Tata McGraw Hill Publishing Co. Ltd., New Delhi, 1991, p. 24.

29. MR R Nair, Foreword to B.L. Maheshwari & D.P. Sinha (Editors), *Management of change through or Human Resource Development*, Tata McGraw Hill Publishing Company Ltd., New Delhi, 1991, p. V.

30. Louis A. Allen, *The Management Profession*, New York, Mc Graw Hill Book Company, 1964, p. 99.

31. William R. Tracey, *Managing, Training and Development System*, American Management Association Inc. Tara porevala Publishing Industries Pvt. Ltd., Bombay. Indian Reprint 1980, p. 173.

32. For further details consult Dr. T.V. Rao, *HRD Missionary*, Exercise 3., HRD competencies check list, pp. 64-67.

33. For full details and elaboration consult Dr. T.V. Rao, *HRD Missionary The Role and Functions of HRD Manager and Departments*, Chapter 4, pp. 16-20. National HRD Netwrok, 1990.

34. For similar views also see G.R. Krishnamurthy—Integrated Management Development in a Multi-unit company—Hindustan Zinc Limited Environment Edited by Dr. S. Ravi Shanker et al. Dhruv and Deep Book, Bombay 1988, p. 19.

35. For detailed analysis and further study consult, *Evaluating Human Resource Development* Edited by Udai Pareek, HRD Research Foundation, Jaipur 1997, pp. 1- 310.

36. S.K. Chakraborty, *Ethics in Management—Vedantic Perspective,* Oxford University Press, Delhi 1996, p. 192.

37. For similar views see M.B. Athreya, *HRD for India Vision 21st Century*—in HRD Vision and Directions for the 21st Century. Edited by ?

38. *Sankaracharya—Katha Upanishad.*

39. Dr. S. Radha Krishna—*Commentary on The Bhagwad Gita.*

40. Dr. Krishna Mohan Mathur—Towards Effective Management—Pathways to Excellence, Gyan Publishing House, New Delhi, 1999. p. 192.

41. For greater details and elaboration see S.K. Chakraborty: *Management by Values—Towards Cultural Congruence,* Oxford University Press, Delhi, 1992, pp. 20-25.

42. For Further details and guidance consult S.K. Chakraborty: *Management by Values—Towards Cultural Congruence* Oxford University Press, Delhi, 1992 and also his other books such as *Human Response Development, Foundations of Managerial Work,* and *Ethics in Management.*

43. Dr. Krishna Mohan Mathur—*Towards Effective Management—Pathways to Excellence,* Gyan Publishing House, New Delhi,1999, pp. 85, 192.

44. Swami Vivekanand—Collected Works Vol. VII, *Advanta Ashram,* Calcutta, 1958, pp. 16-17.

2

The Ethical and Spiritual Dimensions of HRD

Ethics reflects a nation's actions-good or bad—by reference to some criteria relevant to that nation. Ethical behaviour is considered as a blend of moral qualities and mental attitudes. Ethics is generally defined as the discipline dealing with what is good or bad and deals with moral duties and obligations. Personal ethics can be referred to as the rules by which an individual lives his or her personal life. Business ethics is concerned with the professional conduct of the businessmen and has many an aspect—market, corporate behaviour, production of goods and services and other economic behaviour. Ethics, in the true sense of the term, provides the motive force, the supreme propeller in one's behaviour. Ethics, reflecting a character of uncorrupted virtue, honesty, integrity and moral mores, represents the quintessence of civilized relationship between man and man, man and organisation, man and his profession and man and the society in general. Ethical and spiritual development of persons is an important part of HRD. Indian ethos of human development have provided a well-balanced integrated frame in which ethics and morality, a clean polity, selfless leadership, are all recognised as crucial determinants of human happiness. This integrated approach is aptly represented in the four-fold *Purusharth*—

Dharma, Arth, Kama and *Moksha*. The correct meaning of *Dharma* is a code of conduct for human beings, which ensures morality and ethical norms of highest standards. In the present day society, India is facing the following challenges:- (I) How to build ethical and moral values in curriculum ? (II) How to test the ethical and moral behaviour of job seekers ? (III) How to inculcate ethical and moral values in business and management people ? (IV) How to certify the brands bearing the high ethics and moral values of its creators ? (V) How to inculcate Indian ethical values of honesty, devotion to work, non-covetousness, equanimity and *Dharma* ? Our entire education system needs to be restructured, our management training must emphasise spiritual value in business. The modern science has now discovered the unified field which explains the three-dimensional time-space consciousness continuum and the Electro-magneto-gravitational Trimurti of universe. Vedanta referred to unified force as universal cosmic consciousness which is Brahman—having two aspects. Metric or *Saguna* and sub-metric or *Nirguna*. The sub-metric *Brahman* the unified force of *Satwa, Rajas* and *Tamas* is His absolute state of being. Thus, today there is the *sangam* of science, religion and philosophy. Modern science has brought home to us that consciousness is inextricably interwoven with the entire physical universe. During the recent past there has been a great resurgence of groups giving a spiritual dimension to management—be it Christian, Vedantic, Japanese or just secularised meditation techniques to inculcate and develop spiritual consciousness among business people.[1] Amy Gutmann in 1990, while talking to Press said; "Why create a centre for Human Values at Princeton now? The spiritual and intellectual need among students is even greater in 1990 than it was in 1931......What will the centre for Human Values do? The centre will sponsor teaching, research and public discussions that explore the significance, moral values and spiritual teachings in our individual and collective lives." For building and alround personality, spiritual and ethical dimensions need utmost attention. Spiritual dimension is the science of meditation. Christ, Mohammed, Buddha, Zorathushtra and ancient Indian saints all withdrew from the world to spend time in contemplation and spiritual practices. The spiritual teachers of all times have uniformly declared that the vitalising principle in matters is the spirit, and this spirit is universally dynamic and needs awareness. Spirituality implies:- (1) a pure mind, a pure heart: (2) a calm head, a cool brain; (3) smooth, deep, regulated breathing and nervous harmony; (4) peace, light, power, Anand; (5) a core of luminous constancy amidst fluctuating experiences; (6) contacting the inner self which is unchangeable, perfect, whole and luminous, and also identical with the self in everyone else; (7) a weakening of the divisive, selfish ego and strengthening the expansive, inclusive, consciousness; (8) greater giving and less grabbing; (9) diminution of pettiness and meanness, and enhancement of dignity and nobility; (10) putting the faltering human intellect in contact with the infallible supreme or universal or infinite intelligence or creative principle called Brahman or Allah or God.[3] Spiritual development aims at bringing self-awareness that you are pure consciousness—immortal, unchangeable and imperishable. Spirituality is not something tangible. One may not be well-versed in scripture but that does not make one less spiritual. There are highly spiritual people who have never studied the scriptures. Human Resource Development (HRD) cannot afford to ignore or neglect the spiritual and ethical dimensions of human resources. Spiritual development helps reduce stress and expands our horizons, helping in experiencing a subliminal happiness that neither material riches nor relationships can yield. The spiritual/ethical development of the human beings is complete and meaningful only when it is related to the welfare of other people and other forms of life. Attainment and achievement of inner peace, and happiness is an end in itself. The goal of spiritual development is personal and brings forth social transformation. The world is an amphitheater in which there is a close struggle going on between spirit and matter. In Islam, "an act of worship is a means, not a goal. The goal is a true moral and ethical conduct. Anything, which is harmful to human society, must be rejected and must be desisted from. Injustice and falsehood are evils, which must be avoided irrespective of time and place. Anyone who deviates from the path of truth cannot claim to be a worshipper of Allah." The Bible tells that overemphasis on material things can cause spiritual and moral ruin (Timurthy 6.9.12). Spiritual and ethical developments have been some of the unique focus areas of all religions. India is a greatly favoured land in terms of cosmic beneficence according to the Vaastu aspect of its geographical location and is most conducive to spiritual and ethical development of human beings. The *Himalayas* or *Meru Parvat* oversees the whole of India in the likeness of the prime *Sahasrara Chakra* in the human body. The religious practices and *tapas* of so many enlightened yogis and great mystics and the timely appearance of *avatars* and saints over thousands of years have greatly accentuated this spiritual potency. The Vedantic religion is like a gigantic Banyan tree with its refreshing, ever ramifying growth, change and variation and its multiple seats and philosophies enriching it's diversity and all embracing compassion. Spiritual and ethical development can bring total transformation in an individual's personality and the inner change can renew the entire human being, his opinions, and his judgements, his decisions, feelings and even behaviour. In the modern age of liberalisation, globalisation and info-technology some of the following questions related to ethical development can be raised:

(i) Can ethics and morality be taught ?

(ii) How far can ethics and morality be extended to the business and management world ?

(iii) Can a code of ethics or spiritual discipline be imposed on the corporate entity ?

(iv) What are the contributory factors, which can help in the development of ethical dimensions of human resources?

(v) What is the holistic approach to ethical development in the Vedantic Indian tradition ?

(vi) What is the core-value system needed for ethical development and what are its essential ingredients ?

(vii) How can human beings make their lives sublime, enriching themselves, spiritually uplifting themselves, drawing nearer to the divine and awakening within unfolding themselves, enjoying the awakened light ?

(viii) How are core values moulded to make human beings more spiritually uplifted and ethically strong in their convictions ?

Above given questions need our attention.

Spiritual and ethical development of human beings has been always part of the practices of various great world religions. Vedic Indian religion (popularly known as Hinduism), Islam, Christianity and other religions have been emphasising the spiritual, mystical and ethical developments of their devotees and faith-followers. Meditation is a sure way to attain spiritual and ethical development. Prayer is an effective communication with the heavenly father. It is a sincere, sensible, affectionate, out-pouring of the human spirit to god and is spiritually uplifting. "When we pray in a sincere religious manner, whole.heartedly, we link ourselves with the inexhaustible motive power that spins the universe. We ask that a part of this power be apportioned to our needs" wrote Dr. Alexis Cared, a Noble Prize winner. Spiritual development is an earnest endeavour to transcend the perceived, temporary appearances, unrealities and attain the visions and an experience of the supersensuous driven reality, and realise the state of *Sat-Chit-Anand*. Our ethical value orientation should cover the technological, social, psychological systems and must inspire us to do only right and ethical things. The globalisation of the Indian economy has resulted in a serious concern not only for the need for ethical corporate governance but also that corporate governance should conform to international norms and ethics. The modern man seems to have forgotten the divine purpose for which he was created and nurtured, educated and sent to this world. By substituting god with wealth and power as the objects of his worship, humankind today has forgotten the divine self that lies within it as well as evolutionary possibilities. Development of national character should be a part of HRD efforts.

Vedantic Approach to Ethical and Spiritual Development of Human Resources

Vedanta is basically the science of human energy resources.[4]

In his address on "The Mission of the Vedanta" Swami Vivekanand uttered this stirring Vedantic truth: "Arise, Awake, Awake from this hypnotism of weakness. None is really weak; the soul is infinite, omnipotent, omniscient." *The Adhyatma Vidya* is in essence, the method by which human level of consciousness can be raised and a new spiritual dimension added to the physical and the intellectual personality of human beings. Vedantic wisdom envisions human personality in five sheaths. The innermost shell or *Kosha* called *Anand Maya Kosha* is the prime mover which prompts the next higher *Vijnana Maya Kosh* to decide, motivating *Mano Maya Kosha,* instructing *Prana Maya Kosha* to act and finally making *Anna Maya Kosha* (the gross body) to perform for the desired end. For spiritual and ethical development, one needs to cleanse oneself of internal dirt and negative thoughts. The chanting of a *Guru*-initiated *mantra,* which is generally the invocation of divine grace, can help individuals realise spiritual enlightenment and achieve holistic well being. When the body consciousness is negatived by spiritual advancement, the *Jivatman* flies away into the sky of the *Parmathman*—the absolute *sat-chit-anand* and he reaches the supreme goal. Vedantic approach has a claim to universality and eternity, its ethical norms have global perspective for the purpose of the people so that they may control their greed, pride and anger.

The Matrix Showing Vedantic Approach to Spiritual and Ethical Development

1. *Vedanta* is a sovereign science.
2. In each one of us dwells the divine SELF, know thyself.
3. All religions lead to spiritual and ethical development in their true perspectives.
4. The soul is infinite, omnipotent and can be realised by ethical and spiritual discipline.
5. *Vedanta* needs to be taught by enlightened *Guru* coming from *Guru Shishya parampara.*
6. *Vedanta* is basically the science of human energy resources.
7. Four *Purusharth—Dharma, Artha, Kama* and *Moksha* as goals of life.
8. Need to develop a holistic approach to ethical, spiritual and intellectual development.

9. *Vedanta* is a way of life and Vedantic teachings can transform human beings.
10. The five-fold debt system and obligations of human beings.
11. Holistic approaches towards ethic-morality and values.
12. Theory of *Sanskaras* and theory of rebirth.
13. Theory of *Nishkam Karma* and *Dharm Sadhana*.
14. The ethics of decision making and organisation behaviour.
15. Development upto atomic poor natwa (self realisation).
16. Indian model of holistic development.

Swami Gambhirananda with the help of a *sloka* from *Katha Upanishad* has beautifully explained the relationship of various parts of human beings thus; *Atmanam valhinam viddhi, shariram rathameva tu; Buddhim tu sarathi mana pragrahameva cha* (know the individual self as the master of the chariot, and the body as the chariot; know the intellect as the charioteer and the mind as verily the bridle."[5] Purity and control of the mind and its emotions are what ethico-moral conduct fosters for spiritual development. In *Vedanta* practices there is great emphasis on *bhava-shuddhi* or *chitt-shuddhi* e.g. *Yama* and *Niyama* practices of *Patanjali*.[6] Truthfulness, sincerity, honesty, obedience, humility, purity, endurance and consideration for fellow-beings are some of the positive virtues needed for spiritual development. In Vedantic wisdom, Shankara's emphasis on self-realization stems from the eternal philosophy of the integrated life expressed by Lord Krishna in the *Bhagwat Geeta* when he asks Arjuna first to win over the three *gunas* (*Sattwa, Rajas* and *Tamas*) and then to perform action while thus established in being (conscious self). According to *Patanjali*, spiritual development can be easily achieved when man's life is naturally upheld by the five qualities of observance (*Yama*) and five rules of life (*Niyama*) which are as follows

The five *Yama* (qualities of observance) are:

(1) Truthfulness (*Satya*); (2) Non-Violence (*Ahimsa*); (3) Non-Covetousness (*asteya*); (4) Celibacy (*brahmacharya*); (5) Non-acceptance of others; (6) Possessions *(aparigraha)*.

The five rules of life (*Niyama*) are as under:

(1) Purification (*Shaucha*); (2) Contentment (*Santosha*); (3) Austerity (*Tapas*); (4) Study and learning (*Svadhaya*); (5) Devotion to God (*Ishwara pranidhana*).

The different limbs of the body have to be kept fit and strong by various *asanas* (postures) in perfect coordination with the state of transcendental consciousness. The control and tempering of the individual breath is to be achieved through *Pranayama* (breathing exercise for the *Pran*). *Patanjali* included turning away of the senses from the objects (*Pratyahar*) for sense control and *Dharma* (steadiness of mind) through withdrawal of the mind from the realm of the senses. *Patanjali's* exposition of eight-fold *yoga* also recommended meditation (*Dhyana*) for transcending the mental activity to the state of pure consciousness, absolute existence or eternal bliss. The eighth step is the state of transcendental consciousness (*Samadhi*). Spiritual devolopment ultimately leads to the six treasures (*shatsampatti*) which are as under:

(1) *Kshama*—control of mind; (2) *Dama*—Control of senses; (3) *Upasati*—words, thoughts and deeds; (4) *Titikha*—endurance; (5) *Shraddha*—faith; (6) *Samadhanamental*—equilibrium.

Development of national character should be an essential part of our HRD interventions. Spiritual development is a continuous long-term process for an ordinary human being. However, spiritual growth is generally a self-growth through conducive environment and good family and social *sanskaras* can accelerate the process of spiritual growth. Arnold Toynbee has said; "Since we have almost entirely lost this spiritual art of contemplation, it is really another name for the art of living. So now we turn to India. The spiritual gift, that makes Man human, is still alive in Indian souls. Spiritual development can lead to the creation of wisdom-workers."[7] Spiritual development alone can transform the human beings into an integrated personality who is duty-conscious, has intense life-pattern, trully effective in performance and views life and progress cyclically. Spirituality and religion belong to each other but they begin to part company as soon as religion degenerates into ritualism and obscurantism. The goal of spirituality is social and personal transformation.

Swami Rangathananda of the Rama Krishna Mission said, "Nation-building in India can be achieved only when the bricks constituted by our 100 crore people become joined to each other with the cement of renunciation, love and service. The path of renunciation alone can lead our energies in this higher direction-towards realisation of the supreme self." Renunciation is a step forward towards spiritual growth. Meditation is one of the unique pathways to ethical development.

Need for Values and Ethics in Management

There has always been a number of people who cheat, steal, lie, bribe or accept bribes. The problem is one of moral values and moral education, of the individual, of the family, of the school. But there neither is a separate ethics of business nor one is needed.[8] All that is needed is to mete out stiff punishments to those—whether business executives or anyone who yield to temptation. Such things as the employment of call-girls to entertain customers are not matter of ethics but matters of aesthetics. A problem of ethics that is unique to the manager arises from the fact that the manager of institutions are collectively the leadership groups of the society of organisations, although individually a manager is just another fellow employee, a citizen and a neighbour.

The paradoxical situation exists today that many individual businessmen are extremely "religious" in their private lives while in their business, they hardly take account of human sufferings that their actions might cause in society. It is only the moral and ethical conduct, which can resolve the problems in our society. There is a need to draw the *Lakshman Rekha* in business ethics. Ethical and value training is essential for business and management people because it alone can produce balanced and mature managers. Spiritual development has to be basically achieved by the individuals although family *Sanskaras*, social environment and guidance of spiritual guide (*guru*) have vital roles. According to *Bhagwad Geeta*, humility, unpretentiousness, non-injury, forgiveness uprightness, service to the teacher, purity, steadfastness, self-control, indifference to the objects of the senses, absence of egoism, non-attachment, non-identification with son, wife, home and the rest, constant even-mindedness, unswerving devotion to God, consistency in self-knowledge are some of the qualities and values needed to be developed for spiritual development (refer to Chapter XIII-*Slokas* 8-12 of *Bhagawad Geeta*). In Chapter XVI of *Bhagwad Geeta*, Lord Krishna has given an exhaustive list of values, which need to be developed for spiritual development. Fearlessness (*Abhayam*), Purity of heart, steadfastness in devotion to knowledge, charity, restraint of the senses, sacrifice (*Yogna*) study of the religious scriptures (*Swadhyaya*), Asceticism (*Tapas*), uprightness (*Arjavam*), harmlessness, truth, absence of anger, renimeration, peacefulness, absence of crookedness, compassion to beings, non-covetousness, gentleness, modesty, absence of fickle-mindedness, non-violence and harmlessness (*Ahimsa*), truth, even temper and absence of anger (*Akrodh*), Quietude (*Santi*), unmalicious tongue (*apaisuman*), tenderness towards beings, Purity (*soucham*), Fortitude (*Dhriti*), Patience, non-covetousness (*Aloluptvam*), modesty and *sthitipragyta* are some of the recommended values for self-realization and spiritual development. Management *Gurus* world over are now convinced about the severe limitations of the western soulless and mechanical approach. There is a search for spirituo-technical approach. This has become essential to secure perfect harmony of the individual with management objectives through adopting a consciousness approach. So that the innate qualities of individuals as well as groups (springing from finer attributes of human psyche, like spirituality, faith, culture, beliefs, etc.) to attain an equilibrium from which could flow optimum management results.[9] Training and social environment can help individuals in developing above-mentioned values. Such values have universal applications and ensure the greatest good of the greatest numbers. Above referred values have to be instilled in business with a firm conviction that ethics will pay at least in the long run in business and management world. The key task of management is to transform and elevate every act into a sacred process, a spiritual prayer or every step is a pilgrimage. Shri Aurobindo summed up the general theory of work as under: "Make the work you have to do here the means of inner spiritual relish, the divine birth and having become divine, do the divine work as an instrument of the divine."[10] Lord Krishna spoke of *Nishkam Karma* and *Karma Yoga* and it can be termed as transcendental management. The workplace should be transformed into a spiritual and moral gymnasium.

Ethical norms emerge from self-discovery by managers, who have several subtle ways to integrate social cohesion with self-realisation, social responsibilities with individual obligations and individual ethical norms from social morality. In spite of vast difference in various religions, basically ethical norms emerge remarkably identical. In business and management there is a very subtle integration of social and individual values. Ethics is important for business and management and one need not be apologetic or defensive about it. Even while pursing profits in business, one must watch its greater impact on society. The wheels of ethical reprisals are always moving and wrong-doers always get their dues sometime or the other. Every individual has an ethical responsibility and accountability, which he cannot shift or transfer to the organisation or to his superiors or subordinates. Ethics is a matter of execution and action and not of theoretical hair-splitting or ideological discussions. The *summon bonum* of ethical education is individual sensitisation and personal experience. Ethical education requires one to individually and personally apply oneself to every task on hand and find out one's own way to deal with various dilemmas. In areas of human resource development, ethical norms and principles must be followed particularly in matters of promotion, transfers, postings and recruitment. Peter Drucker says; "To be able to manage yourself, you finally have to ask, what are my values. This is not a question of ethics. With respect to ethics, the rules are the same for everybody..." What is ethical behaviour in one kind of behaviour or situation is ethical behaviour in another. But ethics are only part of a value system especially of an organisation's value system."[11] In a climate of liberalisation, when MNC's come, they bring not only massive funds, sophisticated technology, expensive opportunities but also a new culture—indeed a clash of culture, new commercial orientation, new result consciousness and preponderant product concern. At the altar of the new religion of productivity, consumerism and prosperity, let us not sacrifice the man, his values, his cultural ethos and ethics. Let us train and educate Indian managers and businessmen in the ethics and value system of our Vedantic scriptures. We must try to immunise our industry leaders and managers by instilling moral values in them.

Problems in Whistle-blowing

The problems in Whistle-blowing and listening to the inner voice need to be analysed. Ralph Nader and others have listed the following areas for Whistle-blowing:

1. Defective vehicles marketed to unsuspecting customers.
2. Waste of government funds by private contractors.
3. Industrial dumping of pollutants.
4. Discrimination by age, race or sex.
5. Misusing pension funds.
6. Deceptive advertising.
7. Companies and campaign contributions.
8. Adulteration.
9. Government power used for private gains.
10. Non-enforcement of pesticide laws.
11. Corruption.
12. Suppressing of occupational diseases.
13. Monopolist price rigging.[12]

Whistle-blowing is an attempt by an employee or a former employee of an organisation to disclose what he proclaims to be a wrong-doing in or by an organisation, it may be exposing moral violations or unethical practices or may be infringement of certain rules, procedures or instructions of the government. Whistle-blowing is not only permissible but expected when an organisation is harming society or denying justice to the people. Whistle-blowing can be an obligation to society and should not be treated as disloyalty to the organisation which is involved in unethical practices. Many thinkers are in support of Whistle-blowing, as socially desirable and are less concerned in developing public institutions and laws, which could reduce the need for Whistle-blowing. It is necessary to work out strategies on Whistle-blowing and some useful tips are given below:

"1. Identify precisely not only the objectionable activity but also the public interest or interests that is or are threatened and the magnitude of the harm anticipated from non-disclosure.
2. Verify accuracy of your knowledge of the situations.
3. Identify ethical standards as well as laws and regulations that support your decision to blow the Whistle.
4. Develop a plan of action, consider the personal costs and the likely response of allies and antagonists within and outside the organisation.
5. Select an appropriate outside contact."[13]

Code of Conduct for Business People and Managers

According to Peter F. Drucker "Not knowingly to do harm" is the basic rule of professional ethics, the basic rule of an ethics of public responsibility.[14] Business managers still have to learn that it is their job to scrutinise their deeds, words and behaviour to make sure that they do not knowingly do harm to others particularly with respect to (I) executive compensation, e.g., stock options, (II) the use of benefit plans to impose "golden fetters" on people in the company's employment and (III) in their profit rhetoric. Cheating income tax authorities through the device of "after tax compensation" system is also unethical and socially as well as psychologically they knowingly do harm to the society. According to Peter Drucker what managers need to accept as legitimate authority is a principle of morality. They need to ground their authority in a moral commitment, which at the same time expresses the purpose and character of the organisation. The Federation of Indian Chambers of Commerce and Industry (FICCI) held in July, 1995, a national level declaration on "Norms of Business Ethics" and have promulgated the following norms for the business community:

1. To ensure quality of articles manufactured, processed or sold and to adhere to specified standards.
2. Not to manufacture, store or sell adulterated goods.
3. To maintain accuracy in weights and measurements of goods offered for sale.
4. To support free distribution of goods and avert creation of artificial shortage.
5. Not to deal knowingly in spurious or smuggled products.
6. To avoid publishing misleading advertisements.
7. To ensure that warranty of a product or service is based on adequate data or test.
8. To conform to specified standard or accepted norms for ensuring safety of products. Date of manufacture, expiry dates and contents etc. are some of the requirements of law.
9. To provide effective after sale service for consumer durable.
10. To encourage setting up of consumer affair cells in industrial enterprises and chambers of commerce and industries associations.

The Punjab, Haryana and Delhi Chamber of Commerce (PHD), located at Delhi organised a seminar on "Ethics is Good Business." Important features of the code of ethics promulgated by the PHD chamber read as follows:

1. Business must maintain highest standards of behaviour so that their actions and decisions result in the benefit of industry, employees, consumers, shareholders and society.
2. Goods and services must conform to the commitment promised to customers. Business must be realistic and truthful in stating claims.

3. Customers must be given best possible service and treated with respect and fairness.
4. Business must understand and respect the needs, concerns and welfare of the community and society. It should use knowledge and experience for upgradation of quality of life. All business endeavours must combine the qualities of private excellence for public good.
5. Best way of promoting high standards of business practices is through self-regulations.

The code has been designed as an instrument of self-regulation to serve as voluntary guideline towards better quality of life and higher standards of business practices. It should be realised that "customer is not an intruder; he is the reason for your existence." (Mahatma Gandhi). Now the climate has started changing and at the global stage, there is talk of improving "business ethics." Ethical standards impose a measure that goes beyond the standards imposed by law. The real value of an ethical code is that it represents a more explicit and permanent statement of good conduct than implicit expectations.[15]

Another groups of businessmen have spelt out seven principles for projecting the ethical image:

1. Equity before stake holders.
2. Support for innovations and justice.
3. Beyond letter of law towards spirit of trust.
4. Inter-firms cooperation and not increase of competition.
5. Multinational trade beyond isolation towards a world community.
6. Respect environment beyond protection towards enhancement.
7. Avoid illicit project and work towards peace.

These principles were worked at in 1994 at XLRI and are called the Caux Principles. There are very big gaps between pious resolves and application. The basic difficulty with codes of ethics is that they do not establish priorities among the various norms. The priorities are the true values of a firm. It's difficult to convert ethical vision of organisational leaders into operational rules for the managers. There have been many cases of the corporate scapegoat. Sometimes when a breach of ethics occurs there is shifting of blame between the top management and the operational level of managers. If the breach of ethics takes the form of breach of law, this mutual mud slinging is done in public. The concept of an ethical ombudsman is a deep-rooted feature of the Indian normative ethics and can be described as the *Raj Rishi* (a sage who is a king) or the Raj Guru (a sage who is also the teacher to the king) concept.[16] Not paying correct taxes by a company is also unethical behaviour.

Basic Issues Regarding Ethics in Management for Indian Managers

Moral conflicts are often inevitable because the definition of right and wrong is highly diverse and large differences in personal values exist.[17] According to Partha S. Ghosh, a consultant on strategic management, liberal market economy requires three Es: Ethics, Education and Efficacy. In India all the three components are badly lacking. India has failed to take a hard look at cultural attributes—work ethics, intellectual honesty, business transparency, willingness to be fair and honest, and lack of national pride.

Corruption is one of the biggest issues in the business world. Corruption can be dealt with in a multi-pronged manner including activism, free press, better laws, deregulations and effective criminal justice system. There are some basic issues in management in the context of Indian business. Some of the following issues need great consideration:

1. How do we teach ethical behaviour to our young managers ?
2. How do we observe ethics in advertising and promotion of sales ?
3. How do we deal with ethnic, regional, religious, cultural expectations, behaviour patterns and needs in our

business dealings?

4. How do we ensure our public relation departments are credible in the eyes of the public and our clients ?
5. How do we handle a re-engineering situation involving down-sizing?
6. How do we face activists and environmental regulators?
7. Is lobbying for political, legal and administrative changes ethically desirable ?
8. How should we be even-handed in dealing with petty and major corruption within the organisation?
9. Are the codes of conduct mere facades or are they vital instruments to effectively run creative and dynamic organizations?
10. What bold working arrangements have been made in the organisation to eliminate gender disadvantages or gender bias?
11. How can we distinguish between tax planning, tax avoidance and evasion and how far should we be transparent in our tax returns in India and in foreign lands ?
12. How do we handle the onslaught of copyright and patent violations on the one hand and ancient traditions of knowledge as a common property ?
13. How do we handle hegemonic cultural imperialism in the guise of ethics in our dealing with business from developed countries ?
14. What do we do when the government is unable to protect us from terrorists, insurgents or organized mafia gangs ? Should we be prepared to pay protection money to unlawful insurgents/terrorists and mafia gangs.
15. When diverse cultures may operate under different set of community norms, how will you operate as a leader of a multi-national business organisation ?

There can be many more such complex issues, which need to be resolved with a given set of ethical values. Each issue needs a debate, a discussion and indepth analysis.

Factors Responsible for Ethical and Moral Erosion in India

Some important factors contributing to this moral erosion are as follows:

1. Explosion of public expenditure in India due to economic planning.
2. Over-population and increase in younger age group people.
3. Resource scarcity in relation to demand.
4. Laxity in terms of accountability, monitoring and responsibility due to the creation of "soft state".
5. Nexus between politicians, bureaucrats, businessmen and middlemen and percolation of pollution of politics in every aspect of citizen life.
6. Failure of leadership and socio-religious reformers to inspire and fire people's righteousness.
7. Criminalisation of politics and social deviance as a way of life.
8. Failure to inculcation of moral values through schools, families, religious institutions.
9. Tolerance of crime by society and failure of social control systems.
10. Sacrificing of spiritualism at the altar of materialism due to western influence.
11. Rise of "consumerist culture" and vulgar display of money power by the rich.
12. Technological invasions and rise in T.V. advertisements and ill-effect of cinema on young minds.
13. Corruption at all levels and rule of speed money.
14. Near collapse of criminal justice system and delayed justice.

15. Ineffective policing and lack of social control devices.
16. Rise in terrorism, insurgency and Naxalism and its negative impact on young minds.
17. Role of pressure groups in democratic society and its negative impact.
18. Lack of religious teachings and absence of ideal role models due to secular character of our society.
19. Plural society and absence of correct value system in legal, economic and social systems.
20. Defective Taxation system and loopholes in tax payment systems.

Need for Ethical Norms

Spiritual and ethical development is felt necessary today in view of the clashes of personalities, succession feuds, top-level manipulations and boardroom fights in the corporate sector. The question of values and ethical principles faces several challenges from the rapidly changing environment at all levels—the individual, the family, the society, the organisation and the nation. In the corporate sector there is need to bring character development to the centre of our HRD programmes and then only will the quest for true, unsparing excellence can have an enduring base. Management of the senses through sense-control (*Indriya Nigrah*) is a pre-requisite for effective and wise leadership roles in the corporate world. Ego-management and purification of mind can be critical tonics for vitalizing the organisational transformations. Indian organisations can bring human resource development through ethical and moral awakening. Spiritual and ethical growth of human resources can be ensured through the practice of the *Yoga Sutras* of *Patanjali*. For the growth of human resources, the human beings have to evolve the mind, the intelligence and emotions as well as the physical aspects. "Ethical violations occur where individuals, organisations, professionals and societies fail to deal with basic values like honesty, justice and a clear definition of right or wrong. This leads to choices and decisions based on rationality, market imperatives and economic-optimizations rather than ethical integrity."[18] There is a very high degree of agreement among societies, corporations, legal systems and individuals regarding an appropriate ethical paradigm. Blind and greedy profit-seeking and the rhetoric of profit maximisation and profit motive are not only anti-social, they are immoral.[19] Manager of an autonomous institution, a company, must accept that he is a public man and must accept the moral responsibility of the organisation. Business ethics is crucial for sustained business development. Business ethics deals with policy considerations founded on an organisation's values and core beliefs. Managerial ethics treats the managerial response at the time of decision-making and decision executing when faced with a dilemma. This distinction is important and subtle. Values are based on one's innate belief system and therefore it is a thought-based concept. Ethics are behavioural norms or patterns that spring from one's view of good and bad, right and wrong. It is an activity based concept.[20]

Ethical Values and a Framework for Managerial Action

Shri R. Venkatesan, principal economist, at the National Council of Applied Economic Research finds it intriguing that many successful business executives, who can identify their organisational mission, do not think about the purpose of life. However, during the last three decades, there has been a great resurgence of groups giving a spiritual dimension to management—be it a Christian, Islamic, Japanese, Chinese or Vedantic or just secular meditation technique to inculcate and develop spiritual consciousness among business people and corporate managers. The revolutionary "balanced score card" was developed for business management by Robert S. Kaplan and David P. Nortan. All managers and business people need a scorecard approach for themselves. There is an urgent requirement for spiritual and ethical development of corporate leaders and business people. Teachings of Indian Vedantic thinkers can come to their immediate rescue. The Vedantic version with managerial and corporate Ethico-Morality must have spirituality as its core content and can build up value driven management with every worker being *Nishkam Karma*

Yogi[21]. Ancient Vedic invocations of India have essentially been global in their value-premises and universal applicability. *Lok Samastat Sukhimo bhavamtu* (may the entire earth find happiness) has been a philosophical concept of *Bhagwat Geeta*. There are four different levels of ethical intensity namely, global, societal, corporate and individual. Human value and context specific values can be easily identified because human values are beyond corporate, societal, national or international morality and are anchored in the wisdom of humanity as identified by ancient Indian saints. There are certain action parameters, which should constantly inspire the people to perform their duties in accordance with those given parameters. The ideal of ethical relativism is becoming increasingly inadequate and irrelevant in resolving ethical conflicts of contemporary international business. For entire humanity, there are spiritual and moral spaces to explore and adding spiritual dimensions to a scientific frame of mind is becoming slowly acceptable. We need not be afraid to explore new territories and areas of human knowledge and excellence. Austerities, forbearance, self-discipline, purity and constant meditation can help us understand the supper-conscious realities and transcendental knowledge. *Patanjali* eight-fold *yoga* is a practical guideline for us to attain self-realisation. The matrix showing framework of globally applicable ethics is given in the figure below. The quest for spiritual realization must lead us to acknowledge the vastness and limitlessness of phenomena beyond the scope of human comprehension.

Figure Matrix Showing Framework of Globally Applicable Ethical Values and Action- Plan

Vedantic Tenets for *Dharma*

Universal Ethics

(A) Respect for all religions
(B) Every one has immense potentiality (*Tal Tvam Asi*)
(C) Holistic Advait concept of universe
(D) Subjective elements are more powerful than objective ones mind>matter
(E) *Patanjali* eight-step *yoga* approach to life.
(F) Goals of life *Purusharth—Dharma, Arth, Kama and Moksha.*
(G) Truth and honesty
(H) *Nishkam Karma*

(I) *Purity*

Levels of Ethical Intensity

Level One—Global

(A) Human Duties
(B) Concern for environment
(C) Technology transfer integrity

Level Two—Societal

(A) Cultural respect
(B) Intellectual Rights respect
(C) Legal, political and economic propriety

Level Three—Corporate

(A) Market Integrity
(B) Social responsibility
(C) Corporate governance

Level Four—Individual

(A) Bribery/corruption
(B) Information Ethics
(C) Violation of personal norms
(D) Strive for spiritual development

Human Values

(A) Moral imagination
(B) Purity of purpose
(C) Accountability and transparency
(D) Global responsibility
(E) Genuine cooperation
(F) Universal brotherhood and respect for life

Context Specific Values

(A) Host country/home country interest
(B) Business culture
(C) Competitive imperatives
(D) Corporate strategy and practices
(E) Respect other cultures/values

Action Parameters

(A) Global citizenship duties
(B) Generation and communication of Ethical Values
(C) Moral free space
(D) Ethical boundary
(E) Legal/market codes
(F) Reporting responsibility
(G) Integrity in information management
(H) Internal ethical consistency
(I) International codes of conduct
(J) Professional code
(K) Follow Vedantic approach to life

There are saints, mystics, prophets, sages and *jivanmukhta* people who have already trodden the path with great success. *Bhagwat Geeta* and Vedantic wisdom provide pathways to achieve excellence and transcendental knowledge. Teachings of *Bhagwat Geeta* and *Patanjali, Yoga Sutras* prescribe the path to the ultimate emancipation of human beings and for the self-realization of the individuals. Spirituality is part of the information explosion which we are experiencing as a part of our technological progress. We can even download the *Geeta* on the computer, a large number of people are at least giving the benefit of doubt to spirituality. Swami Vivekanand, Swami Dayanand Saraswati, Swami Chinmayananda are among the few *Vedanta* teachers who pioneered the ethical teachings based on ancient Indian scriptures. Vedantic thoughts offer an ethico, moral general theory of *Nishkam Karma* and the doctrine of *Karma*. Even Toynbee has expressed its essence in the following works. "The ethical level of a society at a particular moment depends on the state of *Karma*—account of each of the participants in society..... .The most important objective for a human being, both for his own sake and for the sake of society, is to improve his *Karma*"[22] The Biblical pronouncement "You reap as you sow" captures this very truth of ethico-moral existence.

Ethical Education and Role of Leaders/Managers

Bob Haas, one of the pioneers of ethical management believes that "values do make the corporation. I do not want to work for a company that is not ethical, that pollutes the environment, that charges the consumer unfair prices, treats its employees unfairly, exploits child labour or does any similar thing. Good companies must pay adequate attention to their employees and must have a commitment to values.[23] In current marketing trends, there is a growing emphasis on ethical marketing behaviour. In a survey article on the teaching of both ethical awareness and ethical reasoning to future managers conducted by J. Weber in 1989-90 the general conclusion was overwhelmingly positive that ethics can be taught[24] In the spring, 1991 course outline on Business Ethics and Corporate Social Policy processed by Edwin Epstein at the university of

California, Berkeley Campus, a final caveat had the operating premise that modes of ethical analysis in a business context can be taught. In India, Indian Institute of Management, Calcutta had been doing pioneering work under the leadership of Prof. S. K. Chakraborty from 1983 onwards in the areas of ethics and values, deriving from Indian Vedantic thoughts. In 1992 and 1993 IIM, Bangalore started some credit courses on ethics and value systems. JBIMS, Jamshedpur and T.A. Pai Management Institute, Manipal have been offering compulsory second year courses in this subject for quite a few years. It is disturbing and alarming to note that findings of several earlier studies indicate that ethical standards of business students are lower than those of business practitioners".[25] According to Peter F. Drucker, value conflicts are not limited to business organisation, value conflicts crop up in all organisations and situations. James R. Fisher Jr. says," My assessment is that we have lost our moral compass and our way because we are too full of ourselves and have forgotten what gave us purpose, passion, patience and profundity. The drug culture is a symptom of a leaderless society, not a cause..... Leadership starts with self leadership that is a moral compass which gives clear readings of north, south, east and west.[26] In every organisation the leaders must attract best minds and create a sense of ownership in them, not just by stock options but through spiritual and emotional engagement. Successful managers use all their strength by recognizing, developing and utilizing the physical, mental, ethical and spiritual talents of their subordinates.[27] India's challenge is two-fold today; we have to create a concrete model to surpass the western ones in areas like management, economics, politics and spiritual development. The *Vedanta* and *Bhagwat Geeta* can be the basis for creating this unique model. Secondly we have to create an international consciousness and spread the wisdom of our scriptures around the world. We must try and create a sound value system where we have spread people in public activity, in politics, in business, in management who can serve as role models for others. Spiritual enlightenment, and upholding of *Dharma* alone can give us that knowledge whereby the unheard becomes heard and what is not comprehended becomes comprehensive; what is not known becomes known. No school or university can teach you spirituality, nor can they make you well versed in scriptures. A person's inner yearning for the truth will alone lead him to the path of spiritual growth.

Guidelines for Dealing with Ethical Dilemmas

Even in the present day global economy, there can be some guidelines for dealing with ethical dilemmas. Some of the important guidelines can be as under:

1. One has to set personal example. There are often people who see un-ethical behaviour in others but are unable to admit the same tendencies in themselves. The way you can establish ethics in others is by setting personal example.
2. Create a meaningful definition of honesty.
3. Assess your ethical position and moral climate of the organisation.
4. Formal seminars, workshops, discussions and training sessions are good vehicles to seek agreement on ethical issues.
5. Build ethical thinking into daily activities and have discussions about ethics on the factory floor, in casual conversations and in staff meetings.
6. Establish a legend and establish honesty and integrity in the company culture with motivational inspiring stories.
7. Be willing to pay the price to your ethical conduct.
8. Reward ethical behaviour-reward whistle—blowers and persons who stand for ethical conduct.
9. Designate an ethical conscience.[28]
10. Create an atmosphere where each individual will get an opportunity for the realization of his highest ethical personality.
11. Promotion of genuine public interest through empowerment of people and accountability of individuals for

their actions.

12. Restructuring of the criminal justice system and quick disposal of cases of unethical behaviour at all levels.
13. Emphasise character building and ethical conduct during various training programmes and HRD interventions—critical focus should be on inculcation of moral values and generation of an environment where norm-displacement is abhorred and there is a total social intolerance of corruption, unethical behaviour or compromise of integrity.
14. Active vigilance against unethical conduct—one useful practical method of putting some curb on unethical conducts would be to have active vigilance at different levels in all organizations and citizen vigilant groups at district, state and central levels.
15. Need for character—building measures—what is needed is imparting of eternal character building values at the educational level, as well as ethics in various HRD programmes at various levels. Resurrection efforts are needed through character-building by way of rejuvenation of ethical teachings in educational curriculum, control of visual media to arrest spread of vulgarity and obscenity, raising a group of morals managers, curbs on culture of permissiveness and materialism, transparency in working and accountability at all levels can go a long way in establishing an ethical society.
16. Need for an integrated holistic approach—society should be based on *Dharma*—a code of conduct for human behaviour which ensures morality and ethical norms of highest standards—society should be governed by the Vedantic principle of welfare of the many, the happiness of the many. Religious teachings of major religions should be imparted regularly through electronic and mass media for promoting ethical values and essential unity of all religions.

Concluding Remarks

There is today widespread need for integration of western management skills and systems with Indian cultural ethos and value system. Vedantic ethical vision can provide complete application to managerial and corporate ethical morality. It can teach the contemporary society about the individual leadership, transformation of the work ethos and ethics in organizational conduct. Today there is a need for value driven management which alone can be a remedy to the havoc wrought by the consumerist culture of the modern times. Therefore ethical and spiritual dimensions of HRD need utmost attention in contemporary society. HRD professionals must emphasize ethical and spiritual dimensions of human development during various HRD interventions. Business organizations and corporations have a legal status and are amenable to moral and ethical evaluation. Managers and business people can not overstep universal values like honesty, responsibility etc. in favour of company goals under the argument that personal values are inappropriate as standards for corporate decisions. For managers and decision makers, a general check list of following ethical questions can provide useful introspection:

1. Does my decision treat me or my company as an exception to a convention that I must trust others to follow ?
2. Would I repel customers by telling them?
3. Would I repel qualified job applicants by telling them?
4. Have I been cliquish?
5. Would I prefer to avoid the consequences of this decision?
6. Did I avoid any one of the questions by telling myself that I would get away with it."[30]

Two very practical tips for deciding the criteria for taking ethical decisions have been suggested." If you are ashamed to tell your father or mother that you have been doing the wrong thing." Secondly, "If you feel that you will lower yourself in the estimation of your children by an action, then too the action is wrong." These two introspective statements can give good guidance to the managers when ethical dilemmas arise in decision-making. *Taittiriya Upanishad* counsels: "Whenever you are in doubt, as to what your duty is, and what conduct is appropriate, consult learned masters of religion and scholarship. The chief aim of HRD should be the formation of character and development of a harmonious personality. The goal of our HRD efforts should therefore be to generate a climate in the organizations where ethical decisions are taken and value system is considered important aspect of managerial competence. It is not important to know what is right and ethical, it is more important to do what is right and ethical. This will need clarity of concepts and strong will-power and ability to do what is right and ethical. Integrative ethical management can be seen as a continuous process of establishing ethical awareness, developing ethical judgement and following it with ethical conduct. Meditation and Yoga can help people in ethical development and becoming *Sthithiprayna*." HRD programmers should be designed to fire people's imagination about values and help them to think clearly about principles and how to apply these principles to the real world of management.[31] "Never hesitate to follow the path of truth. Never be reticent in following the path or virtue. Never neglect prosperity, or tread sinful ways. Do not be inactive in the path of progress. Never be lazy in studying and preaching the *Vedas*. Never neglect your duties towards the gods and the forefathers."[32] Says the famous convocation address—given by the *Guru* to his pupil who has completed his education and stands at the gateway of life in the world. India must educate all adult citizens about the essential oneness of spiritual truth, develop correct core values for ethical conduct. To attain lasting mental peace and happiness, the *Mundaka Upnishad* asks the seeker to utilise *AUM* as a bow, fix the soul as an arrow sharpened with meditation and have *Brahman* as the target.

REFERENCES

1. Kehemendra Upadhyaya, "Inner Space—Discourse on Religious and Philosophy "Kundalini awakening, *Times of India* 29th July

1998.

2. Rabindra Nath Tagore, *A Vision of India's History* (Calcutta: Visva Bharati 1988), pp. 44-45.
3. S.K. Chakraborty, *Ethics in Management,* Oxford University Press, Delhi, 1996, p. 276.
4. Dr. Krishna Mohan Mathur, "Vedantic Wisdom and Contemporary Management, Indian Journal of Public Administrations, January-March 1999, Vol. XLV, No. 1, p. 6.
5. Swami Gambhirananda, *Katha Upanishad* (Calcutta Advaita Ashram, 1980) Verse iii- 3, pp. 64-65.
6. For further details see *Swami Vivekananda—Collected Works,* Vol. I, Rajyoga-Verses II-29-32, pp. 260-61.
7. S.K. Chakraborty, *Managerial Effectiveness and Quality of Work-life Indian Insight,* Tata McGraw Hill Publishing Ltd., New Delhi, 1987, p. 20.
8. Peter F. Drucker, *Management Tasks, Responsibilities, Practices,* Allied Publishers Ltd., New Delhi, Reprint 1996, p. 366
9. G. P. Gupta, *Management of Consciousness—A Spirituo, Technical Approach.* Excel Books, New Delhi, 1999.
10. Shri Aurbindo, *Right Attitude in Work,* Pondicherry, Shri Aurobindo Society, April, 1991-94.
11. Peter F. Drucker, *Managing Oneself—Management Challenges for the 21st Century* (Aarper Collins, May 1999), Also Harvard Business Review, March, April, 1999, p. 69
12. Ralph Nader, P. J. Petkas and Kate Blackwell (1972), *Whistle-Blowing—A Report on the Conference of Professional Responsibility,* Bantam Books, New York, 1972.
13. Ralph Nader, P.J. Petkas and Kate Blackwell 1972; *Whistle-Blowing.*
14. Peter F. Drucker, *Management Task, Responsibilities, Practices.* Allied Publishers Ltd., New Delhi, Reprint 1996, p. 369.
15. James Bowman, *Ethical Issues for the Public Manager* in William Eddy *(Ed.) Handbook of Organisational Management,* 1983; p. 79
16. R.C. Sekhar, *Ethical Choices in Business-Response Books,* New Delhi, 1997, p. 148.
17. James Bowman, *Ethical Issues for the Public Manager* in William Eddy (Ed) *Handbook of Organisational Management*—New York, Marce Dekker 1983; p. 73-74.
18. S. K. Chakraborty, *Ethics in Management: Vedantic Perspectives;* Delhi-Oxford University Press, 1996.

19. Peter F. Drucker, *Management Task, Responsibilities, Practices* Allied Publishers Ltd., New Delhi, 1996, p. 810.

20. S. Sadri, D. S. Dastoor and S. Jayashree, *The Theory and Practice of Managerial Ethics*, Jaico Publishers, New Delhi, 1999.

21. Dr. Krishna Mohan Mathur, *Towards Effective Management—Pathways to Excellence*, Gyan Publishing House, New Delhi, 1999.

22. A. J. Toynbee and D. Ikeda: *Choose Life*, Oxford University Press, 1987; Delhi, p. 325.

23. "Corporate Dossier—Bringing Business to Life," Sudeshna Sen and Aruna Vaidyanathan. *The Economic Times*, 28 January-4 February 2000.

24. J. Weber, "Measuring the Importance of Teaching Ethics to Future Managers", *Journal of Business Ethics* No. 99, 1990; p. 187.

25. J. R. Harris, "A Comparison of the Ethical Values of Business Faculty and students"—*Business and Professional Ethics Journal*, Vol. 7 No. 1; p. 41.

26. James R. Fisher Jr., *"Leaderless Leadership."*, Executive Excellence, January, 1999; p. 5

27. Zia Ziglar—*Over the Top.*

28. For similar views refer to Quin G. McKay, "Play by which Rules?" *World Executive's Digest*, August, 1988; p. 66

29. Grover Starling *Managing Public Sector*, Chicago, The Doresy Press, 1986; pp. 146, 147.

30. MR. Hyman, R. Skipper and T. Tansey, "Ethical Codes are not Enough"—*Business Horizons*, March, April 1990; p. 17.

31. For similar views refer to James Bowman, *Ethical Issues for the Public Manager* in William Eddy (Ed) Handbook of Organisation Management, New York, 1983; p. 76.

32. Swami Gambhirananda, *The Taittiriya Upanishad*, Advaita Ashram, Calcutta, 1981.

3

A Macro-Approach to Human Resource Development and the Indian Education Policy

"Education is the Manifestation of Perfection already in man", said Swami Vivekanand. Education alone can help achieving perfection or at least the fullest development of human resources in a developing, plural, democratic, and liberal society.

Human resources development is like a flower in bloom to be experienced but only gardener knows how to make it bloom. Human resource development is a meta value, a set of guiding values for man in social setting, an inclusive concept which is conducive to initiative, fair play and self-development in a healthy work environment, in a dynamic society. The HRD activities generally centre around the basic core areas of the need to ensure the availability of trained, competent and motivated employees, who have the required skills, attitudes and knowledge to cope with the challenges and opportunities of the 21st century. Human Resource Development is widely understood "as a system of frameworks, methods and processes aimed at, systematically discovering, developing and using a person's capabilities at the fullest extent both for individual and organisational growth and well-being."[1]

Human Resources Development can be studied both from macro as well as micro angles. The whole concept and range of HRD has undergone a vast change over the last several decades. HRD is the dynamic process of increasing and updating the knowledge, skills, attitudes and competencies of the individuals to make them more efficient, effective and productive. The massiveness of the social, economic and political changes implies the need for careful allround planning and control of resources at all levels. Viewing man as a human asset would normally cause us to reconceive responsibilities for his development in several ways.[2] Concomitant with the changing social, political and economic environment, there is new shift about the conceptualization of manpower planning and the development of human resources through teaching-learning process.[3] Human Resource Development as a new ministry was formed in September, 1985 with Education, Culture, Arts, Youth Affairs, Sports and Women Welfare as part of the ministry. The conceptual frame of the ministry consists in building up allround personality of human beings. India focussed its attention for five decades on non-human variables, with the hope that these will contribute to the development of the nation and benefit the people, but today we stand disillusioned. India's strategy has to change if we have to take nation forward. We have to lay maximum stress on human assets, make human resources productive, committed and dedicated to the cause of national development. One of the primary tasks of planning should be the harnessing of the country's abundant human resources and improving their capabilities for development with the help of educational skills and knowledge. Education and training facilities will have to be organised for categories of manpower where critical shortages have been identified and in the formation of new skills which are needed to meet the needs of the new environment.

There is acute shortage of qualified and trained professionals in many fields. It has been observed that manpower planning and human resources development has been defective and unplanned. "There is acute shortage of trained electricians, mechanics, fitters and other technicians in the country on one hand and lot of unemployed people on the other hand. The basis of any development is not dams and power stations and industries, but the people who are going to build those dams and run those industries."[4] The concept of development can be broadly defined as both the formal and informal processes by which individuals develop their knowledge, skills, values and attitudes. Development of persons to their maximum potential and the conservation of talent are basic to the human resource development concept. Education is both an ingredient and an investment of human resource development. Human resource development implies development of knowledge, skills, attitudes, values, physical fitness, health and moral character of all men and women and every child of the society. No country can progress without investment in its people.[5] Countries of Europe and Japan which were decimated during the World War II rose to become great economic powers within a short period of time only by the strength of their human resources, discipline, high national character and hard work of the citizens. "This is the time when we must really think about building our biggest resource and our biggest resource today is our people. Today the population may appear our biggest liability, because we are not using it, we are not developing it. But we must change this liability and make it our biggest strength and our biggest resource."[6] Human Resource Development can only come about with a major thrust on education which aims at the development of the mind and development of the human beings. Human Resources Development is a strategy to transform human resources inputs into outputs. The inputs are the people-individuals, groups and the total human educational process of educating people to convert them into acquiring, developing and disciplined people. Human resources harnessing at national level involves not only knowledge, skills and attitudes but also factors like personal dignity and status, ego satisfaction, social participation, psychological processes of motivation group dynamics and team work.[7]

Education develops capital in its multi-dimensional facets.

Human Capital consists of three type of capitals-Intellectual capital (knowledge, skills and expertise), social capital (social relationship network) and emotional capital (resilience for taking action and emotional aspects of human life). Education is a strategy for human development. Education is the core of human development. It can change population into our strength and assets. Overall social capabilities of a nation depend on the level of education of the people which in turn is supposed to determine the knowledge, skills, aptitudes and values of its citizens. This also implies that knowledge, skills, aptitudes and values which the system of education endeavours to develop among the people have a close relationship with national needs and aspirations. An integrated concept of human resource development becomes most useful in the concept of national development. The approach to the seventh five year plan (1985-90) identified that one of the primary tasks must be the harnessing of the country's abundant human resources and improving their capacities for the development with equity. "The persons themselves are the wealth; not gold and silver. The true veins of wealth are purple—and not in Rock but in Flesh. The final consummation of all wealth is in producing as many as possible full breathed, bright eyed and happy-hearted human being.[8] Human Resources Development can be viewed both from macro as well as micro angles. Keeping in view the macro approach to human resource development of the country the Education Policy should have the following objectives :

(a) Make use of untapped human resources;

(b) Improve Human Resource capabilities;

(c) Development of Human Resources with equity;

(d) Alleviation of poverty by providing adequate means of livelihood to the economically weaker section of the society;

(e) Reductions of the disparity of income and wealth;

(f) Improving productivity and creative ability of the H.R.;

(g) Socio-economic development of the country by creating a new work ethos;

(h) Release latent power of women and youth.[9]

Development of human resources implies development of an acquisition of capabilities—Technical, Managerial, Human-behaviour and conceptual. HRD philosophy values human beings and promotes their allround development.

Indian Education Policy makers had a clear vision of the future HRD needs of the country even in the early sixties. The Indian Institutes of Management, Calcutta and Ahmedabad were started in 1962. By the early seventies, Indian Administrative officers were given management training and management concepts were brought into the training institutions of other public systems such as police, income tax and postal services. The Adiministrative Reforms Commission of 1967 emphasised the importance of better systems of training and development of public servants. Government of India established administrative reforms and later opened a personnel department to monitor HRD activities. In 1985 Ministry of HRD was set up. The national policy on education, 1986 (NPE) was passed by the Parliament in May, 1986 and the Programme of Action (POA) was passed in August, 1986. "Challenge of Education—A policy perspective" was an important report brought out by the Ministry of Human Resources Development in August, 1985 as a status report on education and as background material for provoking a nationwide debate, leading to the formulation of the New Education Policy in due course of time. The National Policy on Education, 1986 is a valuable document and aims at intensifying the nation—wide effort in Human Resource Development with Education playing its multifaceted role. The programme of action (1986) has identified the following areas for implementation of the National Policy of Education on priority basis.

(a) Making the system work, and providing quality education to the people;

(b) Decentralisation of management and establishment of district boards of education, district institutes of education and training (D.I.E.T.) provision of autonomy and establishing accountability of institutions, systems and teachers.

(c) Working out the details, mechanisms, funding arrangements for the national system of education; for the development of Indian people;

(d) Manpower planning and demand forecasting, for strategic human resource development;

(e) Media and educational technology with special reference to adult education, non-formal education, open and continuing education;

(f) Development and periodic review of curricula and teaching-learning process;

(g) Strengthening the data base; monitoring and evaluation system.

Education planning has to be closely linked to manpower planning by setting up mechanisms for assessing the needs of the industry, commerce, professional services, science, and agriculture in the context of the technological trends and growth strategies of the nations. In India no statutory agency or organization has either the capacity or the responsibility to undertake the kind of exercise required even in quantitative terms, to link long-term planning of education to match developmental and human resource needs in the country. The major challenge before educational planners is to devise an educational system that would, on the one hand meet the growing demand for secondary and higher education and on the other ensure that the objective of qualitative viability does not get diluted. Most salient features of National Policy on Education—can be briefly enumerated as below:

(1) The concept of National System of Education implies that upto a given level all students, irrespective of caste, creed, location or sex, have access to education of a comparable quality.

(2) It envisages a common education structure of 10+2+3 years for all parts of the country.

(3) The National System of Education will be based on a national curricular frame which contains a common core along with other components that are flexible. The common core will include the history of India's freedom struggle, the constitutional obligations and other contents essential to nurture national identity.

(4) The Nation as a whole will assume the responsibility of providing resources support for implementing programmes of educational transformation, reducing disparities, universalisation of elementary education, adult literacy, by sharing of responsibility between the Union Government and the states in a meaningful partnership.

(5) The new policy will lay special emphasis on the removal of disparity and to equalise educational opportunities by attending to the special needs of women, scheduled castes, scheduled tribes, handicapped and other educationally backward sections and areas.

(6) A full integration of childcare and pre primary education will be brought about, both as a feeder and a strengthening factor for primary education and for human resource development in general. The whole nation must pledge itself to the eradication of illiteracy, particularly in the 15-35 age group.

(7) Reorganisation of education at different stages will be ensured and highest priority will be given to solving the problem of children dropping out of school.

(8) A phased drive symbolically called "Operation blackboard"—will be undertaken to improve the primary school level education all over the country.

(9) The introduction of systematic well-planned and rigorously implemented programmes of vocational education is crucial in the proposed educational reorganisation.

(10) Pace setting schools, symbolically called "Navodaya" will be established on a given pattern at each district level. The broad aims will be to serve the objectives of

excellence, coupled with equity and social justice. (with reservation for SCs and STs), to promote national integration by providing opportunities to talented children, largely rural, from different parts of the country to live and learn together, free of charge, to develop their full potential and most important to becomes catalysts of a nationwide programme of school improvement.

(11) Higher education, in the context of the unprecedented explosion of knowledge, has to becomes dynamic as never before, constantly entering unchartered areas. An effort will be made to encourage the setting up of national research facilities within the University system, with proper forms of autonomous management and coordinated research. A National body covering higher education in general and agriculture, medical, technical, legal and other professional fields will be set up. Open University system will be initiated in order to augment opportunities for higher education and distance learning will be encouraged.

(12) A beginning will be made in delinking degrees from jobs in selected areas. Technical and Management education will be reorganised and expanded to cater for growing needs of industry, trade, agriculture and other professional services. The All India Council for Technical Education will be vested with statutory authority for planning, formulation and the maintenance of norms, monitoring and evaluation.

(13) New Education Policy will make education a forceful tool for the cultivation of social and moral values. Such value education should help eliminate obscurantism, religious fanaticism, violence, superstition and fatalism.

(14) A nationwide infrastructure for physical education, sports and games will be built into the educational edifice. *Yoga* will receive special attention.

(15) The methods of recruiting teachers will be recognised to

ensure merit, objectivity and conformity with special and functional requirements. The new programmes of teacher-education will emphasise continuing education and the need for teachers to meet the thrusts envisaged in the new educational policy. District Institute of Education and Training (DIET) will be established with the capacity to organise pre-service and in-service courses for elementary school teachers and the personnel working in formal and adult education.

(16) Advisory board of education at national and state levels will be established to review educational development and monitor implementation of policies. Indian Education Service will be established to bring a national perspective. The District Boards of education are upto the higher secondary level.

(17) Education will be treated as a crucial area of investment for national human resources development and survival and government will invest six per cent of the national income for education.

(18) The evaluation process and the examination reforms will be suitably modified by introducing semester system and use of grades in place of marks.

New Education Policy has really not been implemented even upto sixty per cent and many resolutions have only remained pious wishes and policies. Education is still suffering from bureaucratic red-tapism. For example, even for starting a secondary school at Delhi, you have to suffer 34 bottlenecks and clearances in the form of school rules. (*Business Today*, June 7, 1999).

National Policy for Children—Government of India adopted a national policy for children (1974) and its commitment for full physical, mental and social development of children is reflected in successive five year plans. The national plan of action has been worked out keeping in mind the needs, rights and aspirations of 300 million children of the country and set a quantifiable time dimension to India's charter of action for children by 2000 A.D. The priority areas in the NPA are health, nutrition, education, water, sanitation and environment. In 1975-76 integrated child development services (ICDS) was launched to improve the nutritional and health status of vulnerable groups including pre-school children, pregnant mothers, and nursing mothers. Under the ICDS scheme till 1992 there were 1.66 crore beneficiaries of this programme and by 1996 there were 2.41 crore beneficiaries.

Our present system of education, with all its imbalance and shortcomings, is a living entity which has vast achievements to its credit. It has sustained the democratic institutions and the administrative apparatus, and has provided the manpower not only for spectacular advances in agriculture and industry, but also in new and emerging areas of science and technology. The educational system, however, presents an uneven, often conflicting picture: of great institutions, with a large number of universities and colleges where all norms of academic conduct are undermined; several thousand of schools in which teachers and students are engaged not only in observance of their expected roles but which radiate excellence; and also those which do not open on time, are unkempt and where the teaching and learning processes have little chance to germinate; large numbers of teachers who inspire their pupils are known for their learning, but also teachers who thoughtlessly ignore their obligations, sometimes altogether absenting themselves from the institution; most sophisticated systems of pupil evaluation, with an examination system which is fast losing its credibility; and innumerable instances of outstanding work done by people engaged in the onerous task of organising adult and non-formal education programmes, as well as large numbers of projects which just do not function. "Challenge of Education" brought out by the Ministry of Education tells us some interesting facts. From 1951 to 1982-83 the educational institutions increased from 2.3 lakh to 7.00 lakhs (5.04 lakh primary schools; 1.23 lakh secondary schools, rest higher education institutions, 52461 degree and post-graduate colleges and 140 Universities) Maharashtra and Andhra Pradesh take the lead with nearly a quarter of the total number of educational institutions. More than half of the total 1,600 vocational institutions are located in Tamil Nadu. The number of teachers in elementary and secondary schools increased from 7.5 to 32 lakhs. During the period 1950 to 1983 there has been a 2.5 fold increase in the number of educational institutions in the country. The growth rates of Institutions of different types during the period 1950-83 are: Primary Schools 2.7 per cent, Middle Schools 7.0 per cent, Secondary Schools 6.6 per cent, undergraduate and graduate Colleges 6.3 per cent. During 1951-84 period the overall growth rate of student enrolment rose to 4.5 per cent per annum in the case of primary level, 6.5 per cent in the middle, 7.6 per cent in the secondary and 10.4 per cent at the higher education level. Present management education in India, leaving some notable exceptions is not found suitable for developing participatory management. Managers learn to mistrust trade unions, suspect workers, and try to acquire methods to control them. It is necessary to institute massive re-education and management training programmes, designed to help managers acquire new perceptions, attitudes, motivation, skills and competencies to respond effectively to the new economic environment and rising expectations of the workforce. This needs a new interface of educational institutions and management schools of the country. *Business Today*, May 7-21, 1998 has brought out a survey of Indian business/management institutes and has tried to rank them on the basis of various considerations like applications per seat, annual library budget, average opening salary, proportion of Ph.D. in faculty, number of students per instructor and course tuition fees. The top ten ranked, respectively are II M. Ahmedabad, Bangalore, IIM, Calcutta, Xavier Labour Relations Institute, Jamshedpur, IIM, Lucknow, Faculty of management studies, Delhi, Jamnalal Bajaj Institute of M.S. Mumbai, Management Development Institute, Gurgaon, SP Jain Institute of Management and Research, Mumbai and Narsee Monjee Institute of M.S., Mumbai. For M.B.A. from prestigious institutions, year after year, corporates invest increasingly stiffer sums in hiring newly passed M.B.A. and then follows orientation and training at the corporate levels. An average MNC invests nearly twice his pay-packet on an M.B.A. in the initial two years. (*Business Today* April 7, 1999). From an esoteric discipline in the engineering studies packet driven in 1970s, through a grudging admission to the pedagogical mainstream in the 1980s, to its current status of the hottest postgraduate course in the post-liberation 1990s, management education in India is becoming increasing diluted and mismanaged. Due to mushroom growth of management education, there are many institutions without adequate infrastructure, untrained faculty and corporate experience, thus resulting in poor quality of product. The basic problems of education in India are-large number of students in proportion to teachers, poor and inadequate infra-structure, demotivated teachers and lack of adequate rapport between students, teachers and parents of students. The pattern of student enrolment reveals that during the period 1950-51 to 1982-83, the growth of enrolment in higher education was as high as 9.7 per cent per annum. Whereas the growth rate for secondary and elementary levels was 7.8 per cent and 5.5 per cent per annum respectively. Vocational enrolment has remained marginal and conformed to a few states. By 1976-77 the vocational programme had taken some shape only in three states. However, by 1983-84 it had spread to 11 states. More than half of the 1600 vocational institutions in the country were in Tamil Nadu. The rapid increase in absolute numbers in formal higher education enrolment was accompanied by a precipitous decline in quality. The facilities in the 5000-odd colleges vary widely and are, on the whole, far below the level of qualitative viability. There are today about 33 institutes of distance education conducted by various Universities in India and each of these Institutions has an enrolment ranging from 10,000 to nearly 1,00,000 students. Not surprisingly the annual rate of growth in enrolment in distance learning during the last 12 to 15 years has been much bigger than that in the formal universities. During 1975-76 to 1982-83, the annual rate of growth in enrolment was 15.2 per cent under distance education as against 3.7 per cent in the formal system. At the postgraduate level the enrolment under distance education grew by 23.8 per cent as against 5.5 per cent in the University departments and colleges. According to an estimate, over 80 per cent of the primary schools have no lavatories and that over 50 per cent lack a proper building. There were 103 lakhs of male and 55 lakhs of female enroled students belonging to scheduled castes in primary and middle level classes in 1983-84. During 1976, by a constitutional amendment, education became the joint responsibility of the Central and State Governments. According to the 1981 census the national average literacy rate which was 16.67 per cent in 1951 has increased to 36.23 per cent in 1981. Eighteen States and Union territories are above the National average. Kerala has the highest literate state with the literacy rate of 100 per cent with the lowest literacy rate of 20.79 in Andhra Pradesh.

Along with the arguably largest pool of scientific and technological manpower resource which is unemployed and unproductive, India may soon boast of a large reservoir of equally useless management professional, produced by the ever increasing number of business schools and management facilities of various universities. At the moment the Indian Business Management School bazar has more than 620 institutions of various sizes. The total intake for MBA and other such programmes is around 40,000 and half of it is in three states, Maharashtra, Tamil Nadu and Andhra Pradesh. There are no checks or regulations of management teaching and these institutions are mostly run by universities and private individuals. There is enormous degree of variation with regard to the syllabus and standards. There are many issues which need analysis and research. Who should be blamed? What has led to such a scenario? How can things be improved? How to stop this dangerous trend? How to ensure high quality management training with qualified staff to teach? What to do with so many jobless MBAs who know very little about management practices? Is our education system to be blamed? Although there is quality management training at Indian Institutes of Management and some other 40 institutes, there is much dilution of mangement education in many of the other management/business institutes.

In human development index, followed by the UNDP, India ranks at an unimpressive 135 out of 175. During the eighth five year plan the main thrust of educational programmes should be towards the promotion of quality and excellence, gearing the education system to meet the challenges of emerging areas of science and technology, providing wider opportunities for vocational training and education at different levels and restructuring the education system to encompass the development of the country's human resources potential. Upto the sixth plan, education was taken to be a social service rather than an input in the development process but now education is being considered to be pivotal in the social and economic development of the country through development of human resources.

HRD For Women and Girls

In the field of education, a number of steps have been taken for promoting women's education and training. The enrolment rate of girls in primary schools increased to 92.6 per cent in 1994-95. The dropout rates among girls at primary level showed a continuous decline from 62.5 per cent in 1980-81 to 37.8 per cent in 1994-95. The support to training and employment programme for women (STEP) scheme launched in 1987 to ugrade the skills of poor and assetless women, provide training and subsequently employment on a sustainable basis in the traditional sectors of agriculture, animal husbandry, fisheries, handlooms, handicrafts, sericulture, social forestry, waste land development etc. Since inception of this STEP programmes sixty-one projects benefiting 3.32 lakh women have been launched in various states.

Teacher as the Human Resource Developer

All teachers are human resource developers and their effectiveness depends mainly on the following factors:

(a) Knowledge of the subject and the level of general scholarship

(b) Efficiency and sincerity in teaching

(c) Character and integrity

(d) Classroom management in terms of discipline, order

and attention

(e) Techniques and innovations in teaching

(f) General behaviour, sociability motivation and overall personality

(g) Readiness and willingness to help and assist students

(h) Philosophy and academic perceptions as revealed through classroom behaviour

(i) General value system and commitment to the cause of education

(j) Ability to inspire students and efforts at moulding their character

(k) Ability for harnessing maximum human resource

A good human resource developer is concerned with the development of the whole child—intellectually, emotionally, socially, spiritually and physically and thus he is concerned with the entire complex organism of his pupils. It is the responsibility of human resource developers to develop the qualities of considerateness, kindness, compassion and universal humanism in their students. Students have to be trained to struggle against ignorance, injustice, oppression and fear. "It is the function of a teacher not to give the pupil what they want but make them want what he gives them," says Dr. Radhakrishnan. "No true commitment to knowledge can be achieved if the teachers do not play a progressive role. What the teachers do, the students follow." A good teacher explains; a mediocre teacher, tells, a superior teacher demonstrates and an exceptional teacher inspires. A good teacher, besides passing on knowledge, skills and values, ignites sparks in the mind of students, developing a thought provoking process in each student which really brings out the best in the child and makes the student really develop himself to his maximum limits. The strength of an educational system depends largely upon the quality of its teachers. A teacher has to give everything that life has to give, through his work, his utterances, his conduct, his demeanour and his commitment to his job. The ideal profile of HRD professional, according to T.V. Rao is as under: "a high desire to learn, knowledge based competencies, listening ability, communication skills, high degree of patience and perseverance, hard working with objectivity in approach and productivity.[10] In India the development of human resources has not received required attention particularly in the case of rural sector where abundant manpower is available—HRD for rural sector is an important means for reducing social and economic inequalities. The organisations factors, corruption, party politics, and problems with delivery system have further limited the effectiveness of rural employment programmes. Indian educational policy should revolutionize the value system by substituting values of meanness, greed, vengeance, aggressiveness, deceit, competitiveness, and exploitation with values of magnanimity generousness, forgiveness, cooperation, compassion, honesty, respectfulness and religious tolerance. Realising the importance of teachers the National Policy on Education has recommended that "the pay and working conditions of teachers have to be commensurate with their social and professional responsibilities and with the need to attract talent to the profession. Efforts will be made to reach the desirable objective of uniform enrolments, service conditions and grievance redressal mechanisms for teachers throughout the country". The system of teacher education needs to be overhauled. Teacher training and in-service training, in the new educational policy, will be provided the necessary resources and capability to accredit institutions of teacher education and provide guidance regarding curricula and methods. A comprehensive, open, participatory and data based system of teacher evaluation need to be established. The teacher evaluation in higher education should consist of four element—supervisor evaluation (20 per cent), self evaluation (20 per cent) peer evaluation (30 per cent), and student evaluation (30 per cent). It is essential to assess the quality of teachers through frequent evaluations, periodical in-service training and reorientation courses. Above given suggestions are greatly resisted and opposed by teachers on some genuine grounds. Although there are many irresponsible teachers, but for each irresponsible teacher, there are many more dedicated ones. Anyone who did economics at St. Stephen's College, New Delhi would shudder at the thought of N.C. Ray being forced to do a Ph.D or attend a refresher course. As long as teaching remained a passion and educational institutions places of worship, the system worked efficiently. But its transformation into a salaried profession has turned the educational institutions into a treadmill. Education is not coterminous with schooling but takes place in most work and life situations. In 1978, a national policy to educate about 100 million adult illiterates in the age group of 15-35 was formulated and on Gandhiji's birthday anniversary on October 2, 1978 National adult edcuation programme was launched by the Janta Government. The National policy on education, 1986 has envisaged Adult Education Centres (AEC) at village and Mohalla levels under District Resource Units (DRUs). Adult Education is a great step in human resource development. At the end of March, 1987, a total number of 13.63 lakh illiterate adults were covered under the Adult Education Programme in Andhra Pradesh. It was envisaged to achieve universal elementary education and eradication of adult illiteracy in the age group 15-35 by 2000. But the target of human resource development by 2000 was rather ambitious and due to many practical constraints and difficulties in the way, it may not be possible to achieve it by the end of 2000 AD.

The Sarvodaya Model of Development

The Sarvodaya model is multi-dimensional and integrative and believes in all-sided development of human personality—a perfect blending of mind, soul and body, i.e., *Poornodaya*. It emphasises the inculcation of the values of freedom, equality, justice and fraternity in a decentralised policy. Decentralisation of economy is central to the Sarvodaya model which supports concept of self-governing village units and emphasises self-restraint, discipline, commitment to duty, simplicity and self-reliance in every economic field at the community level. *Swaraj*, equal respect for all religious, love, spontaneity, voluntarism as the basis of state, open society, humanism, autonomy, social justice, societal trusteeship, sattivic materialism and harmony with environment are the main tenets of Sarvodaya model of development. Mahatma Gandhi and Jai Prakash Narayan advocated the Sarvodaya model of human development.

Challenges and Pit-Falls in Human Resource Development Programmes

Human Resource Development has four dimensions: (i) the physical, (ii) the intellectual, (iii) the social and (iv) the spiritual. As the *Atharva Veda* has said: *"Sharir madyam khalu dharma sadhanam*:—the body is the first pre-requisite of all development. Does our education system provide the necessary inputs to ensure the physical development of the students. The answer, I am afraid is definitely in the negative.[11] Mental training and discipline as well as aesthetic and intellectual development are other dimensions of education which need to be rediscovered and applied to our educational system. Socially desirable values, whether it is cleanliness or punctuality, discipline or teamwork, caring or comparison, need to find a place in our education system. The education system needs to provide a balanced and objective view to our vast and varied religious heritage and secular character. All the four dimensions—the physical, the intellectual, the social and the spiritual—must receive adequate attention if our educational system has to measure up to the tremendous challenges that we face today.[12] The human resource development strategy has to give due importance to all the four dimensions for effective harnessing of human resources for national development. A major cancer eating up the vitals of the present education system is the ugly grip of regionalism, casteism communalism. Eighty per cent of the students receiving college level education have suffered because of total neglect with regard to their development and standards. Many colleges have become virtual slums because of the pressure of numbers. The most critical issue is not of delinking jobs from degrees but of deeply linking work and education, indeed making the place of work also a place of education and vice-versa. At present there are at least twenty million educated unemployed at all levels ranging from primary to post-doctoral. India certainly needs a larger infrastructure of education but it needs to be modified to cater to the changing needs of the society. The education policy should be designed to look for and nurture talent wherever it is available. Vocational and technical courses should become more attractive to the students. Our national effort should be to stop "brain-drain" which is a national scourge. It is estimated that around 1500 physicians and surgeons leave the country annually. Each doctor going abroad means a loss of Rs. 3.3 lakhs. Approximately 6.1 per cent of the engineers and technologists leave the country for greener pastures. An environment congenial to young doctors, engineers, technologists must be created in India so that this brain-drain may be stopped and human resource going out of the country may be conserved and utilized for national development in a more creative and useful manner. In education system, brain-drain is a serious malady whose remedy calls for not cosmetic therapy but a radical surgery, Educationalists have agreed that low school retention and high dropout rates have neutralised the gains from educational expansion and development of the last decades. The greatest single quantitative contribution to be made would be to eliminate dropout from the education system at all levels; 72.1 per cent of the children dropout before they reach Class VIII. Out of hundred children who enter class I, only 28 reach class VIII on the national average. A massive programme of school improvement called "Operation Black Board" has been launched to lure the child back to school. The new education policy gives highest priority to solving the problem of children dropping out of school and proposes to adopt an array of meticulously formulated strategies based on micro-planning and applied at the grass root level all over the country. Some of the important suggestions for HRD in India can be as under:

1. By education and training human resources should be equipped to utilize both sides of the brain combining analytical ability with creativity with a view to bring about a better quality of life.
2. All education and HRD efforts should aim at producing ethically aware and value-literate human beings who have interpersonal sensibilities and skills of effective communication.

3. Research and constant updating of all educational syllabii to keep pace with new economic environment globalisation and liberalisation should be attempted on a continuous basis.

Literacy means only the ability to read and write which is nothing in the modern day world of knowledge explosion. Roughly fifteen per cent of Indians can be considered as educated if we workout their ability to read, write and understand upto about VIII level. Obviously three per cent of our GNP has proved to be quite inadequate. We must step up expenditure on education to six per cent of GNP by the year 1990. Kerala spent thirty six per cent of its revenue expenditure budget on education in 1982-83. Considering the need for continuous updating the professional skills, competencies, knowledge and attitude of the people working in industry and various service organisation, it is necessary that educational institutions, engineering colleges and other professional training institutions should aim at an integrated, wholesome development of professional people by giving them periodical in-service professional courses. Today education in India has been come obsolete in terms of research facilities, curriculum as well as the overall quality of teaching. Technical education is unable to attract and retain talented engineers. Educational institutions do not find teaching any more an attractive job. Various five year plans have not improved the conditions and plight of teachers and educational institutions. Plan-wise allocations to edcuation have shown gradual increase as can be seen from the table given below:

The following three inferences can be easily drawn from the data :

(a) To begin with, elementary education was given considerable importance. Half the funds in the First Plan were earmarked for education at this level. Higher and technical education did not receive much attention.

(b) During the next three plans, elementary education came to be grossly neglected so much so that, by 1969, elementary education came down to where higher and professional education had been pegged earlier and the latter

Table Showing Plan Expenditure on Different Sectors of Education

(Percentage)

Sector	Ist Plan 1951-56	2nd Plan 1956-61	3rd Plan 1961-66	Plan Holiday 1966-69-	4th Plan 1969 74	5th Plan 1974-79	6th Plan 1980-85	7th Plan 1985-90	1990-92	8th Plan 1992-97
Elementary Education	56 (850)	35 (950)	34 (2010)	24 (750)	30 (2390)	35 (3170)	33 (8360)	37 (28490)	37 (17290)	47 (9201)
Secondary Education	13 (200)	19 (510)	18 (1030)	16 (530)	18 (1400)	17 (1560)	21 (5300)	24 (18320)	22 (10530)	18 (34980)
Adult education							9 (2240)	6 (4700)	9 (4160)	9 (18480)
Higher edcuation	9 (140)	18 (480)	15 (870)	24 (770)	25 (1950)	22 (2050)	22 (5590)	16 (12010)	12 (5880)	8 (15160)
Others	9 (140)	10 (300)	12 (730)	11 (370)	14 (1060)	14 (1060)	4 (1080)	3 (1980)	2 (1180)	4 (7510)
Technical education	13 (200)	18 (4900)	21 (1250)	25 (810)	13 (1060)	12 (1070)	11 (2730)	14 (10830)	17 (8230)	14 (27860)
Total	100 (1530)	100 (2730)	100 (5890)	100 (3230)	100 (7860)	100 (9120)	100 (25300)	100 (76330)	100 (47270)	100 (196000)

Not : Figures in parenthesis in millions of rupees.
Source : Education for All by MHRD.

had shot up to almost half of the total outlay.

(c) Since then, a conscious attempt has been made to redress the balance. In the Eighth Plan which has just ended, elementary education received forty-seven per cent, whereas higher and technical education received twenty-two per cent.

In case of technical education, where the pay off is very good, private funding has moved in a substantial way. In the case of higher education, where the pay off is moderately good, while the number of universities has expanded, the outlay has gone down. In consequence, higher education has been reduced to a sad pass. There is good deal more to be said about the pattern of support to different sectors of education. This has created imbalances of various kinds and is coming in the way of having a vibrant workforce when it comes to elementary education. Meanwhile other problems have cropped up. The first one is the sheer inadequacy of funds. Something like forty per cent of all primary schools are one teacher schools. In the backward states, mainly the Hindi speaking states, together with Orissa and Jammu and Kashmir to some extent, the situation is simply atrocious. But in better run states like Kerala, Tamil Nadu, Karnataka, Maharashtra, Gujarat, Punjab, Haryana, etc. the student-teacher ratio is reasonably good. Secondly, in addition to shortage of teachers, there is also a shortage of buildings. Buildings, however, in a hot country like India, are not such an important input as the availability of well-trained teachers. The third factor is that while private enterprise does exist at the elementary level, essentially it is the government which is carrying the main load. Now about two-thirds of the states, teacher can be transferred all over and, as everybody knows, transferring teachers is virtually an industry in which politicians, bureaucrats and corrupt elements play almost equal roles. For more meaningful education, Government must be assisted by various professional bodies like the Indian Society for Technical Education (ISTE), HRD network, Indian Society for Training and Development (ISTD) and Association of Indian Management Schools (AIMS). Quality of human resources is determined by the four variables, namely, population policy, population structure, migration and labour force participation. Quality of human resources is influenced by the status of the following variables : (1) education and training (2) health and nutrition and (3) equality of opportunities and labour market behaviour."[13]

Expenditure on education in India, though sizeable, stands no comparison with even some of the developing countries and the investment in education is inadequate in relation to the fast growing needs of Indian education. The Seventh Plan had indicated that in order to achieve the target of universalisation of elementary education by the end of Seventh Plan, over fifty million children in the age group 6-14 will have to be additionally enrolled. With sixty-one per cent of the students dropping out of the educational system before attaining permanent literacy, very heavy investment alone can correct the imbalances of the educational system. There is an urgent need for allocating larger resources for education both for quantitative and qualitative changes and for achieving the different objectives of education. In India, business education is classified in two streams: (1) The management stream with professional character and (2) the commerce stream with liberal character. During the last thirty years management education has made quantum leaps in India. Management education in India made its beginning with the well known person Report (Carnegie Report of 1959) and Gordon and Howell (Ford Foundation) Report of 1959 which underscored the need for developing strong theoretical foundation and practical orientation of current business needs. Today there are more than 285 institutes/universities/academies providing management education with varying levels of academic and theoretical inputs. Inadequate computer literacy, inadequate research base, heavy curriculam input, information stuffing, superficial coverage of Indian business and international economic scenario, very limited contact with industry and business and half baked Indian case material are some of the common features of Indian management education. Management education in India, barring a few notable exceptions, needs to be upgraded, and modernised and given practical orientation with proper interface with industry. The Indian education policy is an attempt to relink learning with life—An attempt will be made through formal education, through vocational education and through non-informal education to reach and teach every one who is reachable. It has to cultivate secularism, socialism, democracy and nationalism and nurture the correct moral values. Education can not be limited to literacy but must be much broader and go into building the character and personality of the child. Open Universities and distance education through non-formal education provide a variety of modes which will help us to reach every section of the society even at the remotest corners of the nation. The future of the country depends on the development of its human resources. There is wastage of resources (27.6 per cent) due to mounting unemployment of educated manpower. Educational planning should be used as an input for advance programming of manpower outflows. Institutions of higher learning have multiple functions to perform—such as : (1) knowledge accumulation and storing, (2) knowledge transmission, (3) mental development, (4) screening, (5) value-affirming, (6) rationing, (7) national prestige, (8) social control, (9) social order and (10) social criticism. Institutions of higher learning are the main source of supply of human resource for the various tasks of development and maintenance. We have 260 state universities, seven Central Universities and thirteen deemed universities. In 1981-82 the number of colleges were 4886 out of which 3504 were arts, science and commerce colleges. Out of them 804 colleges provided post-graduate teaching. Five Indian Institutes of Technology, four Indian Institutes of Management and five Research Councils for different disciplines form the professional institutions of higher learning. Universities are the main source of supply of officers for our public services especially at the higher levels. The marked deterioration of standards in teaching and examinations and increasing dissatisfaction with the conduct of university administration are matters of great concern. There is scope for qualitative improvement in the administration and management of institutions of higher learning. Radhakrishnan Commission on University Education had rightly observed that "we were everywhere struck by a deep general awareness of the importance of higher education for national welfare and an uneasy sense of inadequacy of the present pattern. The Union Government had decided to launch a national literacy mission at a cost of Rs. 550 crores to promote literacy among adult illiterates during the remainder of the seventh plan and also the eighth plan. The intention is to bring about a qualitative change in the adult education policy and to take literacy to about thirty million adult illiterates between 1988-90 and fifty million between 1991-95. The coverage of adult illiterates under the literacy programme during the sixth plan is expected to be around 22 lakh. The enrolment has increased from 25.9 lakh in 1980-81 to 65.9 lakh in 1984-85. Educational programmes have not been able to mobilize human resources to the maximum extent possible because teachers, due to poor training, insufficient supervision and lack of motivation, seldom put in their best. We have nearly 7.5 lakh educational and vocational institutions which are not fully utilised due to bad planning, poor coordination, lack of proper education atmosphere and out-dated teaching technology. Countries like U.S.A., erstwhile Soviet Union and Japan spend over 6 per cent of their GNP on education while India is spending in the vicinity of 3 per cent. The overall allocation to education in the different plans have been declining from 7.86 per cent in the first plan to all time low to 2.59 per cent in the sixth plan. Educational institutions in a developing country play a significant role in preparing and making available people with right kinds of knowledge, attitude, values and skill base to industry and other service organisations. With the new economic policies, the goals, missions, task structure, technology and roles in organisations are bound to change and the educational policy therefore has a very vital role in harnessing available and potential human resources. The educational policy and the educational institutions should be sensitive to the changing needs of society and modify their curricular to prepare human resources with required knowledge, attitudes, skills and other competencies. The education system and the educational institutions in the country have to do an introspection and to assess their contribution from the point of view of utility and excellence. Unfortunately the present education system is :

(a) Course-oriented and not process-oriented.

(b) Useless-knowledge oriented and not use-based knowledge oriented.

(c) Foreign culture-oriented and not Indian-ethos and culture-oriented.

(d) White-collar oriented and not work-culture oriented.

(e) Examination-oriented and not individual development oriented.

(f) Quantity oriented and not quality oriented.

(g) Teacher-oriented and not student-oriented.

Non-formal education, distance education and open education can emancipate the education from the rigid, suffocating and formal system. The system of non-formal open education can serve the following needs of our society:

(1) to make the dream of Universal education a reality in our country;

(2) to make education more cost-effective and need based;

(3) to give specialised training to millions of artisans and skilled workers to enhance their productivity and technical skills;

(4) to give a new thrust to women's education;

(5) to take the message of secularism, socialism, democracy and development of the nation to the masses;

(6) to augment opportunities for higher education to those who are already working and earning a modest living;

(7) to provide equal opportunities to the Scheduled Castes, Scheduled Tribes and the underprivileged for education at various levels of learning.

Open education is working very well in United Kingdom and it can definitely work well in India if the implementing agencies are fully galvanized, psychologically and organisationally. A variety of modes and channels which will reach out to every section, use new communication technologies. T.V., Radio and other media which is available, are required to support and enrich the non-formal open education system. The primary need of open education is to make it economically viable and socially relevant. India's track record in human development is dismal, according to UNDP 1995 report. Table 2 given below gives a comparative picture of India's expenditure as compared to other countries, on human development.

Table 2. Human Development Expenditure

Country	*Education (as per cent of GNP 1990)*	*Health (as per cent of GNP 1990)*	*Labour force per cent of total Population 1990-93*	*Women's Share of adult labour force 1994*
India	3.5	1.3	38	24
Malaysia	6.9	1.3	38	36
Brazil	4.6	2.8	44	28
Srilanka	2.7	1.8	41	27
Pakistan	3.4	1.8	28	13
Bangladesh	2.0	1.4	47	41
Singapore	3.4	1.1	49	36
Mexico	4.1	1.6	39	28
Thailand	3.8	1.1	56	44
China	2.3	2.1	—	43

Source—India's Social Sector Scenario—UNI backgrounder Vol. XX No. Oct. 26, 1995 Annexure -4.

For developing human resources, teachers and HRD professionals have the most important responsibilities. A good teacher acts as a guide and counselor to his students. According to Arthur W. Comb, a good teacher can be characterised typically in the light of the knowledge of his subjects; his frame of reference for approaching problems; his perception of the purpose and process of learning and his perception of appropriate methods of teaching. The main functions of a good teacher, according to Louis Raths, are; explaining, informing, showing how, initiating, directing, administering, unifying the group, giving security, clarifying attitudes, diagnosing learning problems, preparing curriculum material, evaluating, recording, reporting, enriching community activities, organising and arranging classroom, participating in school activities and participating in professional and civic life. According to Barbara, a good teacher guides and leads his class to discover ways of developing the students; learning skills, he sets standards and helps the students to appreciate what is good performance, he puts the students on their mettle to do the best work they are individually capable of. A teacher has to be a conglomeration of many qualities which he has to cultivate, acquire and aim at with perseverance and patience. According to Health, the teacher in the classroom should serve as a catalyst and guide for each child's learning experiences. Pre-induction training and periodical refresher training to teachers assume great importance in this context. Education can develop human resources by inculcating, and promoting values such as egalitarianism, democracy, socialism, secularism, equality of sea and development of scientific temper in the students. Education in words of Dr. Radhakrishnan, must give a basic meaning to personality and existence and equip students with the power to overcome inertia and foster spiritual sensitivity. It is a matter of great satisfaction that India has experienced a major breakthrough in literacy in the 1990s. Data from latest 1997 survey of the National Sample Survey Organisation shows shooting up of literacy from 52 per cent in 1991 to 62 per cent in 1997 as shown below:

Table 3. Showing Literacy Per cent of Persons over 7 Years

Years	*Rural (%)*	*Urban (%)*	*Total (%)*
1961	22.5	54.4	28.3
1971	27.9	60.2	34.4
1981	36.0	67.2	43.5
1991	44.7	73.1	52.2
1997	56.0	80.0	62.0

The student enrolment in higher education in India, faculty wise is given below:

Table 4. Showing Higher Education Enrolment

Faculty	1975-76 %	1984-85 %	1995-96 %
Arts	44.5	40.0	40.4
Science	19.1	19.7	19.6
Commerce and Mgt.	17.1	21.0	21.9
Education	3.2	2.4	2.3
Engineering and Technology	4.0	4.5	4.9
Medicines	4.3	3.8	3.4
Agriculture	1.2	1.3	1.1
Veterinary Science	0.3	0.3	0.3
Law	5.8	6.0	5.3
Others	0.5	0.6	0.8

"India's greatest challenge today is the development of human resources. India does not suffer from a resource gap, not a technological gap nor a gap in planning, it suffers from a gap in management of human resources."[14] People undoubtedly are the most important of all resources of a nation. A good and effective human resource development plan should ensure that all available human resources are developed to their maximum capacity. Inspite of all planning and pious resolutions, there are the following sadly missed targets in education:

1. Free and compulsory education upto fifth standard (primary education).
2. Adult literacy could not cover 100 per cent adults.
3. Nationally and vocationally relevant higher education which could be linked with professionalism.
4. Proper blending of non-formal and formal education for women and disadvantaged classes.
5. Continuing education throughout the working life for updating knowledge.
6. Streaming the middle school and later vocational skills.
7. Cultural education opportunities.

8. Self-actualising opportunities and post superannuation hobbies.
9. Building of motivated and exemplary teachers.
10. Linking education with practical life.

Population regulation and planning is not only a sociological, psychological and economic issue, it is also related with political directives and national population policy, India was the first country in the world to launch a family planning programme as early as in 1951. Population problem is deep rooted with varied socio-economic and political repercussions. In India even today there is a lot of reservation about imparting sex education at the school level. In spite of best efforts only 50 per cent of the population uses various family planning techniques to control the population as given in the table below:

Table 5. Family Planning Techniques

Percentage of eligible couples using contraception

	Total%	Sterilisation	IUDs	Pills	Condoms	Injectable	Norplant	Trad.
1989/90	40	27.40	3.00	1.20	4.00	0.000	0.000	4.40
1990/91	41	27.61	3.20	1.43	4.10	0.000	0.000	4.46
1991/92	42	27.82	3.40	1.66	4.20	0.000	0.000	4.52
1992/93	43	28.03	3.60	1.89	4.30	0.000	0.000	4.58
1993/94	44	28.24	3.80	2.12	4.40	0.100	0.030	4.64
1994/95	45	28.45	4.00	2.35	4.50	0.225	0.063	4.70
1995/96	46	28.66	4.20	2.58	4.60	0.375	0.100	4.76
1996/97	47	28.87	4.40	2.81	4.70	0.575	0.150	4.82
1997/98	48	29.08	4.60	3.04	4.80	0.800	0.200	4.88
1998/99	49	29.29	4.80	3.27	4.90	1.150	0.300	4.94
1999/00	50	29.50	5.00	3.50	5.00	1.325	0.400	5.00

(Percentage of users, by Method)

Without proper education to the eligible couples about family planning techniques India's population problem cannot be controlled. Formal and non-formal education, vocational training, adult literacy drive, open education system and all other available strategies need to be used in an imaginative manner to achieve maximum development. India is the second most populated country of the world and if its human resources are utilised in an optimum manner, nation is bound to make allround development. All developed societies and economies start with the people. Like a silent revolution development begins in the minds of men. Men have to be galvanised, human resources have to be channelised, people have to be endowed and enriched with new skills, new knowledge, new techniques and new approaches. Human resources should be utilised for challenging, jobs opening, trusting and demanding relationship in the joint endeavour of building the nation. India still have 63.77 per cent of population (1981 census) which is not literate and yet to be educated. Full utilisation of human resources is possible only when the above given percentage of population is also educated and given full opportunities to develop their potentials and talents. The strategies and action plan to achieve the stipulated goal should lay emphasis on coverage of the districts having literacy rate below the national average; coverage of special target groups, e.g., women, scheduled castes, scheduled tribes and other weaker sections of the society. Participation of youth and students in adult literacy programmes; mobilisation of voluntary agencies, mass media, T.V. and radio in particular to carry out formal and non-formal education programmes and implementation of all other schemes is recommended by the National Education Policy, 1986. The strategies and programmes for education should be able to release the latent power of women and youth as also economically weaker population groups so that they can make an increasing contribution to the socio-economic development of the country. In developing countries, like India, HRD has to be synonymous with manpower planning, the whole objective of which is to make available sufficient number of qualified men for skilled positions which are created with onward march of the society.[15] The new Training Policy of the Government of India (1996) is a progressive effort in this direction. It emphasises building competencies and ensures that all are able to acquire these through training programmes at the induction as well as through in-service training at suitable intervals. National training policy (1996) envisages an institutionalised arrangement within each department organisation for overseeing the training function as an integral part of HRD system.[16] However there is a wide gap between promise and performance. There is an immediate need for an appropriate HRD approach at the macro-level with an inbuilt system of training, career development, job enrichment and employee participation to improve the quality of work life and in the process attain quality governance of the democratic, plural society. Professor Amartya Sen has rightly observed : "It would be a mistake to see the development of education, health care and other basic achievements as only resources,— accumulations of human capital—as if people were just means of production and not its ultimate end. Improved education and good health should be ultimately instrumental in improving the quality of life."

Organski, author of *Population and World Power* says: "One of the fears that haunts the West today is that such crowded lands as China and India may continue to grow until they reach a point of such unbearable tension that they will send their people swarming across their borders into relatively empty lands nearby" In U.S.A. both population and prosperity have been going up while in Russia both have been going down. Globalisation without a uniform global population policy could have very servious consequences. Colin Clark, an eminent economist says. "Population pressure is probably the only force strong enough to overcome the intense conservatism of the Indian peasant. In the unlikely event of family limitation, most of the stimulus to economic development would be removed with it" There are several civilizations including Greek and Roman the collapsed due to under-population but no country's civilizations collapsed because of over-population. On the map, China looks much bigger than India. But fact is that India has more cultivable land and more water per head than China.[17] We must look at population as human resources and power and must manage them effectively, efficiently and professionally. Our biggest challenge is to manage our human resources when on May 11, 2000, the billionth Indian has already been born. Let us ensure good education, good nutritions and good quality of life to them by effective management.

REFERENCES

1. Rao T.V. (Editor), *Alternative Approaches and Strategies of Human Resource Development*, Rawat Publications, Jaipur, 1988.
2. R. Wright, Managing Man as a Capital Asset, *Personnel Journal*, April, 1970, p. 294.
3. Dr. Krishna Mohan Mathur, *Human Resource Development in Administration*—April-June, 1987. Vol. XXXIII No. 2, pp. 218-19.
4. Shri Rajiv Gandhi's address at the National Development Council held at New Delhi on April 29, 1986. Courtesy Press Information Bureau, Ministry of Human Resource Development, Department of Education for Text of speech.
5. Gunnar Myrdal, *Asian Drama*.
6. Shri Rajiv Gandhi's address at the meeting of National Development Council held at Delhi on April 29, 1986. Text released by Press Information Bureau, Ministry of Human Resource Development, Department of Education.
7. P.L. Rao, "Harnessing Human Resources for National Development", *The Hindu*, November 4, 1986.
8. Ruskin, *Unto This Last* (A Paraphrase by M.K. Gandhi) Navjeevan Publishing House, p. 30.
9. P.L. Rao, "Harnessing Human Resource for National Development". *The Hindu*—November 4, 1986.
10. T.V. Rao, *HRD Missionary*, 1990.
11. Dr. Karan Singh, "Some thoughts on Education" *Part I—Hindustan Times*, New Delhi, 30th July, 1987.
12. Dr. Karan Singh, "Thought on Education *Part II—The Hindustan Times*, New Delhi, July 31, 1987.
13. Dr. Krishna Mohan Mathur—*Towards Effective Management—Pathways to Excellence* Gyan Publishing House, New Delhi, 1999, p. 70.

14. Dr. Dharni P. Sinha, Padmaja Naidu memorial lecture, "Gaps in Human Resource Management", *The Hindu*, January 20, 1988.

15. Dr. Krishna Mohan Mathur, "Human Resource Development in Administration" *Indian Journal of Public Administration*, April-June, 1987, Vol. XXXIII No. p. 216-17.

16. Rajesh Singh, Behavioural Science Training Imperatives for Managing Change in 1990s. *Indian Journal of Public Administration*, July-Sept., 1997. Vol. XLIII, No. 3, p. 635.

17. K. R. Malkani, "Forget the Numbers Look at Population as Power" *Times of India*, New Delhi, 25 May 2000, p. 14.

4

Human Resource Development in Administration

The challenges of HRD are becoming more complex with the advent of globalisation and liberalisation in a developing pluralistic society like India.

The liberalization of the Indian economy which started in July, 1991, has brought in an environment characterised by, among others : (1) Decontrol and delicensing, (2) Globalisation of competition, (3) Information explosion with communications revolution, (4) Internationalisation fluidity in geo-economic reality, (5) Quality concerns, (6) Denationalisation and Privatisation, (7) Newer skill generation and diversification due to technological invasion, (8) A new freedom from the past orthodox and straight jacketed ideology and protective economic strategy. In a post-liberalisation scenario, some characteristic parameters worth noting in this emerging context are:

(1) Globalisation of human and material resources; (2) Total Quality Approach; (3) Upgradation of Human resources by bridging the learning irrelevancies and obsolescence and narrowing the technological gap; (4) Interacting with the environment by developing the information system and; (5) Quality of life as the focus. Human Resource Development (HRD) is needed for upgradation of knowledge, skills, techniques, creativity, interpersonal relations, team-building,

motivation, education, health, nutrition, and all other quantitative and qualitative development of human resources in a liberal economy. According to Stephen H. Rhimesmith (1993) the core competencies required for global managers can be summarised as follows :

"1. Managing competitiveness by constantly scanning the environment for changes in market, socio-economic and political trends and global competition conditions;
2. Managing complexity by managing trade-offs of many competing interests as well as the inherent conflicts and contradictions of various global organisations.
3. Managing adaptability by developing a global culture with the values, beliefs, systems and norms of behaviour.
4. Managing teams within a multi-cultural sensitivity and demands, cultural sensitivity and managerial skills to lead, supervise and manage people coming from a wide range of different nationalities.
5. Managing uncertainties to deal with constantly changing environment.
6. Managing learning on a continuous basis and building a learning organisation. Liberalisation requires administrators to put due emphasis on productivity, quality, effectiveness, efficiency, latest technology, skill development and customer satisfaction."

In a liberal economy, globalisation throws the following main challenges :

1. Technology and machinery upgradation,
2. Attracting, maintaining and developing efficient, competent and trained professionals,
3. Competitiveness in terms of quality of product and cost,
4. Surviving and maintaining growth in a liberalised environment by systems improvement, cost reductions, innovation and customer satisfaction.

The Concept of HRD

Conceptually HRD is pursuing excellence of people through enhanced knowledge, skills, committed and motivated people participation by creating a climate of certain values. Streamlining of personnel policies is one of the major functional areas of HRD. As per the Human Development Report of UNDP, about four per cent of GDP in India comes from services and service sector is largely managed by the government. Service sector is characterised by the technology, lack of professional management, bureaucratic structures, overstaffing, skill base and practically no HRD orientation. The term Human Resources Development encompasses the three areas of training, education and development. Human Resource Development means (1) a series of organised activities, (2) conducted within a specified time and (3) designed to produce behavioural change[1]. Human resources development, like "broad-spectrum—antibiotic" has multi-coverage and acts like a travelling salesman's cure all elixir. Human Resources Development Systems (HRDS) include performance appraisal, potential appraisal, employee feedback and counselling, assessment of training needs of the various categories of the employees, designing and using special interventions, organisational diagnosis, organisational development, evaluations of various interventions and increasing the motivation of the people for the optimum effectiveness of the organisation. The human resources can be defined as "the total knowledge, skills, creative abilities, talents and aptitudes of an organisation's workforce as well as the values, attitudes and beliefs of the individual involved. It is the sum total of inherent abilities, acquired knowledge and skills, represented by the talents and aptitude of the employed persons."[2] The whole concept and range of human resources development have undergone a vast change over the last three decades. "Human Resources Development represents an intervention strategy with, *inter alia*, the following overall objects, namely :

(a) arresting obsolescence, both individual and organisational (preventive);

(b) bridging proactive insufficiencies of knowledge and professional skill (curative);

(c) shaping adjustments with socio-technological, environmental changes (adaptive);

(d) developing new outlook, an ethological version of quality excellence and accomplishment (promotive);

(e) making a total man with cultural attributes (transformative)"[3].

The HRD concept signifies that personnel administration must carry out manpower research and planning to anticipate longterm labour market needs, manpower distribution through an effective placement service and manpower utilisation to assure full use of the nation's human resources. Human Resources Development can be studied both from Macro as well as Micro angle. An individual in his career undergoes certain life-cycle which has been analysed by Levinson and others. Levinson's model gives us an insight into how to merge various stages of an individual career with various human resources development programmes. On March, 1985 the National HRD Network was formed as an association of professionals committed to promoting the HRD movement in the country. In February 1990, a permanent academic body was formed as "Academy of Human Resource Development" with the underlying philosophy that "every human being has the potential to do remarkable things." The HRD movement has focussed attention of individuals and organisations on how to optimise human resources. On 1st July, 1995 the Academy of Human Resource Development started functioning at Hyderabad. On 4th January, 1996, Individual and Organisational Assessment Centre (OAC) was launched. The activities of the academy can be broadly classified as (1) Knowledge generation, (2) Knowledge dissemination and (3) Capacity building. Prof Udai Pareek, Dr. T.V. Rao and Dr. M.B. Athreya have done some pioneering work in the field of human resource development. One essay written by Dr. K.M. Mathur was judged by IIPA, New Delhi as the prize winning essay in October, 1986 and the title of the essay was "Human Resource Development in Administration" which was later published in its journal by Indian Institute of Public Administration, New Delhi. The explosion of knowledge has suffocated the human personality so much that the majority of people find themselves outstripped by a psychodolic cyclone. There is a revolution of rising expectations in villages and the commitment of social justice have highlighted the burning problems of providing adequate food, shelter and clothing to a large majority of rural people who lived for decades below the poverty line. Politically there is a wave of turbulent tensions because of high promises of all round prosperity without having the hope of their realisation even in a distant future. The massiveness of the social, economic and political changes implies the need for careful all round planning and development of resources at all levels. An enlightened administration dealing constantly with new situations, with economic, social and technological developments, with a constantly changing society increasing in complexity all the time, needs an equally committed, motivated, dynamic and inventive administrative service personnel to handle various levels of administration. The citizens have become conscious of their rights and have become more vociferous and powerful. The goals of administration are becoming increasingly numerous and varied. The administration has to assume many different roles and responsibilities for effective management of various functions. The importance of manpower planning and human resource development in the above context becomes quite clear.

Object of HRD

People are a resource, the use of which needs to be forecast, planned, coordinated and financially controlled in the same manner as any other major resource. In a world that lately seems to be running out of everything, we hear a lot of talk about exploring, discovering and tapping new resources." Traditionally in all countries far more attention has been paid to the development and fuller utilisation of material than of human resources. This can be seen in the fact that while technology advances at an ever-accelerating pace, the scientific study of social behaviour is until recently, still in its infancy...we want to promote a more enlightened philosophy of management which encourages responsible participation of all employees by respecting their dignity as human beings".[4] We can improve administration by utilizing people's minds as well as their hands. People and their brains are the most precious assets. "Nobody in this world works at top capacity. An average person works at about 30 per cent of his capacity."[5] The basic idea of HRD is to improve productivity, output and efficiency of the organisations "by utilising people's minds as well as their hands."[6] Most organizations waste the talents of their people freely as they do not utilize the talents to their full capacity. In all public services and at various levels of administrative functioning there are a number of so-called "low level" jobs such as cleaning people, garbage-men, maids, dish-washers, car washers, parking lot attendants and night watchman. These jobs should be treated as entrance-level jobs-tasks that people perform temporarily as the first stepping stone to shoulder more advanced responsibilities earned by merit and advancement of basic education. Moreover administrators will find that people in such jobs will often show potential and eagerness for growth when they become convinced that promotion opportunities for advancement are real. Administrators must accept management innovations—new ways of organising people, dealing with people, motivating people, respecting people, giving people the opportunity to convert their experience and ideas into better ways of getting a job done. The task of human resource development begins with collection of personal data with a view to appropriately visualise the professional content of the individual vis-a-vis his placement and job requirements in the administrative system. Categorisation of personnel in terms of levels becomes necessary to form the base for accomplishment of human resources development policy. Human resource development policy has to be conceived either as (a) Immediate plan or short-term plan or (b) Long-term plan or (c) An adhoc plan in the areas of human resource development. The matter of providing funds for human resource development is important at the micro-level as well as the national (macro) level. Earmarking of two per cent of the wage-bill in any organisation for human resource development is accepted as an ideal and sufficient provision. The administration and implementation of human resource development policies require lot of efforts, dedication and commitment of the system. Preparation of realistic and meaningful human resource development plans require careful consideration and professional approach. The basic objects of human resource development in administration can be as under :

1. To equip the civil servant with precision and clarity in the transaction of business;
2. To attune the civil servant to the new tasks which he will be called upon to perform in a changing world;
3. To develop resistance to the danger of becoming mechanised by visualising what he is doing in a wider setting and by persevering with his own educational development;
4. To develop his capacity for higher work and greater responsibility;
5. To develop and maintain staff morale particularly because large number of people have to deal with tasks of a routine nature;
6. To inculcate the right attitude towards the public, never forgetting that the civil servant is the servant and not the master of the community;
7. To sustain the human touch not only in direct personal contacts with the public but also in handling correspondence which demands a proper sense of urgency and due consideration of the "man at the other end"[7]. Training, career planning, performance appraisals, job rotation, and varied experience are all parts of HRD processes.

The success of any development programme lies in a number of variables of which training is an important factor. Training, education and development of Human Resource Development in administration are expected to provide the needed stimulus to initiate impulses of change in the administrative apparatus and will lead to improved efficiency, productivity and administrative performance. In fact, of late there has been significant enlargement of the training infrastructure-cum-proliferation, enhancement of financial outlays and consequential numeral increase in the number of training opportunities for administrators.[8] Enunciation of human resource management policy and its effective implementation will go a long way in human resource development.

There are four basic steps in human resource planning:[9]

1. Planning for future needs,
2. Planning for future balance,
3. Planning for recruitment and selection,
4. Planning for development.

Human resource planning should ensure congruence between individual and organisational goals and setting high standards of efficiency. Planning for development aims at increasing the ability of the individuals and groups to contribute to organisational effectiveness. Development programmes are designed to educate employees beyond the requirements of their present position so that they will be prepared for promotion and be able to take a broader view of their role in the organisation. How should the training and movement of individuals within the organisation be managed so that the organisation will be assured of a continuing supply of experienced and capable personnel? The central elements in human resource planning are forecasting and the human resource audit. Forecasting attempts to assess the future personnel needs of the organisation. The human resource audit assesses the organisation's current human resources. In the human resource audit the skills and the performance of each individual in the organisation are appraised. Induction and orientation are designed to provide a new employee with the information he (or she) needs in order to function effectively and comfortably in a given setting. Typically, induction and orientation convey three types of information :

1. General information about the daily routine of the organisation.
2. A review of the organisation's history, purpose and deals with how the employee's job contributes to the overall activity.
3. A detailed presentation, perhaps via brochure, of the organisation's policies, work rules, work culture, and employee benefits and obligations.

All HRD mechanism such as role analysis, performance appraisal, OD exercise etc. should be used to develop employees. Induction and orientation is generally followed by training programmes aimed to improve skills, techniques, knowledge and attitude of the employees. Continuous monitoring of the actual job performed will reveal changes that call for new training. Training for advancement is needed to enable the employee to climb the promotional ladders. Taking over the duties of higher ranked colleagues during their vacations or short absences is another opportunity for informal on the job training for advancement. Erik Ericksons' famous adult stages[10] of adolescence, young adulthood, adulthood and maturity demand progressive and suitable training and development for effective job performance by the individual.

The Levinson's model of evolution of individual career. It describes a series of personal and career related crises that occur in a fairly predictable sequence in service career. The main stages are as under.[11]

1. *Pulling up Roots* : (age 16-22 years)—Individuals complete academic life and enter into service by pulling up roots from parents and embark on the careers with some measure of self-confidence. Those who prolong parental ties, according to Levinson, often under-perform in their careers. This period is period of induction and placement.
2. *Provisional Adulthood* (Age 22-29)— The employee becomes preoccupied getting into the adult world and tries for satisfactory career goals. Training in this period is essential.

3. *The Transition Period* (Age 29-32)—In this period individual reviews his personal and career goals, often moves to his most favourite goal career and pattern of life. In-service training becomes useful at this stage. Performance appraisal, management appraisal and potential appraisals become useful for HRD at this stage.
4. *Settling down* (Age 32-39)—The individual strives towards "becoming one's own man" and subordinates everything to job and career advancement. Job enrichment and job enlargement provide useful stakes at this stage.
5. *The Potential Mid Life Period* (Age 39-43)—These years represent a second transitional period in which individual reviews career progress. A certain pride in one's achievement and experience begins to develop. If the progress has not lived upto early dreams, feeling of resentment, sadness or frustration may cause emotional disequilibrium resulting in excessive drinking, in quitting a job or a "middle aged hippie life style". Professionalism is achieved in this period by internalising the values of the organisation.
6. *The Re-estáblishing and flowering period* (Age 43-50 or upto retirement)—The individual experiences a sense of contentment over past achievements and individual relaxes his competitive drives. He develops social ties and family relationships and learns how to relax.

The age limits are slightly arbitrary and may vary in accordance with countries and places. The above mentioned Levinson model of careers provides a new insight for appropriate training and development plans at each stage for achieving maximum individual and organisational effectiveness, productivity and output. HRD experts can find out training need for each stage of one's career and restructure human resource development plans to help building up individual development.

Various Approaches to Human Resources Development

Indian people have enjoyed the reputation of being learned people and our oldest Indian scriptures "the Vedas" signified knowledge. The holy *Guru-Shishya* tradition (*parampara*) and the Gurukul system of integrated life training signified the ancient Indian human development system. The sermons to Arjuna by Lord Krishna, as contained in *Bhagwat Gita* symbolize the system of learning in a non-formal way through a preceptor. The story of Eklavya mastering the art of archery by observing *Guru* Dronacharya giving lessons to his pupils, points out towards the self initiated learning process through observation. The Indian concept of HRD extends beyond individuals to include dyads, teams and inter-teams; it focuses not only on knowledge and skill development but also on developing appropriate attitudes, values, relationships and physical health. Indian system stresses on spiritual development, ultimately culminating in self-realisation.

Different thinkers and scholars have developed different concepts about human resource development in accordance with the needs of various societies. Sharu Rangnekar has identified these approaches as follows:[12]

A. Queen Bee approach in which one particular individual such as a chieftain, king or tribal leader utilizes all available resources for his own development;

B. Brahmanic approach wherein all resources are primarily used up for developing an elite group or section of the organisation;

C. Input approach which regards HRD as a mathematical equation of an assigned input and corresponding output in a mechanistic manner;

D. Automation approach which believes that HRD efforts can be over-simplified and rationalised with the creation of the ability to work with computers and modern technology;

E. Motivational approach which regards HRD as a means of motivation to all employees for greater productivity and efficiency;

F. And finally, creative approach which insists on creativity and innovations as the main focus of HRD efforts.

G. Human capital approach equated it with human capital formation. Schultz analysed five areas namely health, on the job training, formal education, adult literacy programme and migration of workers.

H. Social Psychological approach of David Mc Clelland in his book *Achieving Society* (1961) gave stress on achievement motivation for human development.

In developing countries like India, HRD should be synonymous to manpower planning, the whole object of which is to make available sufficient number of qualified men for occupying skilled positions which are created with the onward march of the society. Due to corruption, nepotism, caste, creed and other considerations many unqualified and incompetent persons manage to get key positions, while qualified and suitable persons remain discriminated, and unrecognised. The HRD concept starts with MC Gregors Theory of 'Y' and presumes equitable distribution of talents and capabilities amongst all individuals in the administration. HRD in administration assumes the possibility of development of the capabilities of all individuals depending upon the availability of the opportunities for development.

HRD Mechanisms, Processes and Outcomes

There are various HRD mechanisms which can be used by various organisations for meeting the needs and aspirations of individuals and teams in terms of their professional growth, advancement, recognition and self-actualization. Some of the main HRD mechanisms are as under:

1. Role analysis and development exercise;
2. Performance planning, and potential appraisal;
3. Performance analysis and review;
4. Training;

5. Job rotation;
6. Performance counselling and interpersonal feedback;
7. Quality Circles and taskforces;
8. Meetings, conferences and managerial learning networks;
9. Self-renewal and institution building exercises;
10. Career planning and succession planning;
11. Stress audit and stress management;
12. Personal growth laboratories and working education programmes;
13. Communication policies and motivational exercises;
14. Rewards and job-enrichment programmes;
15. Organisation development exercises.

HRD philosophy aims at developing the enabling capabilities of people in administration by developing an environment which provides some amount of initiative, trust, openness, autonomy, risk-taking and commitment to work. The HRD philosophy believes that it is the responsibility of the top level bureaucrat to create a climate of development and trust so that people may give their best to the administration with a sense of satisfaction and growth. It assumes that the government will take care of their basic needs through a series of welfare measures and higher order needs through appropriate management styles and systems. It assumes a healthy and motivating climate in the administrative system so that all individuals are able to develop their potential capabilities and skills under the supportive supervision and coaching of the superiors. HRD is a continuous process that involves development of enabling capacities of various levels of administrators in relation to different organisational tasks, functions and roles. HRD philosophy assumes that every superior provides a development climate and supports continuously the development of his subordinates. HRD mechanism consists of performance appraisals, feedback and counselling, potential appraisal, training, career planning and development, organisation development, job rotation, job enrichment, transfers, rewards, promotions, recreational and cultural activities, educational opportunities, sports activities, and all other developmental activities. In order to solve the complex problems of HRD which are predominantly of socio-psychological nature, a creative approach has to be adopted by the Government by allowing fullest development of all the employees engaged in the task of administration. India is committed to self-sustained accelerated growth of the country and this is a direct challenge to HRD policy makers because of the obvious direct link between administrative achievements of the bureaucracy and economic development. The human resource development programmes have to bring a democratic orientation in administrators. Democratic participation, preference for change and innovations, economic pragmatism, self-effacing role of civil servants and faith in developmental administration are some of the areas which Indian administrators will have to imbibe. The value system of Indian administrators at all levels has to be oriented. Human resource development should ensure proper utilisation and development of all individuals who are engaged at village, district and state levels in the task of administration.. Administration at lower levels in India is gripped in a curious psychological state dominated by the desire for radical self-advancement and fear of being left behind in wilderness and backwardness. Are we making fullest and optimum utilisation of all available human resources ? The question needs a careful analysis and in-depth study. The internal climate and environment of Indian administrators at lower levels requires drastic changes. Spirit of innovation, self-confidence, team spirit, cooperative working and a sense of service to the poor people have to be systematically promoted amongst field level administrators. An HRD climate or culture is essential for developing human resources which is characterised by octapace values i.e. openers, collaboration, trust, authenticity, proactiveness, autonomy, confrontation resolution and experimentation. Wright has put it well—"Viewing man as a human asset, would normally cause us to reconceive responsibilities for his development in several ways. First, upper management would insist upon the completion of approved (capital budgeted) human development programmes. Second, spans of management (ratios of subordinates to superiors) would be narrowed to facilitate the fulfillment of responsibilities both to current matters and to building the value of future resources. Third, managers would be given an incentive to develop subordinates since one measure of their effectiveness would be the "value added" to subordinate employees. Fourth, in response managers would allocate their time and intellectual energies to include the development of the human assets under their direction."[13] Manpower planning and the development of human resources must be seen in the context of socio-economic changes, the political commitments and the nature of political system of the country. Concomitant with the changing social, political and economic environment, there is a new shift about the conceptualisation of manpower planning and the development of human resources through teaching-learning processes.

Manpower planning can be defined as the process by which an organisation or system ensures that it has the right number of people and the right kind of people at the right places at the right time doing things for which they are economically most suitable. The concept of manpower planning at the macro-level involves anticipating the future by manpower projections and then planning, developing and implementing manpower action programmes, largely in the form of education and training, to carry out the implications of the projection.

The Role of Government in HRD in Administration

Firstly it refers to HRD activities in various government agencies and public sector undertakings. Secondly, it refers to the role of government at the macro-level by issuing and implementing various policies, procedures and conditions which affect HRD in various organisations. Training, job rotation, data-bank, manpower forecasting, performance appraisal are some of the well known HRD systems used in administration. Organisational development is one of the most widely used HRD mechanism in administration. Management by objective

(MBO) is a very useful O.D. intervention in administrative systems both at the central and state levels. An integrated HRD system has to provide for the development of administrators and personnel who in turn, have to look after key developmental activities in the country. Our concern in the development of human resources is the "socialisation of the individual to work." socialisation involves change in person and aims at "terminal behaviours". Human resource development programmes are specifically concerned with five kinds of changes. First are changes in skills (the abilities to perform some acts). Next are changes in knowledge (or ideas about something). Third are changes in attitudes (or in the feelings, emotions or beliefs people have). Fourth are changes in an awareness of self (or the present way of seeing one's behaviour). Lastly are changes in motivation to perform (or the desire to act differently)[14]. Human Resource Development in administration is a very challenging and difficult task as development strategy depends on an effective balance in the choices of some of the following critical areas :

1. Selection between three contradictory areas of training—skills, knowledge and attitudes.
2. Relative emphasis between quantity versus quality.
3. In the development of skills, the relative reliance of pre-employment formal training versus in-service or on-the job training.
4. Relative stress on science and technological subjects versus law, arts and humanities in educational field.
5. In the general rationale of human resource development, consideration of individual development versus development of the society.

Both training and development can be classified as on-the-job or off-the-job. Coaching is the most important formal on the job development method—other development methods include job rotation, classroom teaching and sensitivity training. It is foolish to assume that a person wholly lacking in natural environments of leadership can be trained to be a successful leader in administration or an effective manager.[15] Human resource development programmes must take note of people at lower and grass root levels and provide periodical reorientation suitable for their tasks and levels of performance. There are at times contradictions and implicit conflicts in human resource development programmes. Primarily the conflict arises at the level of individual and the organisation which the individual serves. Do we provide HRD programmes to improve the performance of organisational tasks or to fill in the gaps in the individual scale of knowledge, skills, attitudes and behaviour? Do we aim to promote individual excellence or organisational effectiveness ? The human resource development programmes in administration can include exploration of individual and small group behaviour through:

(i) identifying the values and attitudes stimulating innovative behaviour in administration,

(ii) developing incentives for goal achievement, and

(iii) discovering and practicing new behaviour patterns which are conducive to administrative effectiveness.

In the context of development administration HRD programmes should include; (a) simulation of problem solving situations in administrative organisations, (b) exercises for more effective decision-making, (c) application of various models of administrative behaviour to the real life situations of developing countries and (d) application of leadership skills and strategies to stimulate organisational innovations for more effective administration.

In developing countries there are two main difficulties in administration : (a) the rapidly changing and increasingly turbulent environment characterised by its complexity and uncertainty and (b) the divergence of public administration in different state environments leading to difficulties in making generalisations[16]. Human Resource Development becomes an instrument of achieving attitudinal change in administrators and ultimately results in efficient performance and output in the government. Human Resources Development programmes have received great attention in more developed countries like U.K., U.S.A. or France.

Human Resource Development—Needs Analysis

The analysis of human resources indicate the qualitative needs among people and logically leads to planning various types of developmental opportunities and experiences, especially educational and training programmes. The development of human resources if it is to be effective, must be backed up by careful and continuous research. Need analysis has to be a continuous cycle and can be conveniently conceptualised as consisting of several identifiable elements.

The HRD cycle may be expressed as planning (based upon need determination and goal setting), organising (deciding what type of final programme is needed and how it should be structured), implementing (making the programme available and placing participants in it), reviewing (evaluating the results obtained in terms of the objectives set) and feedback (the overall assessment of what should be done next to recycle based upon the cycle just completed) and thus the development of human resources operates not as an open-end sequence but a system.[17] The use of development programmes to achieve organisational goals requires the careful assessment of needs within the organisation; a determination of the goals that can be served by education or training; the people who need it and for what purposes and the content of the programme.[18]

For determining human resource development needs, a three-fold approach can be useful. It consists essentially of the following :

1. Organisational analysis;
2. Operational analysis or contextual analysis;
3. Man analysis and job analysis.

In the context of human resource development in administration, organisational analysis places an emphasis on the study of the entire organisation, its objectives, its resources, and the allocation of these resources as they bear upon organisational objectives. Development needs can be viewed as equivalent to problems and can be identified by determining (1) the stated standards and behaviour desired, (2) the standards inferred from and the behaviour observed and (3) the causes of discrepancies between the expected and the observed. Programmes for the development of human resources (i.e. formalised chances to learn) are provided to remove the causes of failure to attain standards or the desired, behaviour organisational analysis is the initial step for the diagnosis of individual behaviour. A second step is determining the adequacy of the human resources in the organisation by manpower inventories and performance appraisal systems. A third step is considering deviations from managerial standards as shown by unacceptable ratios or scores on direct and indirect efficiency indices. Broad organisational climate and the employees attitude are required to be surveyed for determining requirements of educational or training programmes. Organisational development programmes are really focused upon human resources. Operations analysis is concerned with the problem of what education and training should consist. In the fields of administration it is much more difficult to do operational analysis for high level administrative jobs and it is also difficult to measure the various individual skills, knowledge and attitudes that effect or are inferred from administrative behaviour. Man analysis in the context of administration is the most difficult phase in determining developmental needs because not only are we interested in performance but also the cause of that performance. In the context of administration the measurement of individual job behaviour leads to the injection of innumerable subjective or judgemental kinds of imprecision in measurement. In the field of administration the difficulty in obtaining objective performance records for technical, professional and managerial manpower is accentuated by the time-span problem. Interviews and questionnaire, as means of securing information from an employee or administrator with regard to his developmental needs have been relatively neglected so far in the context of public administration.

The basic need for providing development programmes to public personnel primarily rests on two arguments : (a) to keep employees updated in terms of their knowledge, skills and open attitudes since in recent past administration has become increasingly complex and diverse, (b) The profile of jobs is significantly different today than before, and to prevent employee obsolescence. Obsolescence becomes uncomfortable for these administrators who have stopped learning and count on their former education to carry them through, even though their jobs have outgrown them. In-service training is being visualised as an opportunity for formal training provided at appropriate time intervals in appropriate areas. "An antiquated structure and the leisurely procedures are incompatible with the fulfillment of the Plan tasks. Attention needs to be given towards evolving an administrative set up and modes of functioning which can meet the challenge of the plan. Professionalism in administration must be promoted. The administrator must have the capacity and the initiative to provide active leadership rather than merely react to the views and actions of others"[19]. Administration has a vital role in fulfilling the objective of the Five Year Plans. Human Resource Development can be a powerful instrument for effecting basic changes in the administrative structure. At district, State and Central levels, the personnel administration has to develop a system of early identification of talent, monitoring it through training and placement and improving the quality of support needed at various levels of administration. It has to evolve systems by which equal opportunity is available to people to grow and it must create special rewards to go to those who do better. There are many basic issues of human resource development such as selection, placement, training, education, individual development of talents and these areas need to be carefully examined by the professional human resource developers and specialists in the field of personnel management. The emerging culture in administration set certain norms such as the following :[20]

(i) Playing safe and adherence to rules is important for personal success. Playing safe also includes sending files to many people.

(ii) Poor achievement of results is less important than keeping to rules. Risk decisions are worse than putting the blame on other people.

(iii) Saying no to a proposal is generally safer than saying yes. No committed response will shift the responsibility in decision elsewhere and no serious damage is done to one's own position.

(iv) It is wiser to push the file and a decision to higher authority to avoid reversal of a decision in appeal or under pressure. The complex development needs of the present day administration call for a diverse range of programmes, designed to enhance their understanding of modern management techniques, their knowledge of significant technological and managerial developments, their appreciation of the outlook necessary for makers of policy, their interpretation of behavioural patterns in an organisational setting and their awareness of leadership skill[21]. In the context of human resource development in Government, HRD objectives can be analysed at three different levels; (i) Programme level (ii) Institutional level and (iii) Aggregate level. These three levels, from micro to macro, naturally involve different considerations and attributes.

HRD Developers and Administration

For human resource development in administration, manpower to be developed, available physical facilities, costs and funds allocated, availability of instructional personnel and the urgency of the situation have bearings on the selection of the techniques of HRD. There is indeed an abundance of HRD mechanisms used for developing human resources. The administrative arrangements for the conduct of formal development activities are also important in selecting the methods of instruction and implementing programmes for various levels of employees. There is a need for human resources developer who has three major roles; learning specialist, administrator and consultant. An individual has to perform three sub-roles.[22] Possibility of a human resource developer functioning in one or more of these roles is affected by three factors—the person, the organisation and the problem of developing human resources. HRD developer has to be a professional with adequate training and experience.

Development on-the-job—Organisational socialisation and on-the-job development reinforces the off-the-job training. It can be arranged by assigning new employees to an experienced administrator who explains various methods and techniques of administration by doing it himself and later supervising it when it is being done by the new entrants. Because of the complexity, it is difficult to provide on the job training as in a Vestibule School in the field of general administration. In management of people, administrators have to deal with each individual in a different manner and therefore on the job training for administrator, is rather difficult. HRD developer has to be a curriculum builder, materials developer, instructor and a mentor.

Development off-the-job—In the context of administration, off-the-job programmes like conferences, seminars, management games, group discussions, in-basket exercises, case studies, incident studies, syndicate discussions, role playing, brain storming sessions, laboratory training and other such HRD techniques are generally very useful, informative and valuable. Case method, which was first used in the Harvard Law School in 1880s has been widely used in human resource development programmes in administration as it provides opportunities for trainees to study, discuss and discover the underlying principles in each case. The British have made clever use of living case material in the residential Administrative Staff College at Henley-on-Thames. Many of the development programmes used today centre upon ways to improve some facts of individual communication skill such as speaking, listening, reading, writing and of course, getting along with people—Dale Carnegie Courses and public-speaking courses are well known and widely available. Performance appraisals and potential appraisals are also very useful tools.

The Existing Infrastructure for Human Resource Development in Administration

Government of India now have a separate Ministry of Human Resource Development which covers education and cultural development. There are numerous programmes entirely on human resource development, a number of central and state level Institutions are providing various training programmes to the administrators. Lal Bahadur Shastri National Academy of Administration, Mussorie is conducting following courses—

1. I.A.S. Professional Course (Phase I)—24 week programme for direct recruits.
2. Training Programme for I.A.S. Officers (Promoted or on the select list)—4 weeks.
3. Foundation Course—16 weeks Programme for fresh recruits to All India and General Services Group 'A'.
4. Joint Secretaries Course on Policy Analysis and Formulation—4 weeks programme.
5. I.A.S. Professional Course (Phase-II)—10 weeks for fresh recruits to I.A.S. on completion of their one year district training.
6. Management Development Course—4 weeks for I.A.S and All India and Central Services 'A' Group Officers with 6 to 10 years of service.

The above programmes are thus preparing the I.A.S. and All India and Central Services 'A' group officers of the Centre and State Governments for various duties and responsibilities in the field of administration. There are thirty two General Training Institutions catering for the training needs of various central government employees. There are seventeen State Training Institutions engaged in human resource development programmes for state government administrators of district and state level. There are twenty three National Training Institutions and twenty eight other Training institutions which organise various human resource development programmes for state and district level functionaries[23]. Indian Institute of

Public Administration, New Delhi is conducting a number of Management Development programmes, Management Orientation programmes, Advanced professional programme in public administration and other specialised course on various aspects of public administration. It is very difficult to elaborate or review the various human resource development programmes in administration which are being organised in hundred and one training institutions of the country. The Administrative Reforms Commission's Report on "Personnel Administration envisaged *inter alia* a leading role in the field of training with the following main functions"[24] :

— promote, coordinate and facilitate training.

— formulate policies, regulations and procedures on training and oversee their implementation.

— advise Ministries and Departments on : determination of training needs, instructional techniques, and evaluation of training programmes.

During the last ten year Minsitry of HRD has developed class-links between Universities and academies and various Central/State Government agencies, leading to several very useful human resource development programmes. Programming of training programmes here only means development of feasible plans with fairly identified time schedules, supported by adequate preparation and resources needed to implement plan and thereby creating a relationship between training inputs and the training users. If we analyse the patterns of human resource development programmes we find pre-entry training programmes, in-service training programmes, management development programmes and many educational programmes for public administrators at various levels. Pre-entry institutional training along with foundation course is now a must for I.A.S. probationers and All India and Central Services 'A' grade officers. At state level Provincial Services class I are also getting pre-entry basic courses at State administrative institutions. In several state services, the picture is not very happy due to a heavy backlog of untrained administrators. Although the concept of in-service training to administrators is acceptable to all, to hopefully reach wider segments public administrators is a massive and gigantic task, not only in volume but also in qualitative terms.

A combined foundational training in respect of fresh entrants of higher civil services in India e.g. I.A.S., I.P.S., I.F.S., Indian Audit and Accounts service etc. for four/five months has been started. Courses offered are (i) Public Administration, (ii) Law, (iii) Political Theory and Constitution of India (iv) Planning and Economic Policy, (v) Indian History and Culture and (vi) Hindi which equip the new entrants inducted from various educational disciplines with an understanding of the basic knowledge, fundamental and applied, relevant to the new functional setting as civil servants. New entrants are exposed to the fundamentals of the country's socio-economic and politico-administrative institutions, that is, the ecology of their work place so that they understand the interdependence and interpenetration of the various sub-systems that make the total system in democratic India. Through foundational training new entrants are expected to acquire right kind of values, develop right type of attitudes, inculcate appropriate sensitivity to the needs and demands of the public. The new entrants are catapulted into an expansive and open environment of social moving where interpersonal relationships, sympathy, empathy and other faculties of head and heart are required to be built by their exposure to the totality of socio-cultural existence in a given system. Middle group service officers are also exposed to various subjects of foundational course in their state level/ national training institutions. Basic training of new entrants in professional subjects is ordinarily done in professional training institutions, or staff colleges. Generation of specialised skill, promotion of specific competence and improvement of particular job-oriented technical know-how (or know why) of work, socio-structural dynamics of the particular service cadres, form the essential part of professional basic training. During basic training contextwise as well as conceptually, the departmental professional training is operated at the micro level and prepares new entrants for their professional jobs. The National Academy of Direct Taxes, Nagpur caters to and oversee the training needs of the income tax department. S.V.P. National Police Academy, Hyderabad provides basic training to I.P.S. Officers and Basic Terminal Courses on a sandwich pattern of training. Without basic trainings a public servant may remain an educated man but can never become a human resource in the service of the Government. On-entry training has a vital nexus with aspects like efficiency, economy in learning time, error elimination, personnel productiveness, career development and overall systematic effectiveness[25]. Management Development Programmes (MDP) and Executive Development Programmes (EDP) are essentially in-service, short duration development courses pertaining to character of refresher training of administrators. The general object is to help participants to widen their perspective and conceptual abilities; acquaint them with the latest social, economic and political environment in the country, familiarise them with principles and techniques of modern management and help them to develop interpersonal skills. Often civil servants are imparted refresher training at regular intervals to refresh their knowledge of all that they had learnt in their early careers, or to renew their skills. These courses are conceived as a "consolidation of skill, knowledge and experience" and help trainees in learning the latest development of their specialised professions. HRD philosophy stresses human relationships in a work situation.

HRD at the Grassroot level—The highest priority needs to be assigned to the HRD officials at grassroot level who come into contact with the public directly or indirectly on a large number of occasions. HRD challenges at the grassroot level vary from sector to sector, but the broad objectives of the HRD system are generally as follows :

1. Improve professional and technical competence and skills.
2. Make them perceive the development process in its totality and help in the process of liberalisation.
3. Upgrade their skills for identifying and formulating development projects and make them understand the development approach in the context of new environment.

4. Make them action-oriented and sensitize them to the new needs.
5. Activate them for better coordination at the field level.
6. Comply and execute orders and instructions at the field level.

There is a need for HRD personnel of grass root level to build capacities and provide motivation for planning and management in the context of change in :

(i) Perception of development and globalisation in the new environment,

(ii) Change in value system and basic social values,

(iii) Change in technology and pattern of work.

The challenges involved in the HRD of functionaries at the grass root level can be stated as under :

(i) There is a problem of having adequate infrastructure for HRD for a large number of people. There are an enormous number of functionaries spread across the country.

(ii) Meaningful identification of HRD needs should be made with a view to remove the gaps that hinder optimum performance by employees.

(iii) How the HRD of employees should be followed up and who should do it ? Will it be appropriate for an outside HRD consultant to take follow up action ?

(iv) It is difficult to get adequate number of HRD specialists to train the employee at grass root level.

(v) Most of the HRD institutions involved in grass root development of employees are reluctant to adopt a system of proper feedback and evaluation.

(vi) There does not exist any clear cut HRD policy for grass root employees in most of the organisations of the government.

The grass root level functionaries include patwaris,

agricultrual assistants, foresters, stockmen in animal husbandry department, nurses in health services, clerks in offices and all other categories of employees working interface with citizens at the lowest levels. HRD of such personnel alone can bring about effective change in administrative system. Class III and IV employee (C and D groups) constitute about ninty-eight per cent of the Central Government personnel. It has been roughly estimated that about seventy per cent of the Class III and ninety per cent of Class IV personnel are at present untrained. A review should be made of the HRD needs and existing facilities of Class III and IV employees and a phased programme for improving training should aim at not only improving job skills but also developing proper attitudes towards the public[26]. By and large, HRD in Government has not reached the grassroot levels and inadequate measures have been taken so far.

HRD at grass root level is not attractive as compared to the training of middle and senior levels of functionaries.

HRD for Top Level Administration

There is a general fallacy widely prevalent in the senior circles of bureaucracy that the top level administration do not really need any kind of development and that there is little for them to learn. Knowledge in modern times doubles itself every five years and to just keep oneself abreast with the 'adequacy' benchmark one has to double one's endeavours at equipping oneself with the relevant skills, techniques and knowledge. The Administrative Reforms Commission (India) Report on Personnel Administration has stated that senior management education and preparation should be largely oriented towards policy-making, programme-planning and review and problem solving. The main thrust should be in "overallness" a sense of horizontality, perception of futuristic policy-perspective and a systems approach. The training has to be geared towards policy formulation, integrative outlook and interdependence of sub-systems. The base of the exposure programmes for top level officials who are the senior managers in the making, would naturally consist of headquarters work, policy and planning disciplines, sub-area specialisation etc. and peak of the programmes pyramid would reach for the conceptualisation leading to a sound support system for policy, problem-solving and strategic planning, interactive and productive thinking and input functions such as interest articulation, aggregation and political socialisation.[27] Continuing education provides the civil servants at all levels means to perform competently in their present jobs and widens their mental horizon. The concepts is an indispensable supplement to basic education. Open School and Open University systems are most useful for continuing education. The responsibility for providing competency based continuing education should be shared by the individuals, organisations, educational institutions and the professional bodies. The doors for continuing education after one joins the service should remain open through correspondence courses and evening classes schemes. Open universities with correspondence course systems are doing a great service in this respect. A proper strategy for providing continuing education to all categories of civil servants needs to be evolved. Every encouragement and facility should be given for self development and further education. This should include :

(i) liberal grant of leave for study;

(ii) facilities of leave for attending seminars and conferences.

(iii) encouragement of original work.

(iv) reimbursing part of expenditure on professional books and periodicals."[28]

Reimbursement of expenses incurred on correspondence courses can be a good source of encouragement for self development. The education, training and development of executives, supervisors and other employees in the future will undergo radical changes and strategic shifts. Changes currently underway in thinking about manpower planning, the development of human resources and organisational planning are typical of the times. Development is a life-long process and the minds of the administrators need to be periodically retooled and revitalised.

Computer Technology and Human Resources

A number of studies have pointed out that computer technology reduces unskilled labour and expands the work in such areas as managerial planning, coordination, engineering, research and development.[29] Reinhard Bendix, Seymour Melman, Frederickl Harbison and Charles Hyers have all written on a general theory that technological development demands relatively greater increases in managerial manpower than in clerical manpower. Use of Electronic Data Processing has, according to research studies, decreased overall manpower with the clerical personnel suffering a greater loss than the managerial, both in number and in proportion to the total effected employment. Scholars like Leavitt, Whisler and Shults think that the computer will centralise the process of managerial decision making by taking over much of the decisions previously made by middle management personnel. Computer application in administration may not necessarily centralise the process of decision-making but rather strengthen decentralisation. The improvement in the information content and the standardisation in various reports help the administrators to make more logical and coordinated decisions as a whole. The computer tends to upgrade the affected line job, and tends to rigidify the work environment.

The challenges posed by the new economic environment demand a wholesome development of people and administrations. Human Resources development programmes have to prepare personnel for the tasks of development especially the anti-poverty programme of the Government. Human resource development programmes can be instruments of national integration. After independence the scope of administration has been rapidly enlarged with the object of accelerating rural development, modernising agriculture, building up infrastructure, mobilising the natural resources, rapid industrialization and removal of rural poverty. Administration has to lay greater emphasis on effective empowerment of the people in the rural areas and reorienting the educational system on the model of the rural project at Jawaja in Ajmer (1975) district of Rajasthan. The central and state governments should start experiments of empowering people and intensity monitoring of various scheme formulated to uplift the masses. The enlarged functions and primary responsibilities of district administration today include new activities as community development, employment schemes, family planning etc. Public distribution has expanded today beyond any doubt. The task of administration today is to attain maximum efficiency, efficacy and economy in administrative functions. With the concept of development administration being the primary concern of administrators, there is a qualitative change in the concept of administration today. Drought prone area programmes, integrated rural development programmes and Intensive agriculture development programmes require high level of dedication, spirit of service, integrity and involvement of the administrators. In the context of globalisation and liberalisation, it is necessary that industrial relations, worker's welfare, worker development and quality of work life (including job enlargement, job design and work reorganisation) are given due importance by the administration.[30] Employees commitment can be fostered by providing opportunities for self fulfillment in one's work to everyone in administration.

Difficulties and Problems of Human Resource Development

The tasks of drawing up comprehensive human resource development plans in the developing countries are beset by a number of paradoxical difficulties and problems. Because of the paucity of financial resources the developing countries can hardly afford comprehensive HRD plan for the people. The education and training of a professional man requires eighteen to twenty years of formal education and one year of intensive training followed by periodical in-service training. There are structural imbalances in labour market. Acute shortage of technical people on one hand and large surplus of unskilled grass root level workers exist simultaneously in developing countries. Training needs analysis of various levels of administrators is a difficult task. There is generally inadequate infrastructure for providing adequate in-service training and professional education to all civil servants who are engaged in administration, at regular periods. There is a lack of adequate monitoring arrangements to get feedback of human resource development programmes. The scientific evaluations of various human resource development programmes are not possible due to various in-built problems of evaluation and validation. Although it is easy to ascertain the costs of human resource development programmes, the benefits resulting from such programmes are difficult to measure. Career planning schemes, job enlargement and job-enrichment programmes, and periodical in-service training form important part of human resource development programmes but their total evaluation is rather very difficult in objective terms. Jack W. Tayler has identified the following mistakes which need to be avoided to make HRD programmes more useful :

"1. Although staff department can play a major role in developing and executing human resource programmes, they should not be held accountable for developing human resources. It remains the Line Manager's responsibility to develop the human resources.
2. Failing to equip administrators and manager for their training role.
3. Making a hasty needs analysis.
4. Substituting training for selection.
5. Limiting training to classrooms.
6. Training can be used to change some dysfunctional behaviours of the traineers but using training, to try to change a person's personality is both unproductive and unethical".[31]

It is high time that the basic questions about HRD are properly answered. Why at all should the organisation invest in HRD unless it is assured of commensurate results and returns? Who goes for training and HRD in Govt ? Do we have qualified HRD professionals? Do we have adequate physical facilities for HRD? Do we make correct evaluation of various HRD programmes? Should training be learner-related or teacher oriented? Should not there be a critical appraisal of HRD itself in all its many splendoured dimensions ? The answers to above questions can be very inconvenient, unwelcome and unpleasant. The human resource development programmes have many problems. It is not easy to identify groups which require development in various skills/techniques and knowledge. Appropriate reward system is not built in the civil service system and performance appraisal continues to be subjective. No human resources accounting has been consciously attempted which has resulted in the dwindling of this most valuable asset (viz. man) very fast. There have been increasing efforts on the part of the Colleges, Academies and Universities to offer courses designed to meet the career requirements of civil servants but there has hardly been any move for coordination between academic world and the training division. There is no *modus operandi* to communicate government requirements to training institutions. HRD in Government should be imbibed with serious qualitative concern and professionalism. Today there is a resource gap in training whether it is availability of trainers, of training programmes, or even institutions.[32] Training and Education can be evaluated but development of individual can not be properly evaluated as it is a long-term investment over the years.

The Conceptual Sub-Systems of HRD

HRD Sub-systems—Given below are some HRD sub-systems

1. Role Analysis
2. Selection and Placement
3. Transfer and Rotation
4. Reward and Punishment
5. Appraisal of Performance
6. Feedback and counselling
7. Training and Development
8. Career planning
9. Succession planning
10. HRD data bank
11. Participative devices
12. Other mechanisms

FIGURE - AN INTEGRATED HRD MATRIX (24 A)

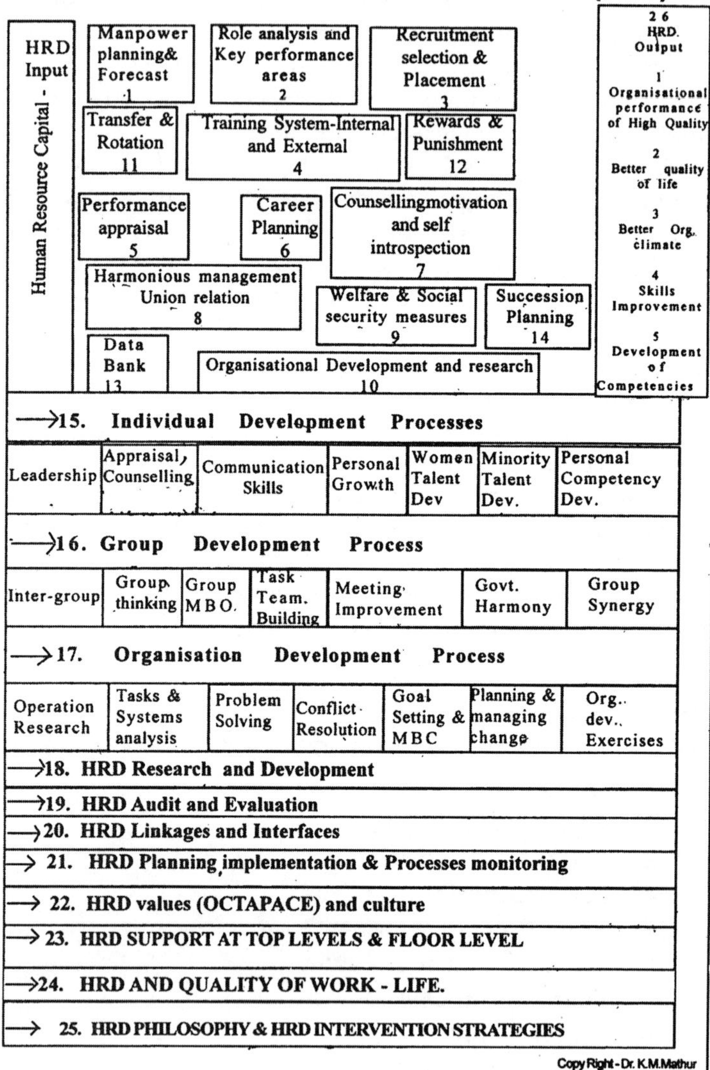

HRD for administration will require development of following skills and values for building HRD climate—

S. No.	*Basic Skills*	*S. No.*	*HRD Values and Climate*
1.	Goal setting	1.	Openness
2.	Appraisal	2.	Collaborative attitude
3.	Counselling	3.	Trust
4.	Reviewing	4.	Authenticity
5.	Learning	5.	Pro-activity
6.	Self development	6.	Autonomy
7.	Visioning	7.	Confrontation and problem solving
8.	Mentoring	8.	Experimentation

There are numerous HRD challenges for professionals in the context of liberalisation and political instability at the centre. Some of main challenges are as under :

1. Balancing HRD systems with the HRD spirit and philosophy and to build a new humanist movement in administration.
2. Increasing Core Competencies for administrators at various levels and providing lower rank functionaries autonomy, growth and individual development.
3. Sustaining vitality and growth of the Indian economy by initiating a comprehensive HRD strategy.
4. Enhancing spirit of competitiveness and total quality management in the Indian industrial enterprises by providing strategic HRD planning.
5. Building synergy among large and small enterprises and their contribution to employment and production by building a conducive HRD climate in the country.
6. Creating visionary administrators and policy makers who are future driven and strategic thinkers;
7. Developing appropriate policy for managing the motivation and morale of employees and to create a larger entity of all employees in administration.

8. Building an international image of Indian products and achieving excellence in various economic sectors.
9. HRD is a total activity and there is strong need for allocating more resources to people lower down in administration.

Administrators of the future will have to reckon with what Toffler described as "the dizzying disorientation brought on by the premature arrival of the future" and human resources development programmes drawn up for future should necessarily need to equip them for this role. To quote Mayo, "The administrator of the future must be able to understand the human social facts for what they are, unfettered by his own emotions or prejudices. We can not achieve this ability except by careful training—a training that must include knowledge of relevant technical skills, of the systematic order of operations ....."[33]. Human Resource Development programmes have to be remodelled and interpreted today along a wide spectrum of economic, political, social and several other parameters. Human resource development programmes have to be suitably strengthened, developed and organised in a far sighted national policy on human resources development in administration. It is a very challenging task that requires an exchange of thought and ideas and pooling of resources among all agencies of State and Central Government which are engaged in the task of development policies. Human resource development is a life-long, whole-career programme and not merely a narrowly conceived, one time, short period work-place phenomenon. It should aim at generating an innate capacity as well as demonstrable capacity to face the future, to overtake events and to tame turbulence in an effective manner. The human resource development programmes must allow people to learn, and create education and development within a sound organisation culture. Participation and mutual goal-setting commitments will result in professionalism and broaden the outlook of the administrators. There will be enormous challenges for HRD in order to help India attain the economic, social and spiritual vision for 21st century. HRD agenda will have to move from corporate to national vision and HRD will have to face the following main challenges :[34]

(a) articulating a shared business vision and help people commit to a strategic plan to achieve quantum jumps in customer satisfaction;

(b) developing quality and cost leadership both to defend the domestic market and also to raise share in foreign markets;

(c) developing indigenous technology and brand names to survive and grow in the regime of intellectual property rights system (IPRS); and

(d) globalising Indian mindset to constantly seek international image of Indian products and achieve excellence in various economic sectors.

The main aim of HRD is to achieve liberalisation and globalisation of economy by building a TQM mindset through customer orientation, process orientation and people orientation at all levels. Successful development administration depends upon the knowledge and utilisation of those factors and processes which motivate change and these changes can be easily brought out if human resource personnel are dedicated. The absence of a constructive and realistic action plan for HRD can make the general development of the country all the more difficult and can frustrate the effective implementation of the developmental plans. A realistic and long-term human resource development plan appears to be a most important pre-requisite for attaining a self-sustained, self-accelerating economy and for implementing the general developmental Five Year Plans. It is essential to undertake HRD action plans which promote positive attitudes and develop harmony amongst individuals and groups which are engaged in implementing developmental administration of the country. Human resource development action plans should aim at development of individuals as well as development of the whole clusters of administrators as a team committed of the high ideals of efficiency, democracy, development, and social justice. HRD can be easily compared to the growth and development of the human resource personnel of a big orchestra. Symphonic music of the orchestra has to be so integrated in the performance that while it should be possible to hear it and appreciate it individually in the total ensemble of the group of instruments in which each instrument maintains its separate identity, it also adds richness, melody and meaning to the performance of the entire orchestra on the whole. The task is stupendous and most challenging indeed yet no efforts should be spared to develop and nurture a big orchestra. The famous proverb that every thousand miles journey begins with the first step is particularly relevant in the context of HRD for administration in the era of globalisation and liberalisation.

REFERENCES

1. Leonard Nadler, *Developing Human Resources*, Second Edition, 1976, Learning Concepts, Austin Taras, p. 3.
2. Leon C. Megginson, *Personnel and Human Resource Administration*, 1974, p. 4.
3. Bata K. Dey—"Training in the Civil Services—Plea for a Holistic Construal"—*Indian Journal of Public Administration*, October-December, 1992, Vol. XXIV, p. 4.
4. Dr. C.D. Deshmukh, *Management and Administration—New Trends*, Training Abstracts, 17—Training Division, New Delhi, 1972, p. 12.
5. Clatt F. Vough and Bernard Asbell, *Tapping the Human Resource—a Strategy for Productivity*, 1975, p. 7, Amacom-New Delhi.
6. C Vough and B Asbell, *Tapping the Human Resources*, p. 172.
7. Assheton Committee Report on the Training of Civil Servants (1944). Quoted in Training of Civil Servants in the United Kingdom—Training Monograph No. 12—Training Division 1972, p. 1.
8. A.P. Saxena, "Accountability in Training of Administrators", *I.J.P.A.* July-September, 1983, XXIX No. 3, p. 539.
9. See Edwin I. Miller, E. H. Burack and Maryann H. Albaecht, *Management of Human Resource*, England Cliffs N.J. Prentice Hall, 1980; Andrew F. Sikula—*Personnel Management and Human Resource Management*, New York, Willey Management and Human Resources Management, New York, Willey 1976.

10. See Krik H. Erikson—Childhood and Society—New York, Norton, 1963, pp. 247-74.

11. For full details, see—Daniel J. Levinson, Charlotte Dcrrow, Edward B Klein, Maria N. Leirnson and Brazton Nc Kee—*The Seasons of a Nan's Life*. New York, 1978, Quoted in James A.F. Stoner- Management, pp. 565-66.

12. Sharu S. Rangekar—"Changing Patterns of Human Resources Development". *Udyog Pragati*. Journal of National Institute for Training and Industrial Engineering; Bombay, Vol. II No. 3, July-September, 1978.

13. R. Wright, *"Managing Man as a Capital Asset, "Personal Journal,* April, 1970, p. 294.

14. Allen A Zell, *Dynamic Management Education* 3rd Rd. Management Education Associated, Seattle, 1966, pp. 2-1.

15. Sir John Fletcher Gooke in Institute of Public Administration in the Commonwealth: the Report of a Conference of Directors.

16. Public Administration in the 1970s. C.Y.W—*International Review of Administrative Science,* Vol. XXXVII No. 3 1971.

17. Jesse C. Mc Keen "Training Records and Information System" in Robert L. Craig & Lester R. Bittel—ed. *Training and Development, Handbook,* Mc Graw Hill, New York, 1967, p. 609.

18. William Mc Gehee and Paul W. Thayer, *Training in Business and Industry,* Wiley, New York, 1961, p. 24.

19. Approach to the Fifth Five Year Plan—Planning Commission. Government of India, 1972.

20. Ishwar Dayal, *Change in Administration—Directions and Organizational Planning,* Training Abstract 26, Training Division 1974 pp. 3-4.

21. Recommendations of the Seminar on the Development of Senior Administrators in the Public Service of Developing Countries, Geneva, 1968, Trg Division Training Monograph No. 18, Government of India, 1972.

22. Leonard Nadler, *Developing Human Resources—Learning Concepts,* Second Edition, 1970, p. 151.

23. For names and addresses of Training Institutions see—Annexure of Compendium of Training Programmes, 1986-87.

24. Report on Personnel Administration Administrative Reform Commission Government of India, April, 1969—Recommendation 26.

25. United Nations—Handbook of Training in Public Service.

26. Administrative Reforms Commission on Training—Recommendation 38—Training Division-June, 1969. Training Monograph No. 2, 1969, p. 44.

27. Bata K. Dey, Training in the Civil Services-Plea for a Holistic Construal, *I.J.P.A.* Oct.-Dec, 83, No. 4 Vol. XXXX, p. 837.

28. Study Team on Personnel Administration August : 1967—Recommendation 121 (p. 249)—Training Monograph. Training Division, June, 1969, p. 54.

29. Frederick Harbison and Charles A Mayers Management in the Industrial world. New York McGraw Hill Book Conf, 1959. p. 24.27 and also William J Wasmith, Simonds, Hilbert & Hak Chang Lee-Human Resource Administration—Problems of Growth and Change Noughton Mifflin, New York, 1970, p. 358.

30. Udai Pareek and T.V. Rao, *Development and Managing Human Resource Systems.* (1985)

31. Jack W. Tayler, "Ten Serious Mistakes in Management Training Development" *Personnnel Journal,* 53, Nov-May, 1974, pp. 357-62.

32. A. P. Saxena, "Some Problems of Resource Gap in Training". Third Annual Training Conference Proceeding, Vol. II, Nov, 1970.

33. K. Nayo, *The Social Problems of an Industrial Civilization,* Cambridge Mass—Narvard 1945.

34. M.B. Athreya (1966), *HRD For India : Vision for the 21st Century,* in D.P. Sinha; Y.R.K. Reddy and Others (Editors), Aligning Human Resource Processes—Challenges of Development pp. 19-31, New Delhi, Tata McGraw Hill.

5

Human Resource Development for Workers

Globalisation is the integration of finance, markets, technologies and Nation-States to a degree never witnessed before in a way that is enabling individuals, corporations, and National-States of reach round the world as one economic unit with free market system. The main components of liberalisation, according to Jiberto and Mommen, are as under:

1. Privatisation of state and parastatal enterprises in order to reduce inefficiencies and government protection monopolies;
2. High interest rates and credit squeeze in order to reduce inflationary tendencies;
3. Trade liberalisation in order to open up the internal market and expose local industry to world market competition and boost foreign trade exchange;
4. Domestic demand management, leading to a lowering state budgets and decreasing expenditure in the social sector;
5. Currency adjustment in order to improve the balance of payment by raising import prices and making exports more competitive; and

6. Free market prices in order to remove distortions resulting from subsidised food taxes on luxury items". [1]

The major objectives of the liberalisation policy are to foster privatisation and globalisation of the Indian economy. July 24, 1991 will be long remembered as a historic day in the annals of Indian economy when Indian model of socio-economic development underwent a paradigmatic change with the decision of the Government of India to follow the policy of economic liberalism. [2] With Liberalisation of the economy, many changes are taking place in the corporate sector and on the socio-economic front. There is pressure on corporate sector to perform—produce quality products and quality services with increased competition, there is need to become efficient cost-effective and acquire upgradation of technology. The world has become a global village today and no nation can isolate itself completely from the rest of the world and survive far too long. Technologies, finances, management systems and even people have begun to move more freely from one country to another. The new economic policies have pushed the country into the race of competitive advantage. Technological improvements, business strategies, quality concerns, structural adjustments and mobility of labour, will all have to be implemented through the people. Recent books such as *The End of Affluence* and *The End of Work* foster a gloom about future job opportunities and people often feel a growing uneasiness about the future,[2a] HRD for workers becomes important in view of the emerging new challenges of liberalisation and globalisation. Therefore human resources the greatest assets. In the context of liberalisation and competitiveness organisations have to make its workers more productive and reduce redundant work-force through redeployment or even retrenchment. How will organisations develop multi-skilled workers and what strategies will be adopted by the corporate world to redeploy its labour force to its best advantages ? The Academy of HRD and National HRD network organised in April of 1993, the national conference on "HRD for workers" at Bhilai to provide a forum for various HRD practitioners and managers to grapple with the challenges, problems and strategies of HRD for workers. The promises and opportunities of HRD for Indian workers have assumed great significance in the context of the new liberalized industrial and economic policy. The increasing challenges of globalisation, competition and growth through expansion, diversification and acquisition have important implications for HRD of workers. It is ultimately the workers who should be the main beneficiary of HRD because they constitute more than ninety per cent of the human resources in almost all the organisations. HRD should be able to develop the five dimensions of human resource namely Physical health, Relationships, Attitudes, Knowledge and Skills (PRAKS). HRD have to take into consideration integration of various sub-groups for achieving organisational effectiveness.

"HRD for workers can be studied under following heads:

1. HRD Strategies for Competitive Advantage of Workers

Udai Pareek defines HRD as encompassing six human units' namely, individual, the role he plays, the dyadic relationship, the team processes, inter-team processes and at the organisational level.[3] With reference to workers, these six focus areas are most relevant for HRD. It is ultimately the worker who really creates wealth and the core of management has to be the "human core." Human Resource development systems have to address to the needs and aspirations of the workman not only as an employee but as a human being in a holistic fashion. For HRD inputs, proper contents and methodology for worker's education and training are needed for building a climate of trust. Workers have to be sensitized to face the emergent business realities of global competition, ISO and need for excellence in product and quality. There has to be a broad consensus about the threats, challenges and opportunities that the above phenomena are throwing up as perceived by the workmen themselves. High level of motivation and trust, reduced absenteeism, better discipline, more cohesive team efforts, greater sense of pride and commitment in the organisation and emergence of a harmonious industrial relations climate are essential for achieving HRD climate of total quality management and total worker's commitment for the corporate efforts. Job-boundaries and skills-boundaries have to go and workers have to be developed for a holistic approach to work.

2. Principles in Designing HRD Systems for Workers

For each organisation, HRD systems have to be designed differently but basic principles and the specific components may remain the same. HRD focus has to be on the following:

(a) Focus on enabling capabilities development of organisational health, improvement of problem solving capabilities, increased employee productivity and development of human resources at all levels.

(b) Balancing adaptation and change in the organisational culture—Role of HRD can be to modify organisational culture and take the organisation forward by enabling organisation to learn anticipating changes and adaptability to it.

(c) Focus to contextual factors—HRD system must make organisations capable of taking care of various contextual factors such as state technology, level of employee skills, union leadership attitudes, employee's attitude towards learning, management approach towards workers, and organisational mission and challenges.

(d) Building linkages with other functions—Long-term corporate planning, marketing, production, budgeting and finance and other similar functions need to be strengthened by HRD system.

(e) Balancing specialisation and diffusion of the functions—HRD should help in strengthening of employees but should also prepare them for other diversified jobs and roles. Line people have to be involved in various aspects of HRD.

(f) Developing monitoring mechanisms—All HRD systems must be periodically evaluated and inbuilt monitoring systems of HRD should be developed by the HRD professionals. Both qualitative and quantitative decisions need to be balanced by the HRD system.

(g) HRD as a total integrated system—Various HRD systems can provide effective human resource development only when entire organisation is covered by HRD in various phases over the years. Geographical phasing, vertical phasing, functional phasing and sophistication phasing should be carefully planned with sequenced phases over a period of time[4] HRD systems are bound to contribute significantly to positive cultural changes, increased productivity and better quality of work-life. HRD has to encompass six human units, namely, individual employees, their assigned roles, the dyadic relationships, the team processes, inter-team processor and at the organisational level to make it a total integrated system.

The development of the employee is not an easy task because he has to face many problems at various stages of his career such as:

1. Recruitment and placement.
2. Job-analysis and role enactment.
3. Job-satisfaction and job evaluation
4. Development of personality
5. Utilisation as human resource
6. Retirement and pre-retirement training for second job.

Development differs from man to man. Productivity and quality are the two areas for concern by all workers. Workers are generally classified into the following four categories and all need to be developed to their utmost capacity:

(a) Work horses (b) Stars

(c) Problem children and (d) Dead-wood

Each type of worker needs different HRD interventions.

(h) Focus on motivational aspects of HRD—HRD must provide inspiration to the employees to do their work with their best ability and commitment. HRD system should help organisations in managing dissatisfaction and frustration by regular counselling and monitoring.

The orientation of HRD professional working in corporate sector has to be different from those working in Government organisations or services to develop a very specific development approach for workers. According to Dr. Mrityunjay B. Athreya, "the ultimate aim of HRD is the full participation of the individual in job and life. HRD aims to move executives and workmen towards fuller participation, so that their potential can be utilised to the benefit of themselves and the organisation." For achieving higher productivity, organisations have not only to meet the basic needs but also employees self actualisation needs.

3. Kautilya's Contribution to Human Resource Development

Kautilya's *Arthasastra* was written in about 310 BC as the minister of king Chandra Gupta Maurya and it contains some ideas on human resources development. Kautilya believed that it is not inscrutable destiny but man himself shapes his destiny (*Sutra* 42). Regarding theory of motivation, Kautilya suggested four-fold strategy of *Sama, Dama, Danda* and *Bheda*. Kautilya believed that in different situations people require different types of motivations. In Kautilya's *Arthasastra* places great emphasis on human advancement, renewal and improvement through training. Kautilya identified the following five basic characteristics of the trainable persons:

(1) Desire to learn,

(2) Effective listening ability,

(3) Ability to reflect,

(4) Ability to reject the false views, and

(5) Intentness on truth and not to any person.

Kautilya had identified six types of competencies and also enumerated methodology of testing them as given below in the table :

S.N.	*Typology of competence*	*Methodology of testing*
1.	Technical/Professional	Use of experts
2.	Intelligence (native) perseverance and dexterity	Direct observation in handing of assignments
3.	Eloquence, boldness, and presence of mind	Direct observations on various occasions of conversation and assignments.
4.	Behavioural ability to bear troubles	Ditto
5.	Uprightness, friendliness and firmness	Ditto
6.	Strength of character	Get report's and make Inquiries

Even today various industrial houses and corporation tend to rely on the above indicated methods of testing for selection of their employees. Kautilya said: From the capacity for doing work, is the ability of a person judged. (Sutra 8.28). He emphasised on the twin qualities of "the skill - in- Action" and "Quest for perfection." *Arthasastra* placed stress on human resource development for building competencies and therefore he can rightly be termed as the origin of modern concept of Human Resource Development. Kautilya recommended rigorous training and self-discipline for achieving human advancement, renewal and improvement. In Sutra 5-4.5 Kautilya observed "Training disciplines suitable stuff.... A science imparts discipline to one, whose intellect has the qualities of desire to learn, listening to the teacher, learning, retention, thorough understanding and reflection. In fact the very first chapter of *Arthasastra* is titled as concerning the topic of training. Kautilya recommended on the job training under the guidance of those who are experienced and experts. He emphasised experienced and qualified experts. He emphasised utility of competent trainers and mentors for HRD of workers. He believed that HRD should be primarily duty-oriented.

4. Rationale of HRD for Workers

The purpose of human resource development is to improve

the intellectual and emotional abilities needed to handle greater responsibilities, through formal or informal means.[5]

Introduction of new technology, growing alienation of workers, declining work ethics, change in aspirations, value system and motivation of employees, complexity of modern corporate organisations in terms of size and diversification and declining trends in productivity provide rationale of HRD for workers. Increasing induction of socially disadvantaged groups, religious minorities, women and other categories in the work-force justify basic programme and HRD for all employees who constitute the biggest junk of the working people. International Labour Organisation has put up an item : "Human Resource Development: Vocational Guidance and Vocational Training" on the agenda of 59th (1974) session of International Labour Conference. International agencies like UNESCO have adopted a number of recommendations concerning technical and vocational guidance for achieving higher productivity. HRD for workers is a well-structured process and strategy by which the workers are helped in a planned and continuous way to:

(a) Develop occupational skills, capabilities and competencies;

(b) Develop intellectual, cultural, social and psychological aspects of their personality;

(c) Nurture higher level of achievement motivation and develop various self management skills and attitudes;

(d) Develop confidence, initiative and teamwork with a view to achieve general enabling capabilities as individuals so that they are able to discover and utilise their own inner potentials for their organisational goals;

(e) Develop an organisational culture which could contribute to the organisational health, dynamism and pride of employees;

(f) To acquire knowledge, perspectives, attitudes, values and capabilities required to perform various tasks and functions associated with their present or future expected roles.

The soft spot of the HRD approach of Pareek and Rao lies in the near total neglect of the worker, who should have been the main beneficiary of HRD.[6] However a number of Indian companies have evolved proactive approaches and long-term strategic initiatives which heighten the need for worker's HRD. Due to various changes in organisational perspectives, organisations are investing more on employees' development programmes and are encouraging them to pursue self-development through various training programmes outside the organisations.

5. Philosophy for Workers of HRD

The art of HRD begins with selection and induction techniques to skill analysis, creating learning opportunities, motivating gambits, management of people, resources and performance and ends with the development and rewarding of employees for post-retirement employment. Competitive advantage through the honouring of employee skills is an important aspect of HRD. Empowerment can not be separated from modern HRD techniques. The reward management and remuneration strategy and practices are vital aspects of HRD philosophy.

The underlying philosophy and goals of HRD for workers can be as follows:

(A) Worker should be at the centre of development and corporate concern.

(B) De-alienation of the worker so that he gets easily mixed with the organisational culture and ethos.

(C) Development of collective and individual personalities of workers as "human beings."

(D) Active involvement and participation in achieving collective goals.

(E) Self-reliance, self-development and self-discipline as expressions of maturity of workers.

(F) Improving overall quality of work life by introduction of innovative welfare schemes.

(G) A meaningful scheme of training for skills envisages a broad spectrum of activities, including the preparation of people for eventual labour market activities through education and training, elimination of certain pre-training and pre-placement problems emanating from frictional bottle-necks, individual inadequacies, rigidities, spatial immobility, etc."[7].

6. Basic Training Programmes for Workers

On the basis of pattern of the Union Carbide India Limited, Calcutta, the objectives of basic training programme for employees can be as under:[8]

"1. Upfront direct communication with each and every employee—specially with the shop-floor employees;
2. Encourage participation and generate excitement at work;
3. Breakdown the barriers and reduce the 'We-They' divide between levels, functions, departments and Union-Management;
4. Initiate a cultural change through training and development for improved awareness, attitudes and skills;
5. Employees should develop a feeling of "Pride, Ownership and Commitment" for own and company work."

The Central Labour Institute under Ministry of Labour, Government of India had the privilege to get associated with HRD efforts launched since 1975 for the personnel at different levels. The Central Labour Institute (CLI) has also played a vital role in terms of spreading "Quality—Circle concept to obtain greater involvement of the workforce.

Generally basic training programmes for employees should be organised by internal HRD managers in the floor office or near the workshop during working hours for short durations of fifteen minutes generally everyday. The proposed approach to such training should include some of the following sensitive topics:

1. Company vision, core values and goals.
2. Company information—history, products, business, scenario and competition,
3. Customers perceptions and both negative and positive feedback of traders, share brokers.
4. Safety precautions at work and home.
5. Introduction to TQM concepts, and company quality control policy.
6. Video messages of chairman and managing directors.
7. Training in the language of employees and participative workshops.
8. Liberalisation and ensuing opportunities and threats to the company.
9. Success stories on employees at shop-floor level and as teamworker by preparing " Par Excellence Films."
10. Audio-Video series on "Know your company."
11. The ill-effects of smoking, drugs, and alcoholism and prevention of AIDS.
12. Safety and health for family.
13. Action-oriented on the job training on Quality centre.
14. Check-sheets for machine and workplace upkeep.
15. Elimination of scraps, wastage and departmental inter-dependence.
16. 5S at work place—sorting, systematising, spic and span, sanitising and self-discipline.
17. Training for attitude change and behavioural modifications.
18. Core competency building and multi-skill development through refresher training.
19. Problem solving and creativity training.
20. Awareness of labour laws and work—culture.

For each company, a need based syllabus has to be prepared and modern methods of training have to be used to make training effective. Each organisation has to carry out a total organisational "Strength Weakness—Opportunities Threats" analysis in terms of the following:

(a) Productivity standards and quality control;

(b) Philosophy, mission and style of corporate governance;

(c) Climate of HRD and opportunities for HRD interventions;

(d) Morale and motivation levels;

(e) Systems and procedures;

(f) Leadership and supervisory standards;

(g) Market situation and globally competitive scenario.

India first adopted an institutional scheme for craftsmen training, enlarging upon the War Technicians Centres in 1950 to include civilian craftsman training. Following the recommendations of several bodies such as the Indian Labour Conference (1951). The Technical Training Committee of Small Scale Industries Board (1956), the Shiva Rao Committee (1957), the Special Apprenticeship Training Committee (1958), the National Council for Training in Vocational Trade (1959), Apprentices Act (1961), training of workers was envisaged to conform to the standards and syllabus prescribed by the Central Apprentice Council.

Employees must have periodical worker-customer interface for getting awareness about quality of their products. Occupational training is a lifelong, post-education process of transmitting and acquiring skills on the job by invitation of the example of colleagues, by stimulation from subordinates and by instruction from supervisors.

7. Productivity Improvement and Personality Development

HRD managers have to play a "positive role in motivating

employees for productivity. In improving productivity the employees have the needs for food, proper working conditions and shelter. Higher - initiative by workers, high levels of motivation and trust, more commitment to their work and successful introductions of total quality management / ISO system, can help in improving productivity of employees. Rigorous cost control system, elimination of wastes, expectation of higher value addition, total attitudinal orientations can go a long way in reducing overall expenses and increasing productivity and ultimately overhead costs. By creating a cooperative attitude, by identifying obstacles and bottlenecks to improve production and removing them, by developing better awareness about total quality improvement and disseminating required technical professional and organisational information, employees can be motivated to improve productivity.

The development programme helps in fostering the organisation's culture and climate. The aim of all development programmes is to make the organisation more effective. Personality development through HRD interventions has to take care of the following core personality dimensions:

1. Extroversion—assertiveness, sociable, outgoing and talkative.
2. Agreeableness—good natured, co-operative and trusting.
3. Conscientiousness—responsible, dependable, achievement oriented, committed to the job.
4. Emotional Stability—relaxed, secure, stress free.
5. Openness to experience—broad-minded, intellectual, imaginative.
6. Creative—constructive in approach, innovative.
7. Self-discipline—control over anger, fear, greed and jealousy.

8. Employees Participation and Investment

Employees participation in management by the workers should mean involvement—both physical and emotional to contribute and take responsibility for achieving the goals of the organisation. Employees participation can be effective only if participation is voluntary. The employee participation can be more effective when employees have free and frank communication with one another in the organisation. The management personnel and the union leaders have to shed their complexes to ensure effective employee participation. The employee participative processes have to focus on the achievements/goals and results of the organisation. The development process of workers can be total and effective when training and other development strategies are result oriented. The new environment call for workers as partners in progress. The concept of "workers—as partners in progress" calls for not only attitudinal change of workers and unions but also of the managements, specifically the Indian counterparts[11]. The real benefit of employees total involvement with the organisation can be derived only when knowledge and competencies of workers are continuously upgraded and they are imparted expertise to analyse the entire series of manufacturing, marketing and servicing steps with a view towards finding and eliminating the irrationality and inconsistencies in the entire system. A holistic employee involvement programme, on the pattern of Hero Honda, needs to include human resource issues, industry trends, business environment and the vision of the future. The employee involvement must be implemented in an environment of making results happen rather than finding fault or blaming.

9. Reducing Cost without Tears

There should be no retrenchment or lay off in the industrial sector for reducing costs. By bringing about a cultural change in the organization with the help of free flow of information and communication, employees can reduce cost by reducing wastages and improving productivity. Management can get meaningful suggestions from employees which could help in reducing wastages. HRD can create better industrial relations and it will reduce absenteeism, low output and work stoppages. It can reduce total overhead production cost by motivating workers to improve their productivity and efficiency.

10. Barriers of Worker's HRD

The major barriers to worker's HRD can be summed up as follows:

1. Management's tepid level of interest in employees HRD;
2. Worker's resistance and disinterest in their own development;
3. Misunderstanding and mistrust of HRD strategies and techniques;
4. Worker's distrust towards management styles and programmes;
5. Adversarial stance of unions towards management, because they see HRD as potential "brain washing mechanisms.

The morning prayer meeting can be an excellent brief meeting for all employees and communication channel can be conducted on the shop floor by each section chief (Kacho in Japanese) preferably beginning with the morning staff. The Godrej Kaizen system works on the principle of empowerment of all employees and is so designed that tangible monetary returns accrue from the improvements thought out by the employees with zero financial implications and zero financial investment.

11. Training at Regular Intervals

HRD plays a vital role in determining training and development needs. The purpose of training is the continuous development of individuals towards their full and unique potential through their life span and thus the continuous development of human resources.[12] HRD through training can make the workers more productive, quality and cost conscious. A series of behavioural training programmes can generate a conducive climate of trust and commitment to the organisation. Training of workers can help in core competency building and multi-skill development with total employee involvement in organisational goals and mission. Training should aim at bringing attitudinal change. Training must use modern methodologies and techniques besides using modern teaching aids and equipment like computers and multi-media projectors; programmes have to be more participant oriented. Training and development of workers must get support from the top management. Training needs of workers and employees have to be periodically examined and training of HRD professionals has to be periodically restructured to keep pace with the demands and expectations of the corporate sector.

12. Counselling

HRD professionals have to obtain feedback about the critical attributes of the employees, personal skill inventories and potential appraisal for future career development. Employees need counselling for their development and counselling must have a developmental approach. HRD counsellors can discuss with the employees the difference between his self-rating and the ratings by his immediate superiors. Counsellors have to discuss the steps that the employee can take for improvement. Counselling can be very useful to workers on topics like family planning, ill-effects of drugs and alcohol and even about career guidance for workers' children. Counselling can help workers in understanding the need for work ethics, organisational commitment and punctuality of time. Counselling consists of the following six steps :

1. Identifying and selecting the problems of an employee or a group of employees.
2. Analysing the problem and its potential causes.
3. Generating potential solutions.
4. Selecting and planning solutions and action plans.
5. Implementing solutions and review actions periodically.
6. Evaluating solutions and getting feedback after lapse of some time.

Counselling is imperative in developing a productive work force.

13. Employee Welfare

Welfare activities are not to be treated as charities making people dependent, but as helping employees to be whole persons. Welfare activities have to bring into its fold not only the employee but his or her family and the significant others who are determining the psychological quality of the employee's life. Human Resource Development efforts of Steel Authority of Inda in scale and scope are tremendous. Bhilai Steel Plant manages a township with a population of over four lakhs by spending over Rs. eighty crores on maintenance of steel township and on welfare facilities for employees and their families.[13] Sundaram—Clayton Ltd. had evolved an HRD philosophy in which " employees are to be adopted into the family and their welfare should be the foremost of the company's concern."[14] Workers must be provided welfare benefits such as medical insurance, disability insurance, holidays and vacations to maintain their motivation and work commitment. Although welfare is only a strong hygiene factor, lack of welfare could certainly be an obstacle of the development of employees. Welfare activities generate a feeling on oneness which is necessary for effective working.

14. Quality of Work Life

All organisations have to make efforts towards improving the quality of work life by developing strong links and family feeling between the people and the organisation. This can be fostered by conducting various social and cultural activities involving employees and their families. Many organisations like SAIL and Indian Railways are providing facilities for education of children of employees and suitable programmes in culture, healthcare and recreation of families. Organisations must look at its workers as a whole person and not an eight hour employee on wages. Recreation and cultural events should be organised with a view to provide platform for individual expression and creativity. Family-get-togethers are occasions for informal interaction and social life. Birthday of employees can be made an occasion for the employees to share tea and some snacks with his shop supervisor and other colleagues.

Employees can be encouraged to plant seedlings and maintain them in the campus with their names exhibited. Quality of work-life programmes generally focus on the environment within the organisation and include the following:

1. Basic physical concerns such as heating and air-conditioning, lighting and safety precautions;
2. Physical amenities such as food beverage facilities, aesthetics and recreation;
3. Motivational and psychological factors such as flexible work hours, challenges at work and varying degree of autonomy.

HRD systems must focus on employee welfare and quality of work life by job enrichment programmes, educational subsidies, recreational activities, health and medical benefits.

15. Quality Circles and Empowerment of Workers

The Eicher Motors Ltd. made use of the strategy of Total Quality Management (TQM) to involve workers in organisational revitalisation by changing the fundamental equations between the workers and the organisation. Quality circle is a small group to perform quality control activities within the same workshop on a voluntary basis. Quality circles stimulate informality and sense of involvement in the work. Quality circles improve inter-departmental communications, develop better understanding between workers, increase knowledge of workers and increase team-spirit. The quality circles are small homogenous groups of people, meeting regularly to identify, analyse and resolve work-problems, with the management philosophy of creating a truly participative work environment for improving quality of products and services.[15] Professor Kaorn Ishikawa (1915-98) is generally known as the father of quality circles for his role in launching Japan's quality movement in the late 1950s. Team work, leadership and communication skills are key factors for the success of TQM journey and workers are the most important actors for completion of this journey. In order to increase the motivation levels of these employees, appropriate HRD interventions are very crucial. Total productivity operations (TPO) were applied in Godrej Soaps Ltd and can be easily replicated.

16. Role of Trade Unions and HRD

Trade Unions can play a developmental role and focus their attention to the psychological and social well-being of the workers. They (Unions) have to give up their traditional roles and opt for development roles as given below :-[16]

Sl. No.	*Traditional role of Unions with focus on economic well-being*	*Developmental role with focus on psychological and social well-being*
1.	Bargainer	Explorer
2.	Negotiator	Trainer
3.	Fire fighter	Educator
4.	Agitator	Counsellor
5.	Grievance handler	Collaborator
6.	Game player	Motivator
7.	Black Mailer	Facilitator
8.	Cross dealer	Communicator

Unions can play important roles in setting the stages, designing, initiating and participating in HRD programmes. Improved communication can help unions in ensuring better quality of work-life and developing internal democracy about farmful effects of excessive drinking, drug addiction, excessive smoking, excessive debt taking, can be done by the HRD in collaboration with the unions. Unions can be partners of HRD staff in development of skills of collaboration, positive assertion, empathy, capacity of organising groups and team building. Real HRD for workers would mean continuous improvement of their social security and other welfare measures. HRD role of unions can be to extend their help in creating a better family life environment and providing education and vacational guidance to their children. Unions can assume HRD role by updating data base on various dimensions of workers needs, aspirations, and problems and project them correctly to the management.

17. Self Development by Workers

HRD should include the art of focussing mind in the present through the practice of *Sadhana* i.e. Living in the present Meditation (*Sadhana*) is an exercise of mind control to develop its capacity to focus on the present with full alertness. Like a playing batsman in cricket, we have to tackle the incoming ball (in the present time). The mind can be trained to live in the present through regular *Sadhana* and become more effective.[17]

HRD for workers has failed in a few organisations because climate for self-development and learning has not been created. HRD philosophy has not been properly articulated and disseminated and HRD functions have been viewed in isolation.[18] Self-development can be encouraged by a conducive HRD climate and encouraging leadership. Skepticism, suspicion and lack of faith in management could abort the fetus of an HRD concept an even before it is even born. Creation of a healthy atmosphere in industrial relations and a positive HRD philosophy are the basic needs for sowing the HRD seeds. Good remuneration, recognition of work, cheap and nutritive subsidised food, good medical facility, recreational facilities can encourage workers for self-development. The Indian contribution to HRD is the due emphasis given to the management of self in Indian culture. *Bhagwat Gita* enjoins that the duty is important and not the consequences. *Gita* touching the essence of managerial psyche says "His mind is steady whose senses are under control." Only a person who has self-control can act firmly without sorrow; self-development has been stressed in Indian scriptures and boldness, forgiveness, fortitude, purity, absence of hatred and pride are said to be the attributes of a noble soul who has learnt self-management through self-development.

18. Free Flow of Communication and Thrust Areas for Action

There should be free flow of communication with workers and they must be explained the following thrust areas for priorities of action:

1. Improve work culture and mutual trust
2. Improve capacity utilisation

3. Increase productivity
4. Improve quality of products
5. Create profits through cost reduction and reducing wastage
6. Aim at customer's satisfaction by quality production.

Communications are very important for workers. HRD personnel must ensure that communications must be timely, should be targeted to specific audiences, should be carefully selected, should be unbiased and modest and must be consistently made to the workers in the language they can understand.

18. OCTAPACE Values and HRD

National Thermal Power Corporation (NTPC) established by the Government of India in 1975 placed its focus on HRD to develop and implement a well-knit personnel policy and a comprehensive personnel programme that was to be result-oriented and to develop an organisational culture which motivates employees to contribute their best towards achievement of the organisational objectives. HRD climate or culture is essential for developing workers and employees of various organisations. The HRD climate can be characterised as consisting of the following:

1. O - Openness or freedom to express one's ideas and opinions;
2. C- Collaborative attitude or team spirit;
3. T- Trust;
4. A - Authenticity or correlation between words and action;
5. P- Pro-action or encouraging some degree of initiative and risk-taking by employees;
6. A - Autonomy or certain degree of freedom of action for each individual;
7. C - Confronting issues with a view to solve them;
8. E - Experimentation of new ideas.[19]

20. Some Basic Issues about HRD Workers

There are many wrong assumptions which have discouraged HRD professionals from effectively carrying out HRD for workers:

1. The results of HRD cannot be measured immediately.
2. We do not know what information to collect for evaluating HRD efforts.
3. Measurement can only be applied to production and sales functions.
4. There are too many variables influencing the behaviour change.
5. We do not need to justify our existence : we have a proven track record.[20]

   It is now proved beyond doubt that HRD system is most scientific and can help in changing cultural values and organisational climate. HRD can improve worker's productivity and can help them in self-development. It can build up team-spirit and improve the work motivation of the employees. Human Resource Development must develop employees and workers, and sharpen their critical attributes and technical/ professional competencies.

21. Liberalisation Policy and its Negative Effects

The Human Development Reports, 1993 and 1996 have revealed "jobless growth" causing unemployment in the contemporary world. Many studies on India revealed that unemployment rose sharply from eleven million in 1990-91 to seventeen million in 1992 and to twenty one million in 1993-94. The rate of unemployment shot up to 5.5 per cent in 1993-94 from 3.1 per cent in 1990-91.[21] At present the nation is generating only six million jobs (2.3 per cent) against the demand of 9-10 million jobs. Due to liberalisation, employment in the corporate sector has become insecure and led to retrenchment rationalisation and displacement of workers. The process of labour displacement is taking place at a rapid pace.[22] The Voluntary Retirement

Scheme (VRS) under the "Exit Policy is being implemented.[23] During 1993-94 a sum of about Rs. 750 crore has been spent under National Renewal Fund (NRF) for 60,000 victimised workers under VRS. During 1992-93 to 1994-95 the NRF financed about 80,000 VRS workers spending about Rs. 1307 crore. In public sector units, dis-investment threatens throwing large number of members of the workforce out of employment. Under liberalisation policy compulsory retrenchment has led to casualisation of labour which enjoyed better social security and protection earlier. The state must not abandon its efforts and dilute its role in the name of liberalisation because state is duty bound to develop the physical and social infrastructure. Raja J. Chelliah claims "inward looking strategy" for the state which should concentrate on irrigation, education, health, flood-control, environment, railways, roads, bridges, space, defense and power.[24] There are many snags in liberalisation and its enthusiastic embrace in USA and United Kingdom during the 1970s and 1980s led to growing disenchantment. The I.L.O. conventions and standards demand incorporation of social dimensions, including social protection, promoting tripartite dialogue and involving social partners in the design and implementation of liberalisation policy. There is no positive comprehensive policy or ideology of the Indian state which claims "many programmes of welfare state.[25] Gunnar Myrdal thinks— that "this lack of a political or social philosophy is not peculiar to Britain. It exists equally in other countries which are generally regarded as welfare states such as Sweden/NewZealand or India."[26] A corporate oriented positive state like United States is not a welfare state at all because its primary aim is to protect the holders of property from the problems of unregulated markets and from potential redistributive demands.[27] In essence, the wealth of a nation or a region is based upon its ability to conserve, develop and utilize its human resources. It takes skilled manpower " to discover and exploit natural resources, to mobilize capital, to develop technology, to trade etc."[28]

HRD should develop those core competencies which can meet three tests, namely, customer value, competitor differentiation and extendibility.

Concluding Remarks

HRD processes and strategies have to develop a holistic approach to develop the workforce for achieving the corporate breakthrough. In order to implement effective career planning, team building, job-rotation and redeployment of workers and employees, all the tools, techniques and systems like training, performance appraisal, role analysis and counselling, have to be developed properly. Dr. Leonard Nadler in the United States in 1969 developed the concept of HRD: as it looks at people from the organisation's point of view. Rao and Pareek's concept of HRD is on the metaphysical plane and sees man as a free creature with his urge for self fulfillment.[29] Kautilya's view of development, advancement and growth for workers needs to be given due recognition. HRD for the worker can only be ensured when top management and middle level managers take due interest in HRD activities and help in building a good HRD climate in the organisation. In the era of liberalisation, constant upgradation of skills, competencies and attitudes are needed in the corporate sector to keep the competitive edge. In the liberalised competitive market environment of today, every organisation will have to ensure continuous development of human resources for gaining technological excellence and competitive edge over other organisations. The major challenge of organisations is to ensure constant upgradation of professional competencies of its workers by developing a human environment, preserving human dignity and showing concern for the working force and retaining them through welfare measures. Core competencies of the workers have to be developed on a continuous basis for survival and growth of the organisations. The art of HRD has to be learnt by all managers in this era of knowledge industries.

REFERENCES

1. Alex E. Fermancez Jibberto and Andre Mommen (eds). *Liberalisation in the Developing World: Institutional and Economic Change in Latin America, Africa and Asia*, London, Routledge, Kegan Park, 1996, p. 6.

2. For the Ideology of Liberalisation and its Interest, please refer to, Prabhat Patnaik, *Notes on the Political Economy of Structural Adjustement*. Social Scientist, Vol. 22. Nos. 9-12. September-December,1994, pp. 4-17.

2a. For details see Jeffrey G. Madrick, *the End of Affluence: There Courses and Consequences of America's Economic Dilemma,"* New York, 1995; Also Jermey Rivkin *The End of work ! The Decline of the Global Labour force and the Dawn of the Post - Market Era* New York, 1995.

3. Udai Pareek, HRD in India, *Problems and Prospects : The Indian Journal of Social Work*, Vol. LR No. 1 Oct. 1992 pp. 457-475. Also Udai Pareek and Rao T.V., *Designing and Managing Human Resource Systems*, New Delhi, Oxford and IBH, 1992

4. For further reading see Pareek U. and T.V. Rao, 1981, *Designing and Managing Human Resource System*, Oxford and IBH Publishing, New Delhi and Rac T.V. and D.F. Pereira—1986, *Recent Experiences in Human Resources Development*, Oxford and IBH Publishing Co., New Delhi.

5. S. Vaswani Marg, New Delhi, 1978, p. 16.

6. D.M. Silvera, *Humna Resource Development—The Indian Experience*, News India Publication, New Delhi, 1988, p. 47.

7. Thakur C.P., *Skill Development and Labour Market in an Industrializing Economy*, Shri Ram Centre for Industrial Relations and Human Resources.

8. P.V. Bhide, *HRD for Shop Floor—Employee Involvement in TQM : The Union Carbide Experience* : in TV Rao and others (Eds) HRD in the New Economic Environment Tata McGraw-Hill Publishing Company, New Delhi, 1994, p. 379.

9. George Tobias and R.S. Queener, *India's Manpower Strategy—Revisited*. Institute of Applied Manpower Research, New Delhi, 1968, p. 62.

10. French W.L., *Human Resource Management*, Houghton Miffin Co Boston, 1986, pp. 337-41.

11. K.V. Rajendran, *Critical Role of HRD for Workers in the New Context*, paper Presented at the National HRD Network Conference, Jan 20-22, 1994 at Bombay in HRD in the New Environment— Edited by T.V. Rao and others—Tata Mc Graw Hill Publishing New Delhi, 1994, p. 338.

12. Dr. Krishan Mohan Mathur, *Administation of Police Training in India*, Gyan Publishing House, New Delhi, 1997, pp. 2-3.

13. For details see DM Silvera, *Human Resource Development—The Indian—Experience*, News India Publications,1998, New Delhi, p. 77.

14. P.V.R. Murthy and J. Gregory, Relevance of Japanese HRD Practices in Sundaram Clayton—*Ibid.* p. 138.

15. Dr. Krishna Mohan Mathur, *Towards, Effective Management Pathways to Excellence*, Gyan Publishing House, New Delhi, 1999, p. 111.

16. Anil K. Khandelwal, "HRD for Workers: Role of the Unions" in T.V. Rao and others (Ed.)—*Alternative Approaches and in Strategies of HRD*, Rawat Publications, Jaipur, 1989, p. 309.

17. Prof. S.K. Palhan, *Enhancing Effectiveness through Living in the Present*, Indian Management, Vol. 38 No. 7, July, 1999, p. 28

18. S. Muralidhar, "HRD for Workers in a Changing Scenario" in T.V. Rao and others (Editors), *HRD in the New Economic Environment*, Tata McGraw Hill Publishing Company Ltd. New Delhi, 1994, p. 346-47.

19. P.V. Murthy, "HRD for Blue Collar" in *HRD in the New Economic Environment* Edited by T.V. Rao and others—Tata McGraw Hill Publishing Company Ltd. New Delhi, 1994, pp. 322 - 24. T.V. Rao, "Role of Chief Executive in HRD"—in *Alternative Approaches and Strategies of Human Resource Development* (Editors) T.V. Rao and others, Rawat Publications, Jaipur, 1989, p. 18.

20. "Does HRD Really Works" N.L. Mirchandani. *The Times of India*, New Delhi, July 1993.

21. For details see Ruder Datt—"Jobless Growth. Implications of the New Economic Policies, *Indian Journal of Industrial Relations*, Vol. 29., No. 4, April, 1994.

22. V.Bhaskara Rao—Liberalisation Policy: Need for People Oriented Approach" *Indian Journal of Public Administrations*, II PA, New Delhi, July - September 1996—Vol. XLII No. s3, p. 322.

23. Kamal Narayan Kabra *Pitfalls of Public Relation Approach*, Main Stream March 5, 1994, p. 33.

24. Raja J. Chelliah—*Towards Sustainable Growth: Essays in Fiscal and Financial Sector Reforms in India*, Delhi, Oxford University Press, 1996, p. 205.

25. William A. Robson, *Welfare State and Welfare Society, Illusion and Reality*, London, George Allen and Unwin, 1976, p. 12.

26. K. Gunnar Myrdal, *Beyond the Welfare State*, 1960.

27. Norman Tumiss and Tcmothy Tilton, *The Case for the Welfare State: From Social Security to Social Equality*. B. Iomingtion, Indian University Press, 1977 p. 15.

28. Thakur C.P., *Skill Development and Labour Market in an Industrializing Economy*, Shri Ram Centre for Industrial Relations and Human Resources, New Delhi, 1978, p. 15-16.

29. D.M. Silvera, *Human Resources Development—The Indian Experience*, New India Publications, New Delhi, 1988, p. 34.

6

Human Resource Training

Human Resource Training has been one of the relatively well-developed functions in Indian organisations. Goldstein (1980) defined training as " the acquisition of skills, concepts or attitudes that result in improved performance in an on the job situation," Training is concerned with the principle and the theories of learning because training is basically linked with the improved performance at some specific task. Debra Cohen in the November, 1990 issue of *Training and Development Journal* cites extenisve research that found a significant correlation between learning and goal setting in the training process. HRD (Human Resource Development) has become a new name for training in many companies. In many organisations training is being conducted just for the sake of it without any specific objective or targetted outcome and training is not job-oriented. Training is telling plus showing plus supervising until the desired change is achieved in the skills, attitudes and behaviour of the employees. Training normally concentrates on the improvement of either operational skills (the basic skills related to the successful completion of a task), inter-personal skills (how to behave and relate correctly with others), decision-making abilities (how to arrive at the most satisfactory course of action) or a combination of these skills. Training can be defined as a learning process where by employees acquire a knowledge, skills, attitudes and human relations abilities to perfom their present and future jobs. Training is an investment in human resources: it is an important means of improving the human potential and increasing the efficiency of personnel. Training in acquiring new found ugrency in the context of globalisation of economy and an information revolution.

Training is acquiring new urgency in view of the great and rapid advances in the field of technology and the resultant equally faster pace of obsolescence in the fields of technology, science and industrial production. The good number and variety of institutions devoted to training at all levels all over the world are the visible symbols of its importance.[1] At the international level, the United Nations for Training and Research (UNITAR), the United Nations Development Programme (UNDP), the International Labour Organisation and several other organisations have been promoting training all over the world. Training is a dynamic well-planned process of human resources development. Training is a planned, continuous effort to improve the employee's competence levels and the organisations work environment. Training is a systematic process of altering the behaviour and/or attitudes of employees leading to enhanced knowledge, changed attitudes and improved skills and techniques.[2] As an intervention strategy, training should have the following overall objectives, mainly:

(a) arresting obsolescence, both individual and organisational (preventive);

(b) bridging pre-active insufficiencies of knowledge and professional skill (curative);

(c) shaping adjustments with socio-technological, environmental changes (adaptive);

(d) developing new outlook, an ethnological version of quality, excellence, and accomplishment (promotive);

(e) making a total man with new cultural attributes operating in the realm of personality, character and behaviour (transformative).[3]

Training is any process by which attitudes, skills and

abilities of employees to perform specific jobs are increased by short-term programmes. The word "training" despite the efforts of some to make it a semantic whipping boy, is accepted as a synonym for all of the forms of knowledge, skill and attitude development which adults need to keep pace with accelerating life involvement and the enlarging concept of man's capabilities. Training is a reciprocal process of teaching and learning a body of knowledge, skills and techniques and the related methods of works[4]. The word training is generally accepted as a synonym for all of the forms of knowledge, skill and attitudinal development which adults need to keep pace with accelerating life involvement in any given profession and the enlarging concept of man's capabilities to achieve excellence. "No training, uninspired by leadership, can produce more than technical competence. No leadership however inspiring, which does not ensure comprehensive system of training is an investment in human resources and is seen as a vehicle of change. Organisational climate has to be conducive to training and training to be effective and job-oriented must get full support and attention of top management. On the job training cannot be replaced by classroom training because eighty to ninety percent of all development takes place on the job.[5] Training and development therefore are complementary and mutually interdependent and are vital aspects of organisational success.

2. The Concept of Training as a Process and its Benefits

Training is a deliberate and planned process of teaching and learning wherein knowledge, skills, techniques, attitudes and experience are acquired by the trainees with the help and guidance of the trainers in a given learning environment. Training, according to modern approach comprises of a series of interrelated, interacting, precisely controlled instructional systems leading to learning experiences that are designed to achieve specific training objectives; and organised into a unified dynamic whole which is responsive and adaptive to the individual trainer while fulfilling specific job-relevant training criteria in a given training environment. Training is a continuous ongoing process which involves the following steps.[6]

1. Develop job standards.
2. Identify needs.
3. Determine objectives.
4. Develop curriculum.
5. Select methods and material.
6. Obtain instructional resources.
7. Conduct training.
8. Evaluate and feedback.

A well executed and well-planned training programme helps in personal growth of the employees and results in wider awareness among participants by enlarging their knowledge and skills. A good training programme should result in improvement in quality of product; improvement in production rate; improvement of efficiency and productivity and improvement of morale. A well-implemented training programme generally should result in reduction in supervisory burden, reduction in machine-breakage and maintenance cost; reduction in accident rate; reduction in manpower obsolescence; reduction in wastage and spoilage; and reduction in learning time. Training is necessary when a person has to move from one job to another because of promotion,. transfer or demotion. Job requirement, organisation viability, technological changes, internal mobility and need for updating are some of the reasons for which training becomes necessary. Training refers to instructions in technical or mechanical operations and is a short-term process wherein employees may acquire knowledge, skills, attitudes and competencies required for their jobs.

Matrix of training shows its components and the various processes of training as a system. These steps are not discrete steps and need not be followed in rigid order but require a great degree of inter-action and recycling and as a continuous process. Various components given in the matrix directly influence level and quality of training.

Fig. 1. The Process of Training as a System and its Components

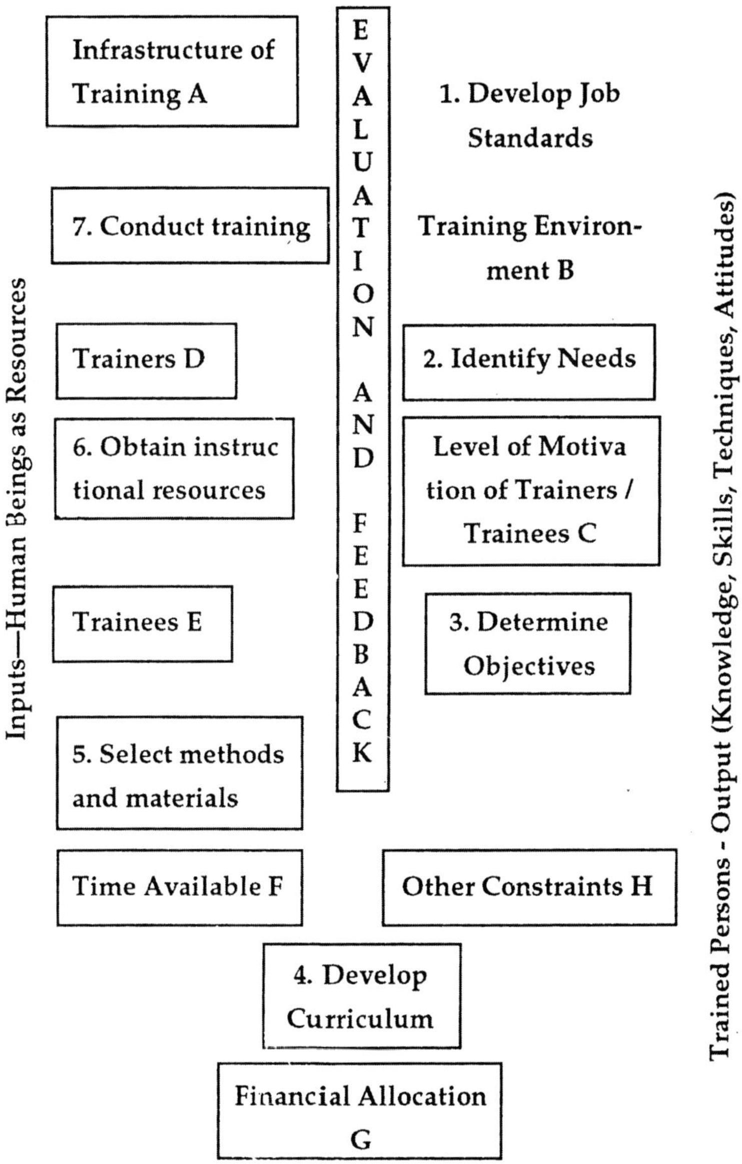

1. Develop Job Standard—Before any training programme is drawn, the training director must know the job description, job analysis, statements of tasks and what is to be accomplished by an individual trainee so that he may develop the training programme accordingly. Training director is a facilitator who develops the training system for meeting the required professional, technical and specialised job standards and requirements of the trainees. Job standards imply what the individual is expected to do and at what level of success he is expected to perform the job.

2. Identify Needs—Identification of training needs is accomplished through observation, group self-analysis, performance tests, interviews, questionnaire and organisational need analysis.[7] Every organisation has changes in procedures, new technologies are emerging all around us and people are constantly changing jobs and thus needs are constantly generated for training of individuals. There are many methods of determining training needs. This can be done in the following ways:

(a) Analysis of an activity.

(b) Analysis of an organisation.

(c) Analysis of individual and groups behaviour.

(d) Analysis of organisational problems.

(e) Appraisal of performance of the individual groups or the departments.

(f) Brainstorming of a group for getting new ideas.

(g) Buzzing by asking an audience of supervisor, managers, and staff as to what the desirable next steps are in the organisation.

(h) Committees and conferences.

(i) Counselling by consultants and internal experts.

(j) Interviews, observations.

(k) Workshops, task force, survey and research studies.

A training specialist is able to identify training needs from:

(a) Analysis of the strength, weaknesses, opportunities and threats (SWOT analysis) of the organisation.

(b) The acquisition of new equipment, new technology, new working procedures and methods.

(c) Under-performance by the employees, evidenced by low output, poor quality, lack of initiative or general incompetence.

(d) Performance gaps between what employees are doing and what they should be doing.

3. **Determine Objectives**—The key to a systematic approach to training lies in knowing what are the desired performance objectives and developing a training programme which provides what is necessary to have all trainees meet all the desired performance objectives in specific terms. As Robert Mager stated "A builder does not select his material or specify a schedule for construction until he has his blueprints (objectives) before him.[8] Mager suggested that training programmes must have clearly stated objectives and must identify them in tangible and measurable terms. The Assheton Committee (U.K., 1944) has outlined the following general objectives of training which, are valid for our country also:

"1. To equip the employees with precision and clarity in the transaction of business.

2. To attune the civil servant to the new tasks which he will be called upon to perform in a changing world.

3. To develop resistance to the danger of becoming mechanised by visualising what he is doing in a wider setting and by persevering with his own educational development.

4. To develop his capacity for higher work and greater responsibilities.

5. To develop and maintain staff morale particularly because large number of people have to deal with tasks of a routine nature.

6. To inculcate the right attitude towards the public never

forgetting that the civil servant is a servant and not the master of the community.

7. To sustain the human touch not only in direct personal contacts with the public but also in handling a proper sense of urgency and due consideration for the man at the other end."[9]

4. Develop Curriculum—The curriculum is the content or subject matter organised in a meaningful sequence. It is desirable to broadly classify curriculum into what one must know, what may be useful to know and what subject should get how much periods and attention. Subject matter, lesson plans, sequence of training etc. all form part of curriculum. Curriculum must match required job standards and the particular level of employees to be trained.

5. Select Methods and Material—It is necessary that the methods and material should be directly related to the learning and should support the underlying principles identified by the trainer. Lecture method, group discussion, case study, observation method, guide scheme, role playing, simulation, syndicate system, in-basket method and incident method are some of the instructional methods which can be used by the trainer to make training more meaningful and effective. Use of training aids, black boards, dispaly boards, flannel board, film strips, films, slides, projectors, tape recorders are some of the useful instructional aids which can build up more interest in training. Teaching material for instructors and reading material for trainees, seminars, symposia, panel discussions and guest talks by eminent scholars can make training more meaningful and instructive. It is difficult to assess the effectiveness of training methods, techniques and aids in isolation from the training courses.[10]

6. Obtain Instructional Resources—Instructional staff plays a very important part in imparting training to the trainees and the quality of training depends on the motivation and quality of instructor. Instructional resources can be from within the organisation or from outside. For effective training, trainers have to be trained in the art of instruction and adult psychology. Evaluation of trainers is necessary so that training may be imparted on correct lines and in an effective manner.

7. Conduct Training—Conduct of training includes a proper co-ordination and interaction between trainers and trainees and careful preparation and supervision of training. Preparation of training programme, availability of training material for staff and trainees, selection of qualified trainers, nomination of candidates as trainees, preparation of training schedule and implementation of training according to given time schedule are all parts of conducting training. Generally each training programme should have one course co-ordinator for effective conduct of training. Physical facilities for classroom, availability of trainers and adherence of time component are important aspects in implementing any training programme.

8. Evaluation and Feedback—Evaluation of training is a systematic assessment of training and can include assessment of trainees, trainers, institutional methods, instructional material, instructional environment and conduct of training programme. According to A.C. Hamblin, evaluation of training can be divided by breaking it into the following four logical steps.[11]

Step 1— Reaction—How well did the trainees like the course?

Step 2— Learning—What principles, facts, techniques and skills were learnt?

Step 3— Behaviour—What changes in job behaviour resulted from the programme ?

Step 4— Results—What were the tangible results from the training in terms of reduced cost, improved quality etc. : ?"

Evaluation of training, in broadest terms implies following types of training evaluation.[12]

(a) Context evaluation—Current operational context, individual difficulties, organisational difference.

(b) Input evaluation—Evaluation of trainers, training methods, training aids, training curriculum.

(c) Process evaluation—Evaluation of training arrangements, training infrastructure, conduct and organisation of training.

(d) Cost evaluation—Per trainee cost and per course cost.

According to Mary Broad and John Newstrom (1992), "most of the investment made in an organisation's training and development is wasted because most of the knowledge and skills gained in training is not fully applied by employees on the job."

3. Formulation of a Training Policy

Training policy of an organisation has to be evolved by the top management, and should contain the organisation's commitment and approach to the training function, provide guidance for design and execution, identify training needs of the organisation and earmark personnel, resources, infrastructure and a broad time-frame for the training activities in the organisation by clearly spelling out its broad objectives, priorities, goals, thrust areas and broad guidelines for execution of the mission of the organisation. A training policy document helps communicate the organisation's intent regarding career planning and succession planning of the personnel at various levels and provides information regarding training programmes to all employees. A training policy should give a clear identification of training philosophy—roles, missions, procedures, priorities, training needs, training activities, long-term and short-term objectives, financial allotment, resources allotment and guidance for the training department on all related matters in the shape of training manuals and training instructions for effective administration and execution. Training should be treated as an instrument of acculturation and attitudinal change.

Formulation of a training policy should be able to provide satisfactory answers to the following questions:

1. What will be the aims, objectives and missions to be accomplished through training?
2. Who will be the main persons responsible for imparting training to persons?
3. Whether formal or informal training will be organised?

4. What will be the main priorities of training and who will determine priorities?
5. What types of training is needed and for what level of employees?
6. What will be the time and place of training?
7. Will training be a continuous process or periodical or casual?
8. What pay, allowances and other perks will be allowed during training?
9. Will training be an in-house activity or outside agencies will be associated?
10. How will training be related to labour policy and promotion policy?
11. Who will evaluate training and obtain feedback and in what manner?

4. **Types of Training Programmes**—Training can be broadly classified into following types:

1. Basic course for new entrants / Induction Training.
2. Refresher courses.
3. Promotional courses.
4. Specialised courses.
5. Training courses for trainers.
6. Executive Development programmes.
7. Vertical inter-action programme.
8. Re-orientation courses or pre-induction courses.

5. Training Environs

Environs of training are those tangible and intangible constituents which exert considerable influence on the complex set of variables involving the trainers, the trainees, campus environment, physical facilities, training techniques and the interrelationship between various factors constituting training climate and can be divided into the following:

Tangible Constituents	Intangible Constituents
1. Physical facilities of training institution	1. Time constituent - duration and season of the course.
2. Trainers, heads of training institutions, incentives and facilities to trainers.	2. Location of training institutions.
3. Administrative and supporting . staff	3. Institutional sub-culture and organisational norms, value system, discipline, turnout, and punctuality.
4. Organisational and administrative set up.	4. Psychology of administrative authorities.
5. Trainees—type and level.	5. Psychology of sponsoring authorities
6. Trg. Techniques and methods	6. Psychology of trainers.
7. Planning, allocation and expenditure	7. Psychology of trainees.
8. Financial allocation and expenditure	8. Motivation for learning and self-development.
9. Training contents programmes and objectives, curricula	9. Interpersonal, inter-group relationships.
	10. Organisational climate and health.

All organisations must provide a suitable HRD environment for effective training.

6. Modern Approach to the Training System

Training is a set of procedures to facilitate learning and one of the primary functions of the training director is to create and manage the environment in which effective teaching / learning activities can take place through interaction of trainers with trainees. There are different kinds of learning and they may require different training processes.[13] Training in any organisation must first answer the following questions: "To whom, by whom, where, when and how shall the training be given?" Thus training needs a systems approach and needs to be carried out on a continuous basis as an ongoing process. Training should help promote, maintain and enhance employees' effectiveness in their present assignments and should prepare them for future responsibilities of higher order. Training constitutes an integral part of the co-existence exercise which cares of its personnel and members and ensures organisational effectiveness and optimum performance. According to modern concept of training each organisation must provide comprehensive and job-oriented training to its employees and create a suitable organisational climate for learning with a bias for self-education, individual development and self actualisation within a given environment.[14] Training, education and development of all three should go together for proper organisational development and development of individuals to their fullest potentials.

In the business world, organisations today are investing substantial efforts, time and money to ensure that their employees are trained to be effective service providers, effective producers of quality goods at reasonable costs and in minimum time frame. What training can do is change behaviour and attitudes. Trainers start with the premise that better selling, management skills, better teamwork can be imparted or improved upon by good and well-planned training programmes. In National Thermal Power Corporation (NTPC) training is visualised as a constant process of reinforcing and upgrading skills through a number of short-term programmes, refresher courses and intensive programmes linked with promotions. Employees are under a lot more pressure and it is upto the company to make learning accessible, fun and interesting and to demonstrate its own commitment. Staffs who have no time to get classroom training can be helped along by their managers sharing skills with them in the workplace.

A more comprehensive way of looking at the training function is by regarding it as a sub-system of the total system of personnel administration. Organisational development is the process of developing an organisational climate and organisational culture and positive modifications are brought about in the members of the organisation through training and development efforts.

7. Main Purposes of Training

Tyson and York have listed the following main purposes of training:

1. Maximising productivity and output;
2. Developing the versatility and employability of human resources;
3. Developing the cohesiveness of the whole organisation and its sub-groups;
4. Increasing job satisfaction, motivation and morale;
5. Developing a consciousness of the importance of safety at work and improving standards;
6. Making the best use of available material, resources, equipments and methods;
7. Standardizing organisational practices and procedures.[15]

Training can heighten the skills, abilities, aptitudes and knowledge of the employees and their motivation by increasing their sense of commitment. Training activities are necessitated by technological advances, organisational complexity and human relations factor.[16] In the post-liberalisation era, training activities in the industrial organisations are generally aimed at making desired modifications in skills, attitudes and knowledge of employees so that they perform their jobs most efficiently and effectively to acquire competitive edge over others. Training becomes necessary when an employee moves from one job to another due to promotion or transfer or change of job. Training is needed for organisational viability, internal mobility, job requirement and technological changes." No organisation can choose whether or not to train employees....the only choice left to management is whether training shall be haphazard, casual and possibly misdirected, or whether it shall be made a carefully planned part of integrated programme of personnel administration.[17] Traning programmes are needed in industrial undertakings: (1) to obtain the specialised skills and competencies to operate the enterprise, (2) to keep turnover up and manpower costs down, and (3) to remain competitive in a highly competitive environment in the present day global economy. It is very difficult to indicate the present status of training in business and industry because it will need the following data:

1. Number of undertakings that conduct training.
2. Number of courses or training programmes offered.
3. Number of staff assigned to various training activities.
4. Training costs, salaries, materials, aids and equipments, maintenance and upkeep of facilities and equipments and other overhead costs.
5. Training facilities of other undertakings utilized by the undertaking.

Actually we know very little about the total training structure of the country because it is so diverse that nobody can easily get an overview of the whole efforts. Regarding training needs, there are many critical issues for consideration. Who should determine organisational and corporate training needs? How should training needs be identified? How often should training needs be identified? Generally determining training needs is the responsibility of the HRD department in consultation with line managers and top level managers.

8. Training and Adult Learning

According to Bower and Hilgard (1981) "Learning refers to a change in the subject's behaviour or behaviour potential in a given situation brought about by the subjects' repeated experience in that situation, provided that the behaviour change can not be explained on the basis of the subjects' natural response tendencies, maturation or temporary states." Continuous learning is vital to the survival of organisations in this borderless world today. For learning to be effective, individuals and organisations must acquire relevant capabilities and successfully apply them to actual work situations. The design of a training system together with the characteristics of the participants and their organisations determine how effectively this transmission of newly acquired capabilities to work setting is achieved. Training can be defined as a planned process to modify attitude, knowledge, or skill behaviour through learning experience to achieve effective organisational performance and to promote growth of human resources. Learning associated with training has been found to emerge from the following nine types of processes:

"1. **Modelling**—i.e. copying or initiating a respected person;
2. **Vicarious discovery**—i.e. observing the conduct of others, its consequences and acting accordingly in similar situations;
3. **Unplanned discovery**—i.e. experiences, trial and error learning on the job;
4. **Planned discovery**—i.e. going into the situations with the deliberate objective of learning from those experiences;
5. Being taught, told or shown an approach or idea;
6. Discussions i.e. the sharing of informations, ideas, feelings and experiences;
7. Storing of information i.e. remembering data during the course or events;
8. Coaching i.e. being guided and encouraged along a determined path towards an objective;
9. Organisational climate i.e. by imbibing the ethos of the system in which one works."[18]

Learning is precisely what training is all about but learning cannot be observed directly. Only "before" and "after" behaviour under various controlled situations can be observed because learning is a process that takes place within the trainees. There are four important dimensions of learning:

1. **Level**—Level of performance or proficiency.
2. **Rate**—How fast can a given level of proficiency be achieved?
3. **Retention**—How well or for how long does the learned behaviour remains in the subject's behaviour at a given

level of proficiency?

4. **Generalisation**—To what degree can the learned behaviour be appropriately applied in various other situations.

Generally learning is a relatively permanent change in behaviour potentiality that results from reinforced practice or experience."[19] Learning process is the process by which trainees acquire changes in their behaviour, improve performance, reorganise their thinking or discover new ways of behaving and learn new concepts and knowledge. There are a number of factors, which bear upon the learning process. Motivation, stimulus, response and reinforcement, feedback, practice participation, transfer or application of learning, perception of trainees, sequence of material to be learnt, individual differences, are some of the main factors responsible for learning. Adult learning has certain characteristics, which need to be taken into consideration.[20] The adult learners require long time to perform learning tasks because their reaction times are slow. Adult learner can easily relate new facts to experience and gets reinforcement in his learning from his past experience. Adult learner wants to be treated as an adult in learning situations. Adult learners have more mental distractions at the time of learning than children do. With age the speed of perception declines and reaction time increases. The adult learner is generally more rigid in his thinking because he acquires a set pattern of behaviour in due course of time. Adult learners have six categories of blocks to learning which are as under:[21]

1. Perceptual—Adults, at times, are unable to perceive the problem.
2. Cultural—Adults have certain cultural script.
3. Emotional—Adults are reluctant to overcome their emotional feelings.
4. Intellectual—Adults lack the mental competence to resolve the situation.
5. Expressive—There are sometimes problems of poor skills of communication.

6. Environmental—Organisational environment at times is not amenable to environment demands. For adults learning there is a traditional distinction between cognitive (intellectual) learning, learning skills and developing attitudes.

The Industrial Training Research Unit have divided learning into the following five types by the CRAMP taxonomy.

"1. Comprehension involving learning theoretical subjects.
2. Reflex learning is acquiring skilled movements or perceptual abilities like typing.
3. Attitude development enables people to change their attitudes and social skills.
4. Memory training is learning information by heart.
5. Procedural learning requires learning systems, procedures, practices and rules."[22]

Since adults become mature in thinking, adult-learning makes the following four assumptions:

"1. His self concept moves from one of being a dependent personality towards one of being a self-directing human being.
2. He accumulates a growing reservoir of experience that becomes an increasing resource for learning.
3. His readiness to learn becomes oriented increasingly to the developmental task of his social role.
4. His time perspective changes from one of postponed application of knowledge to immediacy of application and accordingly his orientation towards learning shifts from one of subject centredness to one of problem-centredness."[23]

9. Principles of Learning

There are certain principles, which need to be followed for developing effective training programmes. Some of the main principles are described below:

1. To be effective, the training must use tested principles of learning that every human being is capable of learning.
2. Training should be conducted in the actual job environment to the maximum extent possible because effective learning results when initial learning is followed immediately by application.
3. An adequate interest in and motive for learning is essential because people are goal-oriented.
4. Learning is active, and not passive.
5. People learn more by doing than by hearing alone.
6. Time must be allowed for practice of what has been learnt.
7. Learning is a cumulative process.
8. The rate of learning decreases when complex skills are involved.
9. Learning is closely associated to attention and concentration.
10. Early success increases an individual's chance for effective learning.

The other nine principles of effective learning are as under:[24]

1. The learner learns what he does.
2. Learning proceeds most effectively when the learner's correct responses are immediately reinforced.
3. The frequency with which a response is reinforced will determine, how well the response will be learned.
4. Practice in a variety of settings will increase the range settings which increase the range of situations in which the learning can be applied.
5. Motivational conditions influence the effectiveness of rewards and play a key role in determining the performance of learned behaviour.
6. Meaningful learning, that is, learning with understand-

ing, is more permanent and more transferable than rote learning or learning by some memorized formula.

7. The learner's perception of what he is learning determines how well and how quickly he will learn.
8. People learn more effectively when they learn at their own pace.
9. There are different kinds of learning and they may require different training process.

10. Factors that Facilitate or Hinder Transfer of Learning to Work Situations

Personality of the individual, his role, and empowerment are individual level factors that help implementation of learning. Inability to change oneself, non-availability of slack time, non-recognition of performance due to demotivations and inability to manage external resistance to change are individual level factors that hinder implementation of change. At organisational level, opportunity for change, empowerment for change, systems for change and critical mass for change are factors that help implementations of learning. At organisational level, existing work culture of fire-fighting and crisis management, lack of resources for experimentations and lack of job related knowledge among employees are factors that hinder implementation of learning. The ability to create a learning organisation requires personal mastery and motivation for change. When effective training and learning preceeds problem solving, quality circles become effective in planning and implementing changes within an organisation.

11. Training Techniques, Methodologies and Aids

Very broadly, various training methods can be grouped in the following four categories viz. knowledge based methods, simulation methods, experiential methods and on the job training methods.

(i) Knowledge based training methods - Basically these methods include lectures, seminars, workshops, programmed instructions, films, T.V., group discussions, presentations and conferences. These methods try to expose participants to concepts and theories, basic principles, pure and applied knowledge of fundamentals. Lecture method is more direct, clear, conserves time and is more controlled by the instructor. A good lecture must motivate group interest, must be developed well and must be presented well after proper analysis of the learning group. A conference method should have a qualified conference leader, must have a carefully selected conference group, with sessions of definite length and frequency with adequate conference facilities. A group discussion is a training technique where a small group of five to twelve persons with a mutual interest in a topic discuss the subject under the direction of a leader to converse and deliberate with the intention of arriving at some useful conclusions. This group discussion method encourage individuals to work as team, helps them to gain group acceptance, helps them to develop self-confidence and provides to them an opportunity to share ideas and experiences with the other group members. Then seminar technique is designed for a group of ten to forty people normally led by an expert in the field and requires preparations by all participants. It develops in-depth systematic study of topic, generates high and active students' participation and is usually led by a recognised expert. Generally a seminar consists of a working paper/key address by the expert, followed by presentations and discussions by other participants' question-answer session, group discussion and summary at the end by the leader in the form of a valedictory session. At times there can be more than one expert and paper presentations are followed by question-answer sessions. Symposium technique stimulates groups by short speeches and this technique guards against oversimplification of topic. In this technique a group of small size meet to discuss a common problem or topic of mutual interest and it is a valid approach for presenting information to a group in an organised manner, clarifying problems and stimulating group thinking.

(ii) Simulation Methods—Simulation methods are useful for real life situations for imparting training through role-play, case method, management games and in-basket exercises. Role playing process as a training technique can be defined "as a method of human interaction that involves realistic behaviour in imaginary situations."[25] The first systematic effort to develop a body of knowledge and skill and to conceptualize the role playing process was made by the Viennese psychiatrist—Dr. J.L. Morens in his book *Who Shall Survive* published by Beancon House, Beacon, New York, in the early 1980s. It is an action-training tool growing out of the relationships and feelings of individuals working and living in real situations. The enactment, spontaneity, real behaviour, feedback analysis and discussions are some of the characteristics of role-playing. For training in subjects like interviewing counselling, human relations skills, leadership training, contract negotiations salesmanship and performance review, role-playing can be used as a very useful training technique. Case method is a very useful method for students for developing independent thinking, discerning in "the ever - tangled skein of human relations." First developed by Christopher Langdell at the Harvard Law School, this non-directive way of helping trainees to think for themselves is quite popular in law, medicine, business administratin and social work. Case report in some forms, case discussion, case analysis and the current situation are some of the important constituent elements of the case method. Case discussions should be free, informal and experimental and should achieve proper coverage and should be carried out under the overall supervision or leadership of facilitator. The case leader should allow discussions in an informal manner and guide the discussion to achieve the objectives. The case method has some basic limitations in that it cannot reproduce the unfolding quality of actual events in all situations. Management games developed by American Management Association are well-documented in the book *Top Management Decision—Simulation* by France, M. Ricciardi, Chiffor J. Craft *et al* published in 1957. The game is built around the model of a business situation and students are divided into teams representing the management of competing companies wherein operating decisions are taken by various teams. A management game is a dynamic training exercice utilizing a model of a business situations; it is exciting and a powerful educational tool. Games can be combined with other teaching techniques such as role-play or case study. In-basket exercise is a simulation training technique designed around the "incoming-mail" of a manager. Under this technique the trainee is given a number of samples of administrative, technical and behavioural problems similar to the things in a basket at work during any day on the job. In-basket or in-tray exercises may vary according to the jobs to be done, the skills exercised, the degree of constraint or difficulty and hidden implications.

(iii) Experimental Methods—Experimental methods include sensitivity training (T -group trg.), transactional analysis achievement—motivation workshops and action learning. Action-learning, derived from the principle of "Learning by doing" was developed by Reg. Revans and in this groups of people find solutions to various organisational problems by identifying their skill, knowledge and attitude deficiencies, their strengths and weaknesses as well as future problems. Action maze is another technique in which trainees analyse a write up narration or descriptions of an incident. Action maze has been deduced from programmed learning and shares some of its qualities. This technique is used for developing one's analytical skills, decison-making capacity and problem solving approach.

(iv) Job-Training Methods—On the job-training, job-rotation, guidance and counselling, brainstorming sessions and syndicate method are some of the popular job-training methods. The most effective way of providing for the growth and development of people in manufacturing organisations is through the conscious coaching of subordinates by their immediate superiors. On-the-job-training is applicable to a wide range of semi-skills, skills and technical jobs as well as to supervisory and management tasks and responsibilities. If on-the-job-training is to be effective, it must be planned, organised, staffed, supervised and controlled very carefully. Competent people must be selected to conduct OJT and required materials, equipment and time must be made available.[26]

Training Aids—Training aids can be broadly classified into three groups, audio, visual and audio-visual aids - materials and equipments. Sounds are normally presented through a radio, tape-recorder, record player, sound track and recorded voices. Black boards, flannel board and graphs, magnetic board, flip chart board and chart-displays and exhibits, poster, graphs, silent video-tape, ediscope or opaque projector, overhead projector, film strips, film slides etc. are useful training visual aids. Audio-visual equipment such as films, television, closed circuit T.V., videocassette recorders are useful training aids because they combine presentation of sound and vision at the same time. Multi-media projector is the latest equipment useful for training.

12. Evaluation of Training

Evaluation of training is a systematic assessment of training so as to study the effectiveness of training and to measure the actual result. A continuous qualitative assessment of training programmes is necessary for making them effective and useful. "Evaluation of Training" in its broadest sense can be defined as "a sub - system which determines the effectiveness of a training system and includes full range of value judgements about training from what trainees think of the programme, of improved quality, efficiency, effectiveness, and change in attitudes and behaviour pattern of the trainees and ultimately in the organization as a whole." Evaluation can be of trainees, trainers, instructional methods, instructional materials, instructional environment and short-term or long-term change in attitudes and behaviour pattern of the organization. Evaluation is an essential phase of the instructional process. The nature, level and contents of the courses, the methods of instructions, the quality and quantum of instructional staff, training environment, relevance of course to the role expectations: all need periodical evaluation and review with the object of constantly making the training meaningful and relevant to the work. An objective and systematic evaluation can serve as the basis for further improvement in teaching as well as learning. Evaluation is generally used in its broadest sense to include the full range of value judgements about all aspects of training to determine the effectiveness of a training programme. Evaluation is an attempt to find out what changes in people, things, employees, procedures and situations have been accomplished through training programmes as against what was actually hoped to be accomplished.

A system of evaluation is necessary :

(a) to find out whether the goals and contents of training programmes are compatible with the mission and current needs of the organisation;

(b) to find out whether the goals and objectives of training are being reached in the most effective manner and if not, necessary modifications may be made;

(c) to provide a feedback to the management about the utilization of training resources and utility of training programmes;

(d) to plan and revise training by adoption of better techniques and design by identifying the shortfalls and gaps in training programmes;

(e) to justify the cost of expenditure incurred on training resources;

(f) to carry out the diagnosis of the trainee's strengths and weaknesses, designing and providing remedial instruction and assessing the individuals' capabilities;

(g) to identify, measure and record evaluation of trainers in objective terms by pointing out their strong and weak points as trainers and giving constructive counsel to them concerning their shortcomings. "The trainers must evolve a methods of receiving feedback from his trainees and wherever possible assessment from his colleagues."

(h) To assess the effectiveness of training methods, techniques and aids in isolation from the training courses.

The scope of evaluation, according to an expert committee should extend to the following:

"1. That the objectives of the training programme are clearly defined and are couched in concrete terms;

2. That the training content is prepared, keeping fully in view the precise requirements of the field;
3. That the training programme is conducted efficiently and effectively;
4. That the trainers are fully equipped not only with the, specialised knowledge of their subjects, but also with the techniques of training; and
5. The trainees acquire not only the job skills, but also the correct approach and attitude to their work.[27]

The nature, level and content of the training programmes, the methods and techniques of instructions and the quality and quantum of the training staff of institutions all need a systematic periodical review and evaluation with the objective of constantly improving the training programmes. The impact and effectiveness of the training programmes upon the trainees and ultimate upon the organization has to be judged and evaluated through field experience, observation, opinion surveys, and feedback from various clusters of the organization. Training programmes, which include attitudinal development, need more comprehensive planning, adequate resources, sufficient time and intensive effort both by the instructors and the students in order to achieve a positive and lasting effect for the organization. Time is a very major factor governing the effectiveness of any training programme. Organizational climate, institutional environment and the training system are also important factors in determining the effectiveness of any training programme. For scientific evaluation of training programmes, in any organisation all aspects of the training system are required to be appraised and evaluated for validity. Criteria tests need to be administered to evaluate training objectives, individual lessons, course material, course duration, course programme, instructional techniques and the quality of instructional staff for a proper evaluation of training programme. However, the need for sound objectives arises again in the area of evaluation. Mager says—when clearly defined goals are lacking, it is impossible to evaluate a course of programme efficiently.[28]

Denaldson and Scannell (1978) offer a more detailed break-down of the ways in which the outcome of the training can mainfest itselt:

1. Direct cost reduction
2. Grievance reduction
3. Productivity of trained versus untrained employees
4. Productivity after versus before training
5. Work quality
6. Quantitative results
7. Accident rate
8. Absenteeism
9. Employee suggestions
10. Supervisory rating
11. Profit
12. Sales Volume
13. Turnover rate
14. Customer complaints
15. Worker efficiency
16. Training period required for proficiency
17. Cost per untrained employee
18. New product development
19. New Customer
20. Public relations

13. Assumptions of Training

The following assumptions implicit in current training practices and approaches, have been identified by Lynton and Pareek:[29]

1. The acquisition of subject matter knowledge by a

participant leads to action.

2. The participant learns what the trainer teaches. Learning is a simple function of the capacity of the participant to learn and the ability of the trainer to teach.

3. Individual action leads to improvement on the job.

4. Training is the responsibility of the training institutions. It begins and ends with the course.

All the above assumptions are really only partly valid. Training, whether qualitative or quantitative, is both formal and informal. It can be planned or unplanned. Learners can learn in many ways and training cannot be the role responsibility of training institutions.

14. Difficulties in Getting Proper Scientific Evaluation of Training

A speaker at the conference of the American Society for Training and Development said that on the basis of a very recent survey of the literature for the past ten years it appears that about one hundred articles or reports for this ten year period have dealt with evaluation of training of which eleven appeared to be respectable evaluations. The question of evaluation of effectiveness of training programmes is indeed difficult.

Major difficulties encountered in securing reliable evaluations are as follows:

1. Evaluation is made generally from a personal rather than objective viewpoint.
2. Failure to recognise the difference between ability and performance of trainers and trainees or in other words what a man could do and what he actually does.
3. Whenever training comes under criticism, like the proverbial doctors, training directors bury their mistakes under the hundreds of corporate variables that affect training outcome. Training directors blame the quality of trainees, the heavy workload, and the supervision that follows thinking and operational environment of the field.

4. Evaluation requires people with time to dig out the facts, people with sophisticated measuring devices and evaluation instruments and people who have courage to admit that training programme was not wholly successful sifting through training records, interviewing all trainees, playing with the statistical tools like mean mode and median and carrying out a comprehensive objective evaluation are not particularly glamorous training exercises and generally dedicated people are not available for such jobs.
5. Due to organizational culture of strict discipline, fear of victimisation and lack of moral courage, trainees are reluctant to give their frank and free reactions in writing. Thus reactions evaluation does not bring out any useful criticism or gaps in training administration.
6. Over-generalization of concept, superficial indication of happiness data (saying pleasant things), justification of expenditure for training by inviting supportive responses are some of the problems of evaluation.
7. Maintaining the anonymity of the respondents does not assure either accurate or useful responses from trainees.
8. One of the problems of evaluation is the failure to differentiate between research and evaluation though current methods of evaluation are emerging from those developed in behavioural and social science research, but the aim of evaluation is administrative and limited. Evaluation has a limited purpose of decision making and its scope is to be confined to its limited objects while the research has much wider scope.
9. Informal evaluation can be based on field trips or discussions and even written evaluation questionnaires if trainees go out to the field and carry out informal discussions with various people. But this practice is not in vogue in India.
10. Evaluation of training becomes difficult when objectives of training are not identified in quantifiable terms.

15. Emerging Challenges in Training

Women are entering the workforce in increasing numbers and will need greater training and orientation. Informal on the job employees training may increase in the service sector—manufacturing and public administration. According to Alvin Toffer, even in the developed countries the pace of growth of technology is so high as to cause severe strains on society. With development of high technology automated machines, high communication and office automation due to computer advancement training activities in these near areas will gain major thrust in post-liberalisation era in various organisations. The current approach to training is to develop a list of competencies which employees need if they are to be productive, and committed to organisational mission. The current interest in competencies was developed by R.E. Boyatzis[30] and the term includes not only skills but also mind-set and personal attributes. General foundation training, business management engineering and technical training have to be dovetailed for all highly paid professional and technical workers. At present the following challenges are most important for training:

1. Competitiveness in terms of quality and cost of product.
2. Experimentation and high quality packing competence.
3. Quality and ISO 9000 certification and its related training.
4. Training for survival in a liberalised global environment.
5. Training for systems improvement and innovations.
6. Training for marketing abilities for maximising sale.
7. Training for customer satisfaction and high quality of service.
8. Training for maintaining growth and position as market leader and creating viable plans for coping with changes.
9. Training for high motivation, efficiency and professionalism.

10. Training for competencies for technological upgradation and innovations.
11. Training for skill development and ongoing self-learning.
12. Training for coping with changing environment, changing customer expectations and changing government policies.
13. Training for development of human personality.
14. Training for total quality management.
15. Training for teamwork and improving vertical/horizontal communications.
16. Training for getting the employees commitment to organisational goals and misson.
17. Training in octapace values—(Openness, collaboration, Teamwork, Trust, Authenticity, Pro-action, Autonomy Confrontation and Experimentation).
18. Training for personality development and entrepreneurship.

Prof. N.K. Singh, former chairman of the International Airports Authority of India says: Training mission should be efficient performance of the entire range of services.... I believe the metamorphosis of change in perception at all levels in an organisation is not the result of the large canvas painted by the chief executive, but of tiny action taken by hundreds of individuals/ employees in the organisation. Such mini-revolutions can bring about the great change and our whole training approach should be based on this concept." Time is the essence in our organisational context and training must continue as an ongoing process in spite of all problems and infrastructural inadequacies. " Training has become more of a perk and less of a competency building instrument in recent years. With increased emphasis on cost cutting, customer service and efficient management of all systems; there is a need for more training to achieve these goals.[31] Today there is a challenge to train the entire workforce and all the employees in addition to train the managers in total quality control and total quality management. The main challenge of training is to aim at building core competence and multi-skill development. Total employee involvement can be achieved through regular training and motivation. For senior level managers, scanning skills, negotiations skills, interpersonal relations skills and info-technology awareness skills are needed. According to Prof. Udai Pareek, "training is the most widely used and yet highly neglected system. Training has become a ritual with huge investments and very little positive pay off. Can't we move away from the number (so many personnel trained) to strategic use of training for developing usable competencies?"[31] This can be done by taking training seriously at the higher echelons of the organisation, by higher budget allocation for training for stronger collaboration between the training system and the organisation.

16. Training for Transformational Leadership

Companies need Chief Executive Officers (CEOs) who can think strategically, inspire trust and motivate, communicate and envision the future. Bernard Bass, the pioneer author of transformational leadership has reiterated four key characteristics of transformational leadership which are as under:[32]

"1. Charisma—Provides vision and sense of mission, instills pride, gains respect and trust;

2. Inspiration—Communicates high expectations, uses symbols to focus efforts expresses important purposes in simple ways;

3. Intellectual stimulation—Offers challenge;

4. Individualized consideration—Gives personal attention, coaches and advises."

Leaders should participate in development programmes, mentor high potential managers, have executives share publicly their mistakes and what they learnt, recognise those who took carefully calculated risks but didn't succeed and promote people who actively share knowledge to help the whole organisation.

The training for transformational leadership is not simple

Exhibit - 2 Linkage of Training with Corporate World

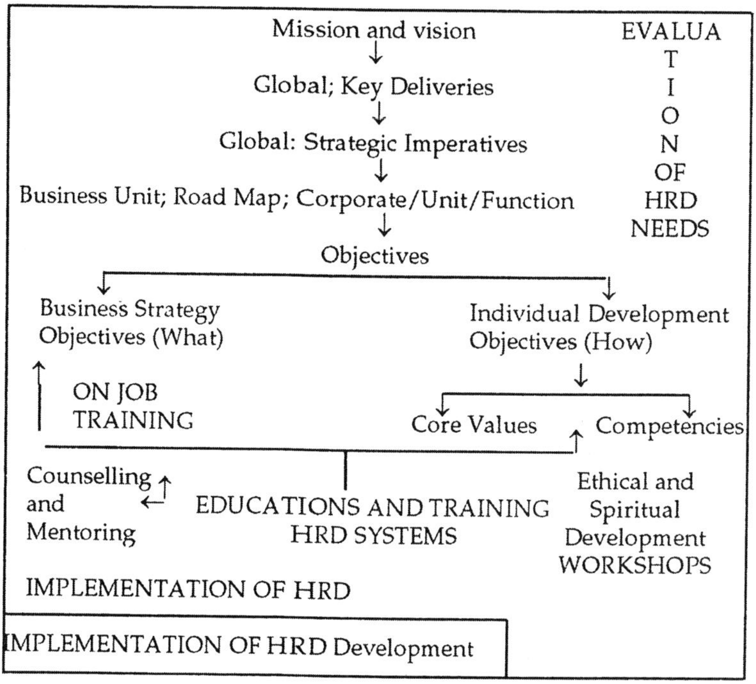

because the main concern of a transformational leadership is to get performance from people beyond expectations by going beyond—the contractual relationship—by inspiring them, stimulating them and paying attention to them as individuals. Training for leadership has to prepare senior managers for both transactional and transformational functions. Transactional functions include policy making, planning, developing systems, monitoring performances, coordination, rewarding, coaching and ensuring achievement of targets by maximising efficiency. Transformational functions include visioning, modelling, setting standards, building cultures and climate, boundary management, synergising, searching and nurturing talents and ensuring organisational learning. The main focus of transformational leadership has to be on HRD institution building, norm building, team building and boundary management.

Organisational learning is "a process by which an organisation acquires, retains and uses inputs for its development and the process results in learning and self-renewal. Training for organisational learning must take care of the five important general areas, namely (i) Experimentation and flexibility; (ii) Mutuality and teamwork; (iii) Contingency and incremental planning; (iv) Use of temporary system of task groups or task forces; and (v) Competence building. Training for transformational leadership can be organised by utilizing external training programmes of various management institutes and other training agencies who specialise in this specific area. Training for leadership must be closely related to the mission and vision of the company. Diagram shown below exhibits how individual performance can be aligned with the company vision:

17. Training for the Corporate Sector

In the corporate sector, new managers are generally selected from freshly passed out MBAs during campus interviews. A survey of campus recruiters conducted by Xavier Labour Relations Institute (XLRI) at Jamshedpur indicated that the CEOs really value the following skills:[33]

1. Ability to work in a team
2. On the job performance
3. Leadership skills
4. Problem solving abilities
5. Adaptability to organisation
6. Interpersonal relations
7. Analytical abilities
8. Entrepreneurial spirit
9. Practical knowledge
10. Realistic career expectations
11. Independence
12. Loyalty to organisation

Since 1993, ICI has been constantly changing its outlook and has recently leveraged technology to foster continuous employee education. Identifying HR mission in 1998, ICI formulated the following mission: "We will facilitate a high performance, seamless and empowered organisation, where the potential of all employees is realised to add value to self and the organisation." ICI identified the following key thrust areas."Consistently provide outstanding customer satisfaction; seek avenues to add value to the organisation through adding value to each employee; pursue operational excellence and build a high performance culture." The ICI has drawn up a dream called IDOLS (Individual Development Online Learning System) to find employees learning whose slogan is "space to pack back your learning."[34] The "IDOLS" allows flexibility, cost-effectiveness, freedom to choose time and place for learning, participant control over the structure of the course, privacy to learn/unlearn in public, free access across the organisation and is aimed to facilitate learning in a virtual environment at the learner's workplace and at a self-determined pace. This online learning system of ICI articulates the following values: Cascade learning across the organisations by sharing knowledge residing within and outside the organisation; listen, understand and respond to customer continuously, define and redefine superior services; establish a service strategy, set standards and measure performance, empower the IDOLS owner (training manager) to work for the customer, recognise and reward learning, to stir continuous employee learning. To minimise access time IDOLS was kept on LAN (Local Area Network). It was decided that IDOLS will not substitute training but would only serve as a basic functional knowledge course for non-functionalists and non-MBAs at all levels whereas training would cater to skill development and advanced knowledge course. As a virtual learning option which enables learning at one's work space and on one's desk top/lap top, IDOLS overcomes the problems relating to dropping out of the course due to last minute business exigencies and reluctance to be displaced from work for a prolonged period, or inhibition to speak in public while attending a course or discomfort with learning at a group space. However, the ultimate measure of IDOLS success will depend on how many employees log in and how much of each course module is used or how many employees ultimately learn from this online learning system to bring it into actual practice. ICI has made a small beginning with a futuristic perspective and later a few more courses can be added in due course of time.

HRD's primary role is to create an environment that facilitates idea generation and execution with a view to harness individual brilliance within the organisational framework. An intensive effort in training generates constructive pressures towards other sub- systems of HRD. When an HRD consultant designed the first training programme of a consumer product company for senior managers, as a workshop on organisational effectiveness and used it as a device for problem solving and identifying those problems which training could help, the following needs emerged.[34]

1. To reduce compartmentalisation and interdepartmental hostilities,
2. To add a managerial competence dimension to the existing functional capabilities of middle and senior executives,
3. To replace expected superannuations of long serving old timers and some seniors on tenure jobs after retirement from the armed forces,
4. To develop a pool of management talent with inter-functional and multi-territory awareness.
5. To enhance skills of goals setting counselling, and appraisal for subordinates developed.

Entry level training is on the priority list of both the young MBAs fresh out of the management institute as well as the firms that hire him. It is the quality of entry level training imparted by the company that matters. The changing business environment has necessitated that companies lay greater emphasis on training entry level professionals. Entry level training aims at helping new entrants understand the working of the organisation, integrate themselves with the corporate mission and of course bring them down to reality. Entry level training familiarise the trainee with the specific culture and philosophy of the company, imparting the right attitude and skills and providing- specific information. Entry level training in companies grooms the young entrants for greater loyalty in the company and good team working. Examples abound of companies such as HLL, Proctor and Gamble, Asian Paints, Marico Industries, Telco, Citibank, ICICI who arrange entry level training for young MBAs.

Training is often found wanting in credibility. It is all very well for trainers to say that a salesman should smile at customers all the time. But be on your feel for ten hours and then it will be seen how well trainers are able to smile at customers. Today training has identified the objective of in "Honadle and Honnah's words"—Capacity building" which means the capacity to find one's own solutions to management problems rather than imposing external ideas upon oneself."[35] In an effort to utilize training for organisational development, Richardson Hindustan Limited conducted training need surveys and later organised need-based training at all levels. Post-training follow-up was done to ensure the implementation of what was learnt was followed. As a result of these efforts RHL has been able to double its sales turnover and increase project order four times in six years without adding people. In Larsen and Turbo Limited (L&T) the main purpose of training is to provide learning opportunities and resources for :

1. Improving performance on the present job;
2. Developing behavioural and management skills;
3. Functioning effectively as an individual.

L&T has excellent in house-training facilities including well-equipped classrooms, library, films and other audio-aids. During the last five years on an average eighty-six training programmes were conducted and about 3000-14000 persons attended big programmes. About 700 persons are deputed every year for outside training programmes. In-service training programmes are based on the following:

1. Training needs specified by immediate superiors and senior managers.
2. Desirability of disseminating recent developments in management concepts and practices.
3. Availability of new programming conducted by foreign experts visiting India.[35a]

In SAIL, the need where training support was needed have been identified as (a) attitudinal changes: (b) utilisation of manpower: (c) modernisation and expansion: (d) efficiency enhancement and (e) orientation of new entrants. In Eicher Motors Ltd. (EML) which has its plants at Alwar, Faridabad, Parvanoo, Pithampur (near Indore); training is carried out effectively based on Japan's effective technique called Kaizen Induction training of three weeks is organised for all employees who join the organisation. This organisation gives top-most priority to training and has Japanese pattern of training with emphasis on customer consideration, do right things first time, making people feel responsible, versatility building on the job training and development training.

State Bank of India has identified its training philosophy which runs as follow—"Training in the State Bank is a pro-active, planned and continuous process as an integral part of organisational development. It seeks to impart knowledge, improve skills and reorient attitudes for individual growth and organisational effectiveness. The main features of State Bank Training systems are:

1. The existence of a proper training structure.
2. Division of training areas between the staff colleges and the training centres.
3. Specialised institutions have been created for rural development and information and communications management.
4. System for assessing training needs and training evaluation.
5. Linkage of training to the corporate plans.

6. Linkage of training to career plans.
7. Focus on programmes in specialised areas.
8. Conduct of special training programmes like stress management-special role transition programmes.
9. Existence of systems of overviewing training function.

State Bank of India organises special courses in areas like International Banking, Merchant Banking, Planning, HRM, Computer System Management etc. Training in SB has been a highly dynamic system, which has played a critical role in facilitating the following things:

1. Ushering in change,
2. Handling people's issues, anxieties and fears,
3. Providing valuable feedback on organisational climate,
4. In improving people's problem-solving and coping abilities,
5. In building the right perspectives,
6. In promoting and building the human competencies,
7. In generating a lot of experiential data,
8. In enabling people to be creative.

18. Management Development Programme

Management Development is a well-planned educative process and encompasses a wide variety of development modules for the acquisition and enhancement of relevant knowledge, wisdom, intuition, insight and skills. According to Elton T Reeves, management development can be defined as "any planned, guided or directed activity undertaken by a manager to help him become more competent in his present position, or to prepare him for heavier responsibilities to come."[36] Robert B. Burr has held that "management develpment is the planned exercise, guided growth, and training opportunities for those who perform the management functions. This includes all members of management from the president through all supervisory levels and staff personnel."[37] The initial evolution of management development (MD) programmes during the World War II was occasioned by a serious shortage of competent managers when the economy was expanding in America because of decentralisation and growth of satellite locations, scientific advances and technological changes, myriad of government regulations affecting wages, hours, working conditions, labour relations and the like.Another important contributory factor leading to the growth of MD was the increased productivity and industrial harmony. The complex changes concerning automation, computerisation, robotisation, emerging and expanding market, elevated role of labour unions and increased interdependence among sub-systems of economy caused forward looking management to reassess their needs for having qualified, effective and professional managers. The beginning of the concept of MD in India can be traced back to 1947 when India got independence and Indian leaders wanted to build up a vibrant economy.[38] MD is largely a twentieth century phenomenon with its most sophisticated development during the World War II.[39] The rapid expansion of technology, higher educational levels, better training and increased sophistication in the business world has made it mandatory to train the management cadre. MD signifies development of mental, critical, physical and moral faculties of a manager to enable him to discharge the managerial functions and to perform managerial roles fairly effectively.[40] Yoder and other have opined that management development (MD) is a programme of training and planned personal development purporting to prepare and aid mangers in their present and future jobs.[41] Management development (MD), according to Dale S. Beech, is a systematic process of training and growth, insights and attitudes to manage organisation effectively.[42] MD is an attempt to improve the managerial effectiveness through a planned and deliberate learning process for the achievement of organisational goals and strategies. Management development programmes generally should focus on the various qualities of a manager namely (I) coherent thinking, (II) problem-solving ability, (III) consensus obtaining ability, (IV) depth of insight, (V) technical and conceptual skills, (VI) reading habits, (VII) capacity to look forward, (VIII) tenacity to live on dissent, (IX) integrity, (X) commitment to the organisation, so that they may improve their managerial competencies and make contribution to organisational effectiveness and excellence. Denning, Hussey and Newman have defined MD as "the total process which an organisation adopts in preparing its managers for the growth and change that occur in their working environment."[43] Management development (MD) has two main tasks: the improvement of management performance and the organisation of management succession.[44] Management Development is a continuous process because changing environment and challenges require constant inputs to managers. According to Rober R.Burr, Management Development (MD) is concerned with "long - range planning and generally consists of the following four main steps :

"Step 1— Organisational analysis.

Step 2— Personnel inventory and performance appraisal.

Step 3— Determining training or Development needs.

Step 4— Planned Development."[45]

Above mentioned four basic elements are essential to the MD but these are not always designated by the same term and sometimes they are combined into fewer or broken down into more steps depending on the nature of organisational structure and role of training department. Generally organisational analysis is concerned with business and market information, general business trends, marketing conditions, competitions, research on new products and socio-economic and political trends. In the light of the above an ideal blueprint for the future managerial structure is built and personnel records showing age, health, education, experience and test profiles will help in advance planning and career development of the managerial personnel. Personnel inventory and performance appraisal can help in earmarking for futrue growth and succession planning. The purpose is to take stock of the present personnel and to determine how they measure upto present and future management standards. Determining of development needs of the manager will depend on the individual's knowledge, skills, and experience and also the organisational needs keeping into consideration various technological, organisational and market requirements. Once the specific long-range and immediate performance development needs are identified, planned development is achieved through various methods. Cost, availability, subject-matter and other factors are taken into consideration for initiating planned development, effective development, needs, opportunities for application particularly in three areas, knowledge, skill and attitude, under proper supervision and guidance. Moorehead Wright, former manager of the General Electric Company Management Research and Development Institute, enunciated the following ten principles essential to success of a programme which are as under:

1. Development is a highly individual matter.
2. Every man's development is self-development.
3. Development cannot be based on specific personality traits.
4. Development is primarily the result of daily work experience.
5. Opportunity for development must be universal.
6. Primary emphasis must be put on development in the present job rather than on the promotional job.
7. Managing is a profession.
8. Decentralized decison making is essential to development.
9. Development is the delegated responsibility of line management.
10. Moral and spiritual values are basic in the development process."[46]

According to Dooher and Marquis, the states involved in a management development programme are as under:

1. Organisational planning to determine the company's present and future needs;

2. Programme targeting to focus the company's efforts on the most pertinent areas;
3. Ascertaining key positions requirements to stress the basic requirements of particular managerial position;
4. Managerial appraisal to evaluate periodically the abilities and performance of individuals with a view to identifying managers showing a promise of further development and meeting their training needs;
5. Replacement of skills inventories to indicate persons qualified for managerial replacements;
6. Planning individual development programmes and provide specific programmes for promising managers; and
7. Appraising existing programmes to ascertain areas of improvement to be incorporated in future programmes.[47]

In the present era of globalisation and liberalisation, MD is neither a choice left to the goodwill of the top management nor a luxury of large multinational corporations. Rather it has become an essential requirement of the organisational systems to develop a realistic and professional approach among managers. MD should not lose sight of its underlying purpose to develop real management skills of real people in a real present day competitive environment. Development must be aimed at the kind of growth in judgement that enables the managers to make hard decisions under actual working conditions.[48] There are a number of different perspectives of management development and different approaches that help us in understanding it in a more comprehensive manner. Some perspectives are as under:

1. Management Development is a continuous process. The rapid expansion of technology requires that the manager continuously update his information to avoid technological obsolescence.[49]
2. MD is an organisational function mainly concerned with the development of managers in the organisation. It

is now agreed that individual development plans; well meshed into organisational development efforts, are a pre-requisite to long-term organisational effectiveness.[50]

3. MD is a means of bringing about changes in the manager's behaviour, attitudes and functioning. It is social influence process of change, dealing with change of attitudes and understanding to affect managerial behaviour, job-performance and operational results.
4. MD constitutes the most important part of Human Resource Development.
5. Management Development (MD) utilizes the education and training to develop the manager's potential as leader and enhance the organisation's as well as for their personal growth.[51]
6. MD is core of organisational success and MD motivates the managers to use their talents for higher productivity.[52]

Management Development programmes must cater to the needs of each organisation. Skill and capability development process can be initiated through a systematic approach as suggested in the exhibit 3 below.[52a]

Exhibit 3 Skill and Capability Development Process

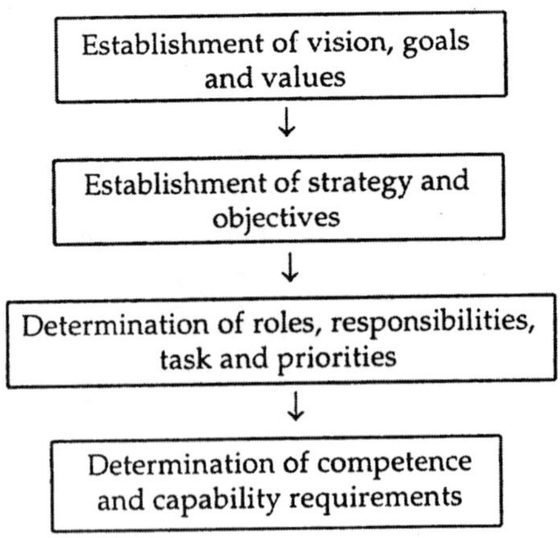

Assembly of groups and teams with relevant / complementary competencies

↓

Identification of deficiencies, gaps and support requirements

↓

Provision of counselling, facilitation, Process and technology support

↓

Evolution of form of organisation, patterns of work and approaches to learning

↓

Identification and selection of learning and transformation partners

↓

Organisation learning and development

According to H.F. Merill and E. Marting, the objectives of the management development are to secure the following valuable end-results:

1. Improvement in technical performance;
2. Improvement in supervision and leadership at each level;
3. Improvement in interdepartmental coorperation;
4. Highlighting an individual's weakness;
5. Attracting good people;
6. Facilitating sound "promotion -from within" policies and practices;
7. Ensuring that the qualifications of key personnel are enhanced and utilized;
8. Creating reserves in management ranks;
9. Making an organisation more flexible by increasing

versatility of its members;

10. Improving organisational structure;
11. Stimulating junior executives to do better work;
12. Keeping the company abreast of technical and economic conditions; and
13. Broadening key men in the middle cadre.[53]

The fundamental objective of the management development is to ensure that managerial cadre grows gradually to full maturity and can effectively lead the organisation to greater heights of productivity, excellence and competitive edge over others, taking into consideration growth of individuals and providing them self-actualisation motivation. The objectives of management development are to ensure that managerial and equivalent professional specialists; positions are filled by capable, suitably trained and motivated employees, according to the needs of the organisation and that the best use is made of the experience and ability available, to enable individuals to find satisfaction in their work and achieve a realistic ambition.[54] Watter S.Wickstorm, after carrying out a survey of about 200 firms in 1961 identified three main objectives of management development :

1. Improvement in the performance of present managers as the most important objective.
2. Helping selected managers prepare for advancement, and
3. Preparing all managers to adapt to changing conditions.[55] Management Development, as a planned process, is designed to cater to the individual and group needs of top level, middle level and functional level managers, keeping in view the organisational requirements.

According to Dr. Udai Pareek and T.V. Rao, the management development comprises of (I) environmental analysis, (II) management manpower analysis and planning, (III) succession planning, (IV) identification, (V) placement, (VI) career counselling and planning, (VII) training and education.[56] According to Stephen P. Robbins, method of developing managers are:

"A. On the job management development techniques include (I) Coaching, (II) Understudy, assignments, (III) Job rotation, (IV) Committee assignments, and

B. Off the job management development techniques include (I) sensitivity training, (II) transactional analysis (III) lecture courses, (IV) simulation exercises."[57] On the job techniques include coaching, job rotation, delegation, planned reading programmes. Off the job techniques include the incident method, the case study, role playing, in-basket method, management games, sensitivity training, syndicated methods, transactional analysis, brainstorming, observation towns etc. Management training has now spread to all levels of the organisations. Self-training and self -motivation can be the greatest rewards of a sound training approach.

Another research survey carried out indicates that corporate training programmes fail to add value to corporate strategies and common reasons for failures are as under :

1. Training programmes are not linked specifically to strategies, problems and challenges in the corporate world.
2. Training programmes are designed to create understanding and awareness but not competence.
3. Programmes focus on individuals rather than operating units.
4. Participants attend programmes for reasons other than personal or organisational needs.
5. Programmes fail to help trainees confront reality.
6. Training is unable to simulate real life in the corporate sector.
7. Training has failed to get top management support in many cases over a period of time.

19. Training for Knowledge Management

Today we live in the knowledge age. Knowledge is not just about information technology, biotechnology, robotics, pharmaceuticals, generic engineering and all those so-called domains of high technology. The world is at the threshold of a transition from an industrial to a knowledge society. The society has seen a shift in emphasis from atoms as the basis of everything to bits. Peter F. Drucker coined the term "knowledge workers" in a 1959 book *Land Marks of Tomorrow*. In India an increasing number of companies will have to depend for their value on the development, use and distribution of knowledge based competencies. Examples include technological know-how, product design skills, understanding customer needs, and problem-solving expertise, personnel creativity and ability to innovate. In the leading organisations of the future, knowledge will be created, stored, disseminated and accessed without any apparent complex interfaces. As a pioneer in the field of knowledge management Dr. Karl Erick Svieby has developed one of the first methods of measuring intangible assets in the 1980s and has written several books on knowledge management including *Managing knowledge, The invisible balance sheet;* and *The new organisational wealth, Managing and measuring knowledge based assets*. Dr. Erick Svieby believes that the difference between a company's market value and book value can be directly attributed to its intangible assets. Knowledge is in some ways the opposite of capital. Knowledge shared is knowledge double; unused knowledge deteriorates. These two differences between knowledge and capital are so powerful that economists like Brain Arthur and Paul Romer believe them to be transforming world economies.[58] Bill Gates vision of "knowledge works without limits" in essence is an environment where those who work with knowledge are empowered with the information and tools they require anytime, anywhere. When the knowledge revolution is hitting the Indian society, government and the people must train themselves and develop a vision to revolutionise the way people create, share and use information by providing exciting new technologies and products to give them the competitive edge. Governments need to take the initiative of introducing IT education at grass roots level and at other higher levels of education. All organisations and companies have to revise their training courses so as to include training in information technology. Management education and management development programmes have to include knowledge management in their various syllabii and course inputs. Although web-based training is mainly a matter of self-help, technical tutorials can help. Corporate training departments should take a serious look at formulating a development strategy that takes advantage of their medium.[59] There is need to arrange comprehensive knowledge management training to the corporate sector middle and senior level leaders so that "a shared space for emerging relationships" may emerge between various users of information technology.[60] It is necessary that in India not only industry and business, but also government organisations and service sectors should recognise the need for training in knowledge management. Managers must rise above daily worries and think in more cosmic terms because management practices as we know them along with many of our own theories have lost that utility, and individuals must try to manage themselves in the years to come.[61] Our business and industrial sectors must integrate information technology into every aspect of business from human resource to sales and services, marketing, finance and customer care. In short, management must treat IT pretty much the way consultants advised them to treat quality in the early 1990s.Researchers have noticed that training has not been able to achieve its desired objectives due to "Trainers Traps", Punch for appreciation by trainers, defensive behaviour of trainers and at times, aggressive behaviour. Some of the negative tendencies and behaviour of trainers, emerging from the Indian training scenario have been noticed by many researchers. Many trainers play tricks, politics and games to keep learners in good humour but these negative attitudes and behaviours of trainers spoil the learning climate of the organisations. Budgeting and controlling training costs and proper selection of qualified and experienced trainers are issues which are difficult to be resolved easily. Most of the training institutions face problems of top support, shortage of accommodation and staff, unqualified trainees. In many organisations training institutions are the dumping grounds for the unsuitable, demotivated and indisciplined persons.Training is a limited instrument and has its many limitations in terms of its effectiveness and efficacy. A mismatch exists between the premises of training and the reality of training because training has been treated as an Aladdin's lamp to deal with all the ills and problems of the organisations. Administrative deficiencies, role dilemma, systems defects and resource inadequacy are four maladies which cannot be cured by training alone.[62] Training has many limitations and it cannot compensate for lack of will or lack of interest of the employees to perform their duties. Many organisations develop functional blindness because they cannot see their problems. Liberalisation and globalisation have changed the way companies have to do business and in order to remain in business answer may lie in regular training programmes and attitudinal orientation of the employees. The changes that training can bring about are broadly at five levels:

1. Increase of effective behaviour.
2. Decrease of ineffective behaviour.
3. Use of additional behaviour for enhancing effectiveness.
4. Improving existing behaviour for enhanced effectiveness.
5. For maintaining the winning edge in the competitive world by updating required competencies and info-technologies.

There is lack of mutual distrust between line managers and trainers in many organisations. Corporate line managers generally do not believe their human resources can deliver the training employees need. The trainers believe line managers do not know how to lead in certain crucial situations. Oxford Training Review Study, 1977 shows that line managers doubt whether HRD Trainers are capable of delivering the training in a number of vital areas; acting as internal consultants, facilitating group events, facilitating group training, tailoring training to specific requirements, helping to plan career development for staff and choosing external training providers. Managers also doubt trainer's ability to transfer their own skills, so as to enable them to continue developing their teams on their part. Trainers say line managers have little understanding of how to lead teams that do not report directly to them. Nigel Purse, chairman of the Oxford Training believes that both groups are concerned that the skill needed to develop tomorrow's effective people, not embedded in today's managerial culture."Line managers, says Nigel Purse," are right not to have a huge amount to confidence in many training professionals. Many fail to get close enough to the business, so they are never in a position to focus on what they deliver. Many fail to build relationships with senior managers in the business but without their support training programmes won't be effective." Oxford Training Review Study of 1997 recommends that training should be customised and delivered just in time, featuring short high-impact programmes dealing with live business issues. The report urges HR managers to ensure that "training issues are on the agenda when business strategy is formulated and that training policies reflect business aims. Trainers must demonstrate how they can add value.They must also be brave about explaining the need for soft skills."[63] HRD managers, before designing a training programme must know business strategy and development needs of the employees so that training is progressive, dynamic and pro-active: since, business calls for negotiations between parties, negotiation skills need to be developed. Negotiation is the basic means of getting what your want from others. It is a fundamental, generic human activity, a process that is often used in business deals like mergers and acquisitions.Therefore all managers should get training in negotiation skills. Besides training, the role of personality, culture, interpersonal and group dynamics and experience, insight and subject matter expertise, among other factors have immense bearing on the outcome of the negotiation. India presents important cross-cultural differences worthy of consideration because of vast regional differences and diverse religious convictions. Indian corporate world must therefore organise training in negotiation skills at middle and senior level managers. Some management institutes have recently done pioneering work in this field. Training of human resource managers itself is a big challenge. A recent survey shows that one in five of those managers questioned say there are no experts when it comes to keeping their work force happy. This research carried out by Robert Half International shows that while sixty-seven per cent admitted to having limited motivational skills, only twelve per cent felt they excelled in this area.This research shows the training needs of the H R Managers. Managers need to be trained so that they may develop their personalities and acquire "self-actualisation". Personality is the core structure on which development takes place. As one advances in age, there is a change in professional and personal needs.An effective training programme must be geared to individuals and initiate a process of developing individuals for their journey towards the state of "self-actualisation", the highest need identified by Maslow. In their endeavour to help people on this journey organisations gain higher levels of professional commitment and Ededication towards achieving organisational goals. Continuous learning must continue in organisations and this is what Tom Peters referred to when he said "learning organisations will survive in the future". Dave Ulrich has recently said "globalisation requires that organisations increase their ability to learn and collaborate and to manage diversity, complexity and ambiguity."[64]

20. Training for Values and Ethics

Training for values and ethics is one of the difficult challenges of corporate sector because of the following main issues:

1. How to build ethics and moral values in training curriculum?
2. How to test the ethical and moral behaviour of job seekers and even admission seekers to higher institutions of learning?
3. How to teach ethical and moral values to people who lack values and ethics?
4. How to separate ethics and values from religion in a

secular, democratic and plural society?

5. How to ensure faithful adherence to values and ethical principles by corporate leaders?

Roberts Bob Haas, one of the pioneers of ethical management, believes that the most important quality for a manager is to create an organisation that will be successful in the long run. Ethics is a very potent weapon which can be used by the government to promote "Made in India" brand abroad especially considering that in the knowledge age, tangible forms of brand promotion may have to be replaced with more subtle and intangible tools and concepts.Training for values and ethics can be imparted through integration of insightful lectures, selected readings, meditation and workshops on corporate values.It is through spiritual orientation and the depth of silence that people can derive their vision, lead and build quality of work - life. There is a need for bringing Indianness in Indian management. Training for values and ethics can be a main integral part of management education. Knowledge of self, honesty, obedience, purity of thoughts and teamwork are values, which need to be taught to all managers.Bhilwara Group of Industries (Delhi), Hindustan Copper Ltd. (Malanjkand), Indian Petrol-Chemical Corporation Limited (Baswada), Bharat Electronics Ltd. (Bangalore), TELCO (Jamshedpur), Indian Oil Corporation Ltd. (Delhi), Indian Oil Corporation Pipelines Division, Shri Ram Fibres Ltd. Madars, Godrej and Boyce Ltd. (Bombay) TISCO (Jamshedpur), Bharat Heavy Plates and Vessels Ltd. (Vizag), Oil India Ltd. (Dulliajan), Bharat Heavy Electrical Ltd. are some of the organisations which have widespread educational programmes or values. The three modules have been organised on mind purification (*Chitta Shuddhi*) in terms of the following major seven Indian thoughts:

1. From Lower self to Higher self.
2. Dis-identification and Reidentification.
3. The Theory of *Gunas* Dynamics.
4. The Theory of *Karma* (Cause and Effects).
5. The Theory of *Sanskaras* (or Residual Impressions).

6. The Theory and Method of Work.
7. The Giving Model of Motivation.[65]

The first module is on "Performance Effectiveness", the second on Leadership and Teamwork and the third on "Managing Stress, Communications and Counselling", organised with some gaps for assimilation and experiencing by the participants. Prof. S.K. Chakraborty has been organising these training programmes with great success. Based on Indian Culture and Society, the following values have been identified for Indian managers.[66]

1. The individuals must be respected.
2. Co-operations and Trust.
3. Jealousy is harmful for mental health.
4. *Chitta-Shuddhi* or purification of the mind.
5. Top quality products service.
6. Work is worship.
7. Containment of greed.
8. Ethico-moral soundness.
9. Self-discipline and self-restraint.
10. Customer satisfaction.
11. Creativity.
12. Inspiration to give.
13. Renunciation and detachment.

Above - mentioned profile of human values are anchored in the transcendent aspect of human life which Indian managers should imbibe, understand, explore and implement. Most of these ethical principles, if properly observed, can bring excellence, leadership transformation in the organisation Bosses, can boost poor group morale by training employees in conflict management as well as by organisation emphasizing the importance of communication with co-workers. More importantly employees and managers must learn to be flexible. More and more organisations are asking employees to leave the isolation of their cubicles to collaborate with co-workers, spawning innovative ideas and increased productivity. According to Debra Connelley, "people have to learn to respond to other perspectives not with a knee jerk but by waiting to hear out information before they make a decision." Ethical behaviour would effectively control the tendency of extremism in business and therefore ethical value orientations during training should cover the technical, social and psychological systems and formal and informal cultures. The word "ethics" derived from the Greek word "ethos" means a system of moral principles, the basis for deciding right and wrong actions. Values represent the standards or ideals about what a person, object, event or activities "ought to be." Values at the individual level include faith, self-respect, open-mindedness, creativity, devotion towards work, tolerance, courtesy, honesty, truth, non-covetousness, equanimity etc. Values that can be imparted at the organisational level should include harmony, discipline, brotherhood, social conscience, cooperation, mutual trust, team-spiritedness, efficiency, morale etc.

21. Concluding Remarks

Training is a continuous journey of organisations for achieving excellence, better productivity, total quality control and increasing competitive edge of the employees. There is an urgent need to start formal training of *Vedanta*, ethics and social responsibilities to all the employees of the corporate world. Indian psycho-philosophical concepts of *Vedanta* and transcendental meditation can offer great depths and richness for the development of training of the corporate employees. The Indian concept of *Chitta Suddhi* (Purification of Mind) and *Sadhana* (Meditation) can go a long way in coping with organisational stress and modern life challenges of the corporate world.[67] More and more it is being realised that the value of an organisation resides in the people and the knowledge they create. Knowledge workers are more mobile than ever before. Sharing knowledge with the co-workers should be a part of their job and they must be recognised and rewarded for sharing their knowledge with others. A recent study shows that eight out of ten staff do not know what expertise their colleagues have and therefore information sharing will boost efficiency in the corporate world.

REFERENCES

1. A comprehensive list of such institutions is available with the United Nations Institute for Training and Research, New York.
2. K.M. Mathur, *Internal Security Challenges and Police in a Developing Society* R.B.S.A. Publishers, Jaipur, 1989, p. 29.
3. Bata K. Dey—"Training in the Civil Service Plea for a Holistic Construal"—*The Indian Journal of Public Administration* Oct- Dec. 1982, Vol. XXIX p. 4 - Quoted by Dr. K.M. Mathur in *Administration of Police Training in India* Gyan Publishing House Delhi, 1987, p. 3. Also refer Bata K. Dey—"Civil Service Training and Career Management in India - *The Indian Journal of Public Administration,* No. 3 pp. 557-58.
4. Cloyd S. Stemmetz *The Evolution of Training* in Training and Development Handbook - American Society for Training and Development. Edited by Robert L. Craig and Lester R. Bittel, Mc Graw Hill Book Company, New York, 1967, p. 15.
5. Frank Docringer, *Developing Top Executive,* PA Special report, 41. The Presidents Assoication Inco, January - Feb, 1970, p. 6.
6. Leonard Nadler, *A Process of Training - Leadership Resources,* Inc, Washington, 1968. p. 3.
7. Dr. K.M. Mathur, *Administration of Police Training in India,* p. 23. For details see pp. 40-43.
8. Robert F. Mager, *Preparing Instructional Objectives,* 1962, p. 3.
9. Quoted by Committee on Police Training—M.S. Gore, Chairman, Government of India, Ministry of Home Affairs, p. 11
10. Committee on Police Training, Government of India, M.H.A., p. 91.
11. A.C. Hamblin, *Evaluation and Control of Training,* McGraw Hill, London, 1947. Also A.C. Hamblin—*Evaluation of Training in Industrial Training International,* Nov. 1970, pp. 33-36.
12. Dr. K.M. Mathur, *Administration of Police Training in India,* p. 244.
13. Colvin P. Otto and Rollin O.Glascer, *The Management of Training,* 1970, p. 111.
14. Dr. K.M. Mathur, *Administration of Police Training'* p. 5.

15. S. Tyson and A. York—*Personnel Management made Simple*—London Heincann, 1982, p. 178.

16. B.M. Bass and J.V. Vanghan, *Training in Industry—The Management of Learning*, London Tavistock Publications, 1969.

17. Paul Pigors and Charles A Myers, *Personnel Administration*, p. 377.

18. Paul Temporal—*The Nature of Non - Contrived Learning*. Management Education and Development, Vol. 9, 1978, pp. 94-95.

19. Richard M. Steers and Layman W. Porter *Motivation and Work Behaviour*, New York, McGraw 1975, p. 478.

20. For details consult K.M. Mathur, *Administration of Police Training in India*, Gyan Publishing House, New Delhi, 1987, p. 30-31.

21. Paul Temporal, *The Nature of Non-Contrived Learning*. Management Education and Development, Vol. 9, 1978 pp. 94-95.

22. Industrial Training Research Unit Chooses an Effective Style: a Self-instructional Approach to the Teaching of Skills, Cambridge. ITRV 1976. E and RM BELBIN—*Problems in Adult Retraining* London, Heinemann, 1972.

23. Knowles, M.S. Andragogy, An Emerging Technology for Adult Learning, The Modern Practice of Adult Education.

24. For elaboration consult—Calvin P.Otto and Rollin O Glaser, *The Management of Training* - Addison - Wesley Publishing Company Massachusetts, 1970, pp. 106-12.

25. Raymond Corsini Malchom Shaw and Robber Blake, *Role-playing in Business and Industry*. The Free Press of Glance, New York, 1961.

26. William R. Tracey, *Managing Training and Development Systems*, Taraporevalla Publishing Industries Pvt. Ltd, Bombay, 1980, pp. 43-44.

27. Conference on Training - Feb '69 sponsored by Training Division, MHA -IIPA, 1969, p. 117.

28. Major Robber F., *Preparing Instructional Objectives*, California, p. 3.

29. Lynton R.P. and Pareek, Udai—*Training for Development*, Richard D. Irvin Illenous, 1987, p. 6.

30. R.E. Boyatzis, *The Competent Manager—A model for Effective Performance*, Wiley Chichester, 1982.

31. T.V. Rao—*Changing Role of HRD in the Liberalised Economy in HRD in the New Economic Environment*, Edited by T.V. Rao and

others—Tata McGraw Hill Publishing Company, New Delhi, 1994, p. 9.

32. Bass, Bernard M—*From Transaction to the Transformational Leadership: Learning to Share the Vision,* Organisation Dynamics, winter 1990, pp. 19-31

33. R. Sukumar, Human Resources—*Wanted Multi - Skilled MBS - Business Today,* Dec. 7-21, 1997, p. 109.

34. Author is grateful to H.C. Ruben Selvadoray for providing useful inputs through his paper Transcending Boundaries ICI's on line learning system" - appearing in *Ascent- The Times of India,* 14th January, 2000.

35. M.B. Althreya *Integrated HRD System - Intervention Strategies in Alternative Approaches and Strategies of HRD* Edited by T.V. Rao and others. Rawat Publications, Jaipur, 1989, p. 382.

35a. Biswajett Pattanayak : *Human Resource Training* Wheeler Publishing, 1998, Allahabad.

36. Elton Reeves *Management Development and the Line Manager,* American Management Association, New York, 1969, p. 10.

37. Rober B. Burr "Management Development" In *Training and Development Hand Book* - American Society for Training and Development, Edited by Robert L. Craig and Lester R. Bittel, MC Graw Hill Book Company, New York, 1967, p. 363.

38. M.V.V. Raman, "Management Training and Industrial Productivity - In *Management Development and Training in Public Enterprises,* (editors) R.K. Mishra and S. Ravishanker, Ajanta, Delhi, 1983, pp. 163-69.

39. Elton Reeves—*Management Development and the Line manager,* American Management Association, New York, 1969, p. 10.

40. Inchak Adize—*How to Solve the Mismanagement Crisis,* Los Angeles, MDDOR, 1980.

41. Dale Yoder, H.G. Heneman, J.G. Turnbull and C.H. Stone. *Handbook of Personnel Management and Labour Relations* - McGraw Hill, New York,1958.

42. Dale S. Beech, *Personnel: The Management of People at Work,* Mac Millan, New York, 1980, p. 382.

43. R.W. Denning, Hussey and P.G. Newman, *Management Development: What to Look For,* Harbridge London, 1978.

44. Bernstein Lesley, (ed.), *Managment Development,* Business Books Ltd. London, 1968, p. 1

45. Rober B. Burr, "Management Development" *In Training and Development Hand Book* - American Society for Training and Development, Edited by Robert L. Craig and Lester R. Bittel, Mc.Graw Hill Book Company, New York, 1967, p. 363.

46. Moore head Wright, "How Do People Grow in a Business Organisation?"

47. Dooher M. Joseph and Marquies Vinien, - *The Development of Executive Talent*, American Management Associations, New York, 1952, pp. 29-30.

48. Charles P Bowen - Jr., Let put Realism into Management Development. Harvard Business Review Training and Developing Executives, Reprint series No. 21196, 1973, p. 58.

49. Colvin P.Otto and Rollin O. Glascer - The Management of Training - A Handbook for training and Development Personnel - Addison Wesley Publishing Company, Philippines, 1970, p. 376.

50. L.D. Goddstein, "Management Development and Organisational Development", *Business Quarterly*, winter 1971.

51. E.C. Eyre *Mastering Basic Management* - Mac Millin, London, 1984, p. 155.

52. Rensis Liker, *New Patterns of Management*, MC Graw Hill, New York, 1981, p. 7.

52a. Coulson, Thomas Colin, *The Future of the Organisations*, 1997, London Kogan Page.

53. H.F. Merill and E. Maring, (ed.), *Developing Management Skills*, American Management Association, New York, 1958, p81. Quoted by Dr. K.M. Mathur- *Towards, Effective Management, Pathways to Excellence*, Gyan Publishing House, New Dellhi, 1999, p. 50.

54. David Ashton and Mark Easterly Smith, *Management Development in the Organisation: Analysis and Action* - Mac Millan, London, 1979, p. 4

55. Watter S. Wickstrom, *"Why Companies Develop Their Manager"* Management Record, National Industrial Management Record, Vol. 23, No.11 Nov. 1961, p. 6-8.

56. Udai Pareek and T.V. Rao, *Designing and Managing Human Resource System*, Oxford and IBH, New Delhi, 1981, p. 9.

57. Stephen P. Robbins, *Personnel- the Management of Human Resources*, Engle Wood Cliffs, Prentice Hall, 1982, p. 224.

58. *The Economics Times*, 19th January, 2000. Master Mind - Karl Erik Sveily - Indexing Intangibles.

59. Steed, Colin, *Web-based Training*—Grower, London, 1999.

60. Cortada J.W. and Woods JA, (Editions), *The Knowledge Management Yearbook 1999-2000*, Butter Worth Heinemann, 1999.

61. Peter F. Drucker, *Management Challenges for the 21st century*, Harper Business, 1999.

62. K.M. Mathur, *Administration of Police Training in India*, Gyan Publishing House, New Delhi, 1987, p. 44.

63. Marget Coles, "Bosses Put Boot into the Trainer"—*The Sunday Times —Times of India, Ascent*, New Delhi, March 18, 1998.

64. Dave Ulrich, "A New Mandate for Human Resources"—*Harvard Business Review*, January - February, 1998, p. 126.

65. S.K. Chakraborty, *Management by Values—Towards Cultural Congruence*—Oxford University Press, Delhi, 1991, p. 95.

66. *Ibid.*, pp. 19-20

67. For similar views see Dr. K.M. Mathur—*Towards Effective Management - Pathways to Excellence*, Gyan Publishing House, New Delhi, 1999, pp. 169-97.

7

Counselling and Mentoring

Counselling is a discipline, and a product of the educational system—particularly the vocational training. The core of counselling, Smith (1966) believes, lies in: (I) faith in humanity, (II) concern for persons, (III) belief in the potentiality of human being for realizing their selfhood and their developing responsibility for themselves; (IV) groups and institutions which embody and implement the values to which they subscribe.[1] The goal of counselling is to help individuals overcome many of their problems such as educational, vocational, marital, parental or personal. According to Rogers (1942) effective counselling consists of a definitely structured permissive relationship which allows the client to gain an understanding of himself to a degree which enables him to take positive steps in the light of the new orientation.[2] As a concept counselling is an interactive process, conjoining the counsel who needs assistance and the counsellor who is trained and edcucated to give this assistance. (Perez 1956).[3] Patterson characterised counselling as "the process involving interpersonal relationships between the counsellor and one or more clients, in which the former employs psychological methods, based on systematic knowledge of the human personality in attempting to improve the mental health and performance of the latter.[4] Blocher explains it as "helping an individual become aware of himself and the ways in which he is reacting to the behavioural influences of his environment. It further helps him to establish some personal meaning for this behaviour and to develop and clarify a set of goals and values of future behaviour.[5] Gustad (1953) has observed, "counselling is a learning oriented process carried on in a simple, one to one social environment, in which the counsellor, professionally competent in relevant psychological skills and knowledge, seeks to assist the client, by methods appropriate to the latter's needs and within the context of the total personal programme, to learn how to put such understanding into effect in relation to more clearly perceived, realistically defined goals to the end that the client may become a happier and more productive member of society."[6] This is most comprehensive and generally accepted concept of counselling. In the context of HRD, counselling is the means by which HRD staff helps trainees and new entrants through purposeful conversation and providing practical solutions of work related problems. HRD facilitators and task force must understand the roles of mentors and counsellors. New entrants and young workers, supervisors and junior managers generally develop themselves by working with the persons whom they admire. They gradually build a trusting relationship with their supervisors and managers who nurture, support and guide their subordinates. This dyadic relationship for employee development focuses on establishing confidentiality, trust and mentoring involves help and support by a mature senior person (in experience, expertise, competence and status) to a younger one through the organisational processes of communication, counselling and monitoring in an environment of trust, healthy relationship and comradeship. Feedback and counselling is an integral part of HRD activities in many organisations. Several organisations in the past have conducted employee counselling programmes as a part of performance appraisal training.[7] Counselling has a wide range of applications and is useful for those who are involved in; (a) business and administrative training; (b) management training; (c) higher education; (d) workshop facilitation; (e) the human potential field; (f) the health professionals; (g) customer relations training; (h) personnel training; (i) public relations; (j) clinical psychological counselling and (k) school education. Counselling is a dynamic process in which two or more people meet to explore personal problems and to identify solutions to work related problems or practical solutions to life. Definition of counselling usually involve some or all of the following :

"(I) two people are present, the counsellor and client relate well;

(II) the process leads to action on the part of the client;

(III) the counsellor is a person who listens with an empathic relationship;

(IV) the counsellor sticks closely to the client's problems;

(V) the client feels free to say what he likes;

(VI) the atmosphere of mutual trust and confidence generally exists;

(VII) rapport is essential and personal growth of the client usually occurs;

(VIII) resolution of problems is an expectation."

Counselling Skills

The various steps of the counselling have been shown in the diagram below:

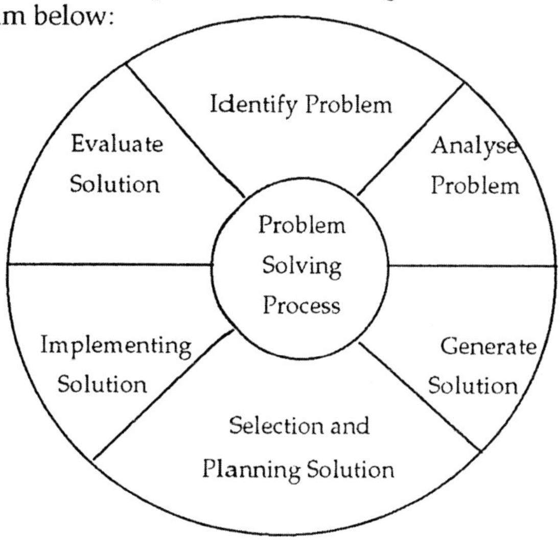

Counselling skills can be further explained as follows:

1. **Identifying and Selecting Problem :**

   (a) Select Employees; (b) Understand Performance Deviation; (c) Understand Areas of Strength Improvement.

2. **Analysing Problem:**

   (a) Potential causes; (b) Inadequate knowledge information; (c) Skill deficiency; (d) Hard data; (e) Testing.

3. **Generating Potential Solution:**

   (a) Inform; (b) Explain; (c) Coach-explain, demonstrate, practice, evaluate, feedback; (d) Train; (e) Counsel; (f) Counselling of project/assignment; (h) Mentoring.

4. **Selecting and Planning Solution:**

   (a) Selection of Solution; (b) Action Plan Solutions;

5. **Implementing Solution:**

   (a) Review action periodically

6. **Evaluating Solution:**

   (a) Evaluate and feedback.

Carfuff (1969) suggested that a climate of trust must be developed in counselling in which empathy, warmth and genuineness are present. Listening, giving information, making suggestions, drawing out, challenging and supporting are some of the main categories of counselling skills. When a counselling relationship develops, the following stages are generally identified:

(I) Getting started when the counsellor and client meet and get to know each other;

(II) Introductory talks explore the existing background about the work and the company (organisation);

(III) Identifying the issues;

(IV) Coping with feelings and emotions;

(V) Identifying possible solutions through brain-storming sessions;

(VI) Agreeing to a plan of action;

(VII) Implementing the plan and its monitoring/evaluation over a period of time.

In the context of increasing role efficacy, the role of counselling is to help the individual realize what prevents him from being effective and taking necessary steps to have a higher role efficacy. Such counselling may become a part of performance counselling.[9]

Objectives of Counselling

The basic purpose of counselling is to develop the employees. The objectives of the counselling involve the following:

1. Helping emplyees to understand themselves and their SWOT analyses—Strengths, Weaknesses, Opportunities and Threats and help them to realise their full potential.
2. Providing them with opportunities to acquire more insights into their behaviour and analyse the dynamics of such behaviour.
3. Enhancing their personal and interpersonal effectiveness through required feedback.
4. Assisting them to have better understanding of the environment.
5. Motivating them to set goals for further improvement.
6. Assisting them to review in a non-threatening way their progress in achieving various objectives, goals and targets.
7. Helping them to generate alternatives for dealing with various problems and definite action plans.
8. Providing them with empathic atmosphere for their sharing and discussing tensions, problems, concerns and conflicts.
9. Providing them with a support system, which may enable them to lighten their stress, burdens and challenges and to seek guidance and wise counselling.

Counsellors and mentors have to listen to the various types of feelings of their clients. Generally feelings may be hostile, guilty, resentful, anxious, despaired, pressured, happy, depressed, miserable, confused, discouraged, uneasy, relieved or mixture of some of these. Questions can serve many purposes; they may assist in getting more information, establishing mutu-

Exhibit- I. Showing Various Responses of Counsellors

Effective and helpful	*Unhelpful and dysfunctional*
(A) Empathic	(A) Alienating
—Levelling	—Continuous stress on conformity
—Rapport building	—Passive listening
—Identifying failings	—Not encouraging creative acts
	—Lack of verbal response
(B) Supportive	(B) Critical
—Recognising	—Criticising
—Communicating availability	—Repeated mention of weakness
—Trusting	—Belittling
	—Reprimanding
(C) Exploring	(C) Directive
—Questioning	—Prescribing
—Reflecting	—Ordering
—Sharing	
—Probing	
(D) Closing summarising	(D) Threatening
	—Giving no option
	—Pointing out only one-acceptable way
	—Quoting rules and regulations
(E) Concluding	
—Contracting for follow up	
—and help	
—Monitoring and feedback	

ality, stimulating thinking, and clarifying various matters. Questions can be critical, leading, testing or resenting questions. There can be open questions, clarifying questions or trusting questions. Counsellors use responses some of which are useful and helpful, and some other responses can be dysfunctional or unhelpful. Empathetic, supportive and exploring responses can be more effective and helpful. Responses that alienate the employee, criticise him or order him are more likely to be unhelpful and dysfunctional. Various verbal behaviours in counselling situations that characterise these responses are shown in Exhibit I given below.

Counselling is helping people to grow and develop in the organisation and the process of counselling has broadly three phases, namely, Rapport Building, Exploration and Action Planning. Rapport building phase involves generating confidence in the employees to open up and frankly share their perceptions, problems, concerns and feelings with the counsellor. Exploration helps the employees to search various dimensions of their problems or discover unidentified problems and bring to light some unnoticed issues. Counselling generally ends with specific plans of actions for the development of the employees. Job rotation, role clarity, identifying a training need or increased responsibility etc. can be some of the likely outcomes in such action plan. The sequential process of performance counselling in given in Exhibit II.

In the first phase of rapport building, attempts should be made to build up a climate to acceptance, mutuality, openness and support. In the exploration phase, the counsellor attempts to assist the employees to understand themselves and their problems better. In the third, action plan phase, the counsellor and the employees work jointly and plan specific action programmes for the development of the employees. There are various sub-phases, which have been explained in the exhibit briefly. There is a comprehensive book on performance counselling by G.L. Morrisey titled *Appraisal and Development Through Objectives and Results* (Addison-Wesley, 1972). A comprehensive model of performance appraisal has been suggested by

U. Pareek and T.V. Rao in their books titled *Designing and Managing Human Resource System* (Oxford and IBH, 1982 and *Performance Appraisal and Review: Operating Manual and Trainers Manual*, 1978 (Learning Systems, 1978).

Exhibit II

Showing Sequential Process of Performance Counselling

Phase	*Helpful Behaviour*	*Hindering Behaviour*
Phase-I		
Rapport Building		
A-Attending	Rituals	
	Conversation on personal matters	Discussion of behaviour from the start
	Smile	
B-Listening (to)	Physical attention (posture)	
C-Feelings	Eye contact	
D-Concerns	Response (verbal and non-verbal)	Distraction
E-Problems	Keeping out telephones noise, disturbances etc.	Attention to other things, telephones
F-Acceptance (empathy)	Communications of feelings and concerns	Lack of response passive listening for a long line.
	Para-phrasing of feelings and concerns	
Phase-II		
Exploration		
A-Exploring	Mirroring or para-phrasing open questions	Criticising, avoiding or hedging

B-Problem Identification	Encouraging to explore Questions to explore possible problems Encouragement to generate information Identification of a probable problem	Suggestion of a problem
C-Diagnosis	Exploratory questions Generating several possible causes	Suggesting the cause
Phase-III		
Action Planning		
A-Searching	Question on possible solutions Generating alternative solutions	Advising
B-Decision Making	Questions on feasibility, priority pros and cons Discussion of one solution Discussion of an action plan Contingency plan	Directing
C-Supporting	Identification of need help Monitoring Contract on help	Promise of general help

Mentoring

Dr. David Clutterbuck, a mentoring consultant, says, "A mentor is someone who helps develop the individual's potential, capability, judgement and wisdom. It is a more personal involvement than coaching, which aims at increasing competence of skills." Mentoring can be done either by an outside mentoring consultant or a senior executive of the organisation itself. Helping junior colleagues to develop their potential can be a good career move for a senior executive. It is the unusual senior manager who, early in his or her career did not have an older, more experienced mentor higher up in the organization. This mentor took the protege under his or her wing and provided advice and guidance how to survive and get ahead in the organization. Mentoring is, of course, not limited to the managerial ranks.[10]

The basic objective of mentoring is to provide opportunities to new entrants and young employees to share their problems, concerns and feelings and get both moral support and guidance for their development. The objectives of mentoring involve the following:

1. Building up and nurturing a relationship of trust, cordiality and confidence.
2. Modelling behavioural norms for the young employees.
3. Listening to the personal, family, social and job concerns of the young employees.
4. Assisting them to search alternative solutions for their problems.
5. Sharing own relevant experience by the mentors.
6. Developing and maintaining long lasting personal and informal relationship.
7. Responding to the emotional needs of the employees without making them dependent on the mentor.
8. Mentoring, as a unique organizational process, needs to be institutionalized with clearly stated objectives.

Mentoring is gradually becoming more and more popular. According to Dr. David Clutterbuck "There is a growing trend for company bosses to have mentors and a belief that someone should supply the challenge the top persons can't get internally. One top executive told me that every time I meet my mentor I drive away thinking how dare he say that to me ? Then I get two exits down to motor way and think, but, of course he's right." Mark Rigby, who has been mentoring graduates for nine years, says; "One of the people I am helping has a strong accounting background, whereas mine's in sales and marketing. We have different strengths and weaknesses, so while I guide and help him, I see a different way of approaching things. Mentoring lets me see the quality of people coming in, so that I can monitor their progress and ask them to join my team. It is very rewarding when you have helped someone to achieve an ambitious career move. It is a real thrill."[11]

Any organization, which seeks to use mentoring as an HRD intervention strategy, has to find out answers to the following main questions.

1. What is mentoring scheme for ?
2. Who is it aimed at ?
3. What is the tenure of this scheme ?
4. What are the ground rules ?
5. What is the basis of choosing the mentor and the mentees?
6. How many times the mentor should meet his mentees in a year ?
7. What type of senior people should be assigned the task of mentoring and whether it should be voluntary ?
8. What should be the areas of focus at the meetings and the scope of the mentoring programmes in terms of what issues mentors have control over and what they do not?
9. Should mentors serve as "role models" for their mentees?
10. What type of training or inputs should be given to mentors to perform their jobs as mentors effectively ?

The success of mentoring as HR initiative depends broadly on three factors; the competencies required for a job, how these competencies develop over time and how they work together to achieve the stated goals. In practice most programmes falter because mentees expect mentors to be able to solve their work and non-work problems. Sometimes mentors believe their responsibility extends to helping the mentee irrespective of the nature or the context of the problem. Mentoring is essentially a developmental tool that encourages individuals to work to their potential. In mentoring system confidentiality is the key to ensuring productive mentor-mentee relationship. As far as the measures for the success of the mentoring system are concerned, such measures are available in the People Capacity Maturity Model (PCMM) and can be used with suitable modifications. It consists of the following two measurements :

Measurement One—to determine the status of mentoring activities, measure the : (a) number of mentoring relationships established in the organisation; (b) rate at which senior employees apply to become mentors; (c) efficiency with which these new mentoring relationships are established; (d) frequency with which mentors and mentees interact; (e) number of problems identified and improvements made in mentoring relationship.

Measurement Two—To determine the value of mentoring activities, measure the: (a) growth of core competencies in individuals or groups being mentored; (b) ability of individuals or groups to use the resource of the organisation; (c) performance of individuals or groups; (d) carrier development of individuals; (e) alignment of individual-group and team motivation along with the objectives of the organisation.

Octavia Jennings says; "Mentoring requires a talent for non-verbal communication and counselling skills, such as empathising, reflecting, summarising, analysing and encouraging." Dr. Robert Mc Henry, chairman of Oxford Psychologists Press says; "A good Mentor knows how to listen and to ask probing questions. Those skills can be picked up quite quickly. But mentoring is time-consuming; though you might spend only a couple of hours together each month, the preparation and aftermath builds it to atleast a day a month for each person you are mentoring. If you are changing jobs, you may doubt that you have gone into the area you want to specialise in. The mentor gave me a broad outlook, saying, don't panic, acquire skills and knowledge and just enjoy it and get exposure to as many opportunities as you can."

Mentoring, as an interactive process holds considerable promise for improving the employee's motivation and shaping the attitudes and responses of the employees. Mentoring is necessary and useful for all employees at each stage of their carrier although the focus and the manner of mentoring may change for one carrier stage to another. The true potential of mentoring is, almost always, never realised because organisations do little in this regard except designating a few managers as mentors. In the corporate sector, organisational efforts towards institutionalising mentoring are limited to running a couple of workshops for the designated mentors about mentoring skills. The identification of suitable mentors in itself is a challenging task[12] High performer does not necessarily make a good mentor. Successful mentoring calls for appropriate skills, values and temperament. A successful record of performance can add to the credibility of the mentor's interventions. Mentoring cannot succeed in isolation in a hierarchic, power-centric and distrust culture of the organisation. Mentoring presupposes a degree of openness and a culture of mutuality. The clarification of roles and the management of expectations are most critical for the success of mentoring in any organisation. Mentoring should not be viewed narrowly and kept at peripheral distance nor should it degenerate into a paternalistic one. Organisations can take several proactive steps to optimally benefit from mentoring. Mentoring can be used in a meaningful way in developing employees. Being called upon to be a mentor, could be made part of the recognition mechanism of the organisation. In the corporate sector, mentoring can be successful in the following organisational context:

1. Mentors need to be invariably free from within the

organisation for new entrants.

2. Mentors should be trust-worthy and confidentiality is essential between the mentor and the mentee.
3. There should be an organisational climate, which recognises those mentors who contribute to the development of the mentees.
4. Mentors should be capable of playing the roles of facilitator, coach and counsellor at the same time.
5. The expectations of the relationship must be clearly defined and known to both the mentors and the mentees.

The success of mentoring could be measured by the frank and free opinion of the mentees. Mentoring should be informal but must become a part of the HRD initiatives. In the corporate sector, mentoring is basically a development-oriented initiative and facilitates an environment in which an individual grows both as a person and as a professional. Mark Rigby, who has been mentoring for eleven years of his fifteen years with one mentoring centre says; "Early in my career, I was given a mentor who could share my concerns and understand whether they were serious or just a phase. A line manager will help you to decide if what you are doing is right for now and where to go long-term but will have to balance keeping your focussed in the team by giving the skills and experience to compete more, being one step removed, can give you a much better overall view. When you share an idea with a mentor, you get a more favoured opportunity to consider it and may then realise you need to discuss it with your line manager."

A successful mentoring programme is generally built on modelling concepts from social learning theory that is, a mentor's impact comes from more than merely what he or she explicitly tells a protégé. Learn to convey the attitudes and behaviour that the organisation wants by emulating the traits and actions of their mentors.[13] They observe and then initiate mentoring operations in the realm of the intangible. Mentoring does not readily lend itself to parameters which are either instantly measurable or have direct impact on its business results.

Organisations must use mentoring as an HRD initiative because it generates a feel good factor within the organisation and gives protege a large mission and a role model to emulate. Nowadays lots of senior executives are getting specialised mentoring services for their professional development. Joe Jaina says; "People seeking mentors write self-advertisements describing their background, job-history, personality, style and ambitions and the sort of people they would like to work with. Then they wait to see who picks them up. We are trying to give people control over their careers and to get a view of the company through the eyes of talented young peoples."[14] In development of professional careers of musicians, artists, film stars and businessmen, mentoring has a very crucial role to play in the present day world. In different situations, the mentor can be a boss or superior, a spiritual teacher, a top performer, a work related guide instructor, a career counsellor, a trust worthy character, a giver of higher impetus to one's total existence and the chief executive. In work shop organised by a management teacher about eighty seven per cent of talented engineers said they themselves needed a mentor and as many as ninety-three per cent evinced interest in themselves being mentors.[15] Generally a person senior in hierarchy-by-age is most commonly a mentor. According to W.G. Bennis, "I know of no leader in any era who hasn't had at least one mentor; a teacher who found things in him he didn't know were there, a parent, a senior associate who showed him the way to be, or in some cases, not to be, or demanded more from him than he knew he had to give."[16] The predominantly senior-based promotion policy in large Japanese firms ensures that the essential spirit of mentorship by the elders of the youngsters is nourished within the organisations, structure in Japan.[17]

A Case Study

(Mentoring in an Organisation)

Lotus Software Solutions Ltd. had been a progressive organisation, which regularly selected young and competent managers. Sammeer Parashar had been the Chief Executive Officer of the Lotus Software Solution Ltd. for the last ten years.

Vipul Kamath was the forty-three year old head of Human Resource at Lotus Ltd. Introduction of Mentoring in Lotus Software Solution Ltd. was his idea. He believed that it was the ideal foil to the other hard HR tools the company had adopted. Despite no prior real-life experience in spearheading such an initiative, Vipul Kamath had launched a full-fledged programme in early 1997. Initially he had considered hiring a specialist firm but soon realised that mentoring had to be an internally owned process if it was to work successfully. Sammer Parashar, Lotus Software Solution Ltd's fifty-four year old CEO, had, in his characteristic hands off fashion, empowered Kamath to do what he thought right. However many other senior executives had not welcomed this unprepared initiative. Vinod Rathore, a forty year old who headed the financial services software strategic management unit had been the most vocal critic. He firmly believed that mentoring needed to be a properly structured process if it was to serve any useful organisational purpose. Unless mentors are properly trained and prepared for their roles, the whole exercise can not be expected to be very useful. Without adequate preparations, Lotus Software Solutions Ltd. had launched a full-fledged mentoring programme. Sameer Parashar was at a loss because the employee turnover in his company stayed high, failing to gain any insights into his employee's aspirations, Sameer Parashar watched helplessly as his talented flock joined his competitors. Since all the standard sops-such as liberal foreign assignments, Employees Stock Options Plan and a flexible work environment were in place, he thought that the problem had something to do with mentoring. Was the mentoring at Lotus Software Solutions too casual, opaque and bereft of any perceived benefits ? Did the belief that people could work it out among themselves, need to be replaced by a well-planned structured mentoring system ? Lotus Software Solutions Ltd. has its market in international world. Naresh Sharma was the Vice-President (Marketing) of Lotus Software Solutions. He had been a successful executive hot-shop and was having tough time convincing Sheila Tripathi to carry out given organisational instructions. Sheila Tripathi was a highly qualified thirty-five year old System Architect and was required to be sent to Germany. Naresh Sharma exclaimed: "I think you ought to go," trying to calm down an agitated Sheila Tripathi. Both had long heated discussions over many rounds of tea and snacks, trying to resolve a sticky issue. Lotus Software Solution's biggest customer in Germany, FITZ SCHULZ GMGG wanted Sheila Tripathi to visit Potsdam the following week to make some changes in a Business To Business (B2B) Software Solutions Lotus had developed for it. But Sheila Tripathi had her own personal and family problems. Her mother-in-law was seriously ill and her son ten year and daughter thirteen year had their school final examinations scheduled for the same week. She felt that her place was by their side at home for obvious reasons.

Naresh Sharma was the mentor of Sheila Tripathi and it was his job to provide her guidance, advice and suggest the way out. Barely a month into his new role as mentor, he realised that mentoring was not going to be as easy as he had initially thought it would be—what options and solutions could he offer to Sheila Tripathi. Sheila argued in a very aggressive and rebellious manner, "Why don't you send Rajendra Purohit instead ? "He worked on the project with me" repeatedly argued Sheila. Naresh Sharma reasoned by saying "I could have sent Rajendra Purohit but client insists on having you there because you were the Chief Architect and also know German language very well." "Don't my family problems mean anything to you and the company". Sheila Tripathi asked, her face flushed, Naresh Sharma tried to explain the position by saying that the company and your boss do not want to do anything that will strain the company's relations with the key customer. Of course problems of employees also have to be looked into.But priorities have to be made and at times, hard decisions need to be taken. Vijay Chandolkar was the immediate boss of Sheila Tripathi. He was an insensitive superior who was only interested in task completion in utter disregard to the personal problems of the subordinates. Sheila was not ready to go and talk to her boss—Vijay Chandolkar because she knew the expected outcome of such a transaction. Sheila had actually made up her mind and said: "Listen, Naresh Sharma, I will go to Postdam but under protest." You can tell Vijay Chandolkar and all those high ups who matter that, as soon as I am back, I am going to resign and look for another job." She further said; "This is not an emotional or rash decision on my part—This is not the first time, I have had to turn a blind eye to my family needs and sort things out for the company. Naresh Sharma was unnerved by this meeting. Although he has known Sheila for the last two year he had never seen her so much upset before. Naresh Sharma informed Vipul Kamath about the whole incident and warned him about the likely resignation of Sheila from the organisation on her return from Potsdam. Vipul Kamath gasped; "Sammer Parasher CEO will kill me. If she resigns, it will be the sixth in three months. Besides Sheila Tripathi is the star of our new systems architecture. I have to figure some way out. She has to be retained at any cost." Sameer Parashar CEO, after hearing about Naresh Sharma's conversation with Sheila said; "We just can not afford to lose her. Not when we are poised for a big leap." Sameer Parasher, after some thought over the entire episode said, "Let us send Rajendra Purohit to Potsdam instead of Sheila and I will talk to the client. And tell Shiela that she can work from home if she wants to when her kids have their exams."

Sameer Parashar, CEO, had worked hard making Lotus Software Solutions Ltd. a good company to work for. The company was originally a distributor of Software packages in its early years but it had climbed the value chain rapidly. In mid-1997, Lotus created a fast track carrier path for seventy-five engineers, who it called doubled HP (High Performing and High Potential people). By the mid of 1990s, Lotus was providing a variety of solutions, having built up considerable domain knowledge in the core segments.

Lotus had pioneered solutions like customer relationship management packages for companies in airlines and hotel industries. As a system architecture specialist, Sheila Tripathi, who had joined Lotus in 1996 had played a key role in developing these packages. Senior officials of the Lotus were planning to make her General Manager (Architecture) the next month although CEO had so far not formally announced it. The immediate concern of CEO was about the four new clients they could not hope to service without the expert guidance and supervision of Sheila Tripathi. "If she leaves us, we cannot complete our four new projects and it is difficult to get a replacement even half as good at short notice", thus CEO was in no position to lose Sheila Tripathi. CEO was worrying about the future of the company any how to retain highly competent, professionally committed, high performing and high potential people. "Is mentoring breaking down in our organisation ? CEO was asking.

The financial and other details of Lotus Software solutions Ltd. are as under:—

Year	*No. of Employees*	*Net Profits in Rs. Crores*	*Turnover in Rs. Crores*
1990-91	24	1	15
1991-92	53	3	32
1992-93	72	8	52
1993-94	105	11	88
1994-95	140	18	126
1995-96	186	23	189
1996-97	220	32	259
1997-98	280	43	326
1998-99	350	53	415
1999-2000	340	58	440

In Aprit, 1997, CEO had launched a stock option plan that was extended to forty employees. By early 1999, close to twenty-five per cent of the 300 plus work-force had been covered. Around the same time, the company governing body had decided that each of its engineers would work on at least one overseas project every two years. In mid-1997, Lotus started other initiatives focussing on empowerment and motivation. Vipul Kamath had insisted that mentoring could be clubbed as a soft option that could build a culture of teamwork, open communications and trust. The result of this combination of initiatives was that employee turnover fell from a high of twenty-five per cent in January, 1997 to eighteen per cent in early

1999. Employee satisfaction index rose. The worry was however was that the attrition rate in double HP category at twenty-five per cent a year was still rather high. It was a matter of concern and anxiety. Vipul Kamath did not think there is anything wrong with the concept of mentoring. Lotus had defined the mentee as a high performer who needed personalised attention. CEO Sameer Parasher enquired whether they had erred in not spelling out the rules for this relationship of mentoring? Sameer Parasher, CEO, made a sign of interrogation and said "A well-meaning decision but may be, our fundamental approach was wrong or misplaced: The working environment in the company was of strict bureaucratic rigid hierarchy, cut throat competition, distrust, lack of transparency and rather suffocating. New entrants felt isolated in this non-comparative work oriented culture. There have been occasions when bosses of mentees were not happy with the relationship of mentees with mentors and at a few occasions some bosses grumbled about this informal mentoring system. A need was felt to get a proper feedback on mentoring system.

About a month later one Dr. Rishma Mathur, an independent consultant and management expert was hired to find out the results of various initiatives. Dr. Mathur submitted her report after making proper study of the whole situation. Managing mentoring, it was evident, was more complex than it had originally appeared. It was felt that mentoring can be successful if it is launched after proper planning and orientation. Mentoring can be successful only when mentors are properly trained, motivated and professional.

The basic issues that emerge in the case study are as under:

1. Was it a fact that mentoring was not linked to Lotus Software HR framework properly ?
2. Why the rules and responsibilities of various participants in mentoring system were not properly articulated ?
3. Why the objectives of mentoring were not properly spelled out ? Could senior executives carry out mentoring

without orientation and training ?

4. Why the broader components of mentoring were not properly focussed ?
5. Could the results and impacts of mentoring be measured in quantitative terms ?
6. Why the rate of attrition in Lotus was not coming down in respect of high performing, high potential performers?

REFERENCES

1. M.R. Smith (Ed.), *Guidance Personnel Work*, Future Tense, New York, 1966.
2. C.R. Rogers, *Counselling and Psychotherapy*, Boston Houghton Miffui, 1942, p. 18.
3. Jospeh F. Perez—*Counselling Theory and Practice*, Reading Addison—Wesley, 1965, p. 15.
4. C. Patterson, *Counselling and Psycho Therapy—Theory and Practice*, New York, Harper, 1954, p. 13.
5. B.H. Blcoher, *Development Counselling*, New York, The Ronald Press, 1966, p. 15.
6. J.W. Gustad, *The Definition of Counselling*, in R.F. Berdie, (Ed.) Roles and Relationships is Councelling, Minnesota, 1963.
7. T.V. Rao, *Changing Role of HRD in the Liberalised Economy*—HRD in the New Economic Environment, Edited by T.V. Rao, D.M. Silveira & others, p. 9.
8. Philip Burnad, *Counselling Skills Training—A Source Book for Activities for Trainers*, Viva Books Private Ltd., New Delhi, Madras, 1995, p. 18.
9. Pareek U. and T.V. Rao (1981), *Resigning and Managing Human Resource Systems*, New Delhi, Oxford and 1BH.
10. Stephen P. Robbins, *Organisations Behaviour—Concepts; Controversies; Applications*, Prentice Hall of India, New Delhi, 1998, p. 77.
11. *The Times of India—"Ascent, Wise up to Benefits of Mentoring—The Sunday Times*, May 19, 1999, p. 1.
12. Santrupt Mishra, A Holistic look at Mentoring, *Business Today*,

March 22, 2000 p. 142.

13. Stephen P. Robbins, *Organisations Behaviour—Concepts; Controversies; Applications,* Prentice Hall of India, New Delhi, 1998, p. 78.
14. "Wise up to Benefits of Mentoring", *The Sunday Times, The Times of India—Ascent,* May 19, 1999, p. 1.
15. S.K. Chakraborty, *Ethics in Management. Vedantic Perspectives.* Oxford University Press, Delhi, 1996, pp. 158-59.
16. W.G. Bennis, *On Becoming a Leader* (Reading; Addison Wesley, 1992), p. 91.
17. S.K. Chakraborty, *Management by Values—Towards Cultural Congruence,* Oxford University Press, Delhi, 1992, p. 190.

8

Evaluation of Human Resource Development

Human resource development is a continuous and systematic process in which the employees of an organisation are methodically helped in a planned way:

"1. To acquire, sharpen or improve capabilities and competencies required to perform various functions, tasks and roles associated with their present and future expected roles and responsibilities;

2. To enhance and develop their capabilities and competencies as individuals so that they are able to discover and exploit their inner potential for their own and/for organisational development purposes; and

3. Develop and foster an organisational culture where superior-subordinate relationships, teamwork, and collaboration among different sub-units are strong and contribute to the organisational growth, corporate excellence, dynamism and pride in employees, with the help of various mechanisms like performance appraisal, feedback, training, education, job rotation and career planning, and other such HRD intervention strategies.

HRD managers have the responsibilities for designing

and implementing various HRD mechanisms in an integrated way for synergistic impact. HRD managers have to constantly evaluate and monitor various systems and mechanisms for effective results. Human resource development aims at achieving organisational viability and initiating the transformational process for survival, growth and achieving competitive edge. HRD cannot solve all organisational problems but can enhance skills/attitudes, knowledge, aptitude and value-system of the employee in the desired directions. The purpose of evaluation of HRD is to bring to the fore "weakness and failures... strengths and success of various HRD processes and interventions for managerial feedback and corrections for achieving excellence". HRD should prepare employees for new realities and become multi-skilled in the broadest sense of the term. Human resource development should be concerned with applications-oriented learning and should prepare people for the future roles. Human resource development has both Macro and Micro approaches and evaluation has to take care of both. According to Prof. Ishwar Dayal they are:

1. "Man-centered Approach is guided by humanistic considerations and viewed as a philosophy, a belief that development of people in every organisation is a prime responsibility of management.
2. Reciprocal approach which comes from partly humanistic and partly business interest and which regard development of people as the most important asset for either improving or sustaining performance of the organisation.
3. Selective approach which consists of identifying persons who have to move to higher and more responsible positions and grooming them for future careers."[1] In case HRD outcomes are not realised in an organisation at a very satisfactory level, then one needs to evaluate the qualitative and quantitative inadequacies of the

HRD processes in that organisation. HRD is not equivalent to training but extends beyond individuals to include dyads, teams and inter teams: it focuses not only on knowledge and skill development but also on developing appropriate attitudes, values, relationships and physical, social and spiritual health. It includes coaching, mentoring and performance appraisals. HRD professionals have to stop equating HRD with training and education and think more creatively about low-cost alternatives for employee's development at national and even international level. Education, health, urbanisation, brain-drain, nutrition, employment generation are subjects related to human resource development at national level. Human Resource Development has a positive ethical and philosophical connotation when applied to people and it integrates the needs, aspirations and dreams of the individuals into the strategic objectives and mission of the organisation. It has both Macro and Micro level approaches. HRD systems have roots in the concept of quality of life and they emphasize psychological growth of the individuals besides security and well-being. For the successful implementation of HRD, besides top management support, a well-designed HRD programme, and a well-designed implementation strategy; regular evaluation and monitoring of HRD programmes are also important. The present chapter proposes to focus on the methodology and approaches to evaluation of HRD. The various components of evaluation of HRD have been covered at the conceptual level. Is HRD being driven by the employee than the resources of the organisation? Is employee feedback sought? Is the feedback used constructively in improving HRD? Is there any proper and scientific evaluation of HRD programmes? Whether HRD is meant for only hotel-relaxation, and diversion? Some of the issues have been discussed in the present chapter.

Evaluation -Definition

Evaluation is used in its broadest sense to include the full range of value judgements about outcomes and results of human resource development, from what employees of the organisation feel about the programme, to what is ultimately gained by the organisation in terms of its output, performance and quality of products. The purpose of evaluation activities is to find out whether the goals and contents of HRD programmes are compatible with the mission and current needs of the organisation and to find out whether the goals are being reached in the most effective and efficient manner. Warr (1969) defined evaluation as the systematic collection and assessment of information for deciding how best to utilize available training (HRD) resources in order to achieve organisational goals."[2] Hamblin defines it as "any attempt to obtain information (feedback) on the effects of a training programme and to assess the value of training in the light of that information."[3] Evaluation, in simple terms, can be defined as the assessment of value or worth of an HRD activity in terms of some criteria of results (may be reaction, extent of learning, change of behaviour or results) in the light of the available information. Evaluation helps to pin point the need, as a diagnostic tools for organisational analysis, to report the comparative effectiveness of different changes, techniques or different instructors, to record the results of change efforts, to get more insight about the individual and the organisation and to know the overall effectiveness of HRD Training.[4] Evaluation is the process of determining the effectiveness and efficiency of HRD Systems and their components by noticing variations from plans and the causes of the variations and identifying alternative means of improvement. Absence of feedback can prove very costly. *Ethan M.Raisel,* talking about his experiences while working with *Mc. Kinsey* and company found that clients were often no better at diagnosing themselves than a doctor's patients.[5] One has to listen to all levels of personnel to get adequate and frank feedback of HRD efforts. HRD should focus not only on the present but also on the future, otherwise the Peter Principle enunciated by Lawrence Peter may come into play and in the hierarchy, the managers may rise to the level of their incompetence.[6] People have to be given training and development to become multi-skilled and professionally equipped to take on future challenges, and prepare themselves for the new realities.[7]

Requirement of Effective Evaluations—A good evaluation system must include the following characteristics.[8]

1. A clear statement of the expected results of the change experience should be in observable terms including the time-frame over which specific HRD results can be measured.
2. The development of relevant reliable yardsticks which measure progress towards the stated HRD objectives.
3. Application of the yardstick in terms of time spent implied by the objective.
4. Establishment of an evaluation design of HRD which distinguishes the effects of changes from those of other intervening contaminants.
5. Establishment of various sources of information required to evaluate the change experience in terms of objectives of the HRD.
6. Specifications and examination of those underlying personality and situational factors which explain the identified change caused by HRD.

If it is to be effective, evaluation must be conducted in accordance with accepted and proven principles and procedures.[9] Evaluation must be planned in advance, it must be a continuous process, specific, verifiable and objective —Evaluation must result in usable information and must be administratively feasible. Evaluation must be conducted in terms of objectives and purposes. Human resource development (HRD) professionals have been talking about the need for evaluation through numerous articles and presentations at various national and international conferences and have urged to evaluate the results of their efforts. "Evaluation is a very complex, time consuming, continuous and tedious job. It is likely to be biased and subjective if not carried out on scientific lines by experts.[10] The objectives of the HRD programmes may relate to improvement of work culture, optimum use of corporate facilities, improvement in productivity, profit maximisation with customer satisfaction, technological upgradation, reducing wastage, increasing safety and improving the quality of work life. Evaluation of HRD is not an easy exercise since it involves questions of criterion validity and reliability, test construction and the practical problems of getting an objective assessment of HRD processes and interventions. Evaluation can be used for the following purposes:

1. To improve the delivery or design of the learning events created by HRD processes by assessing HRD effectiveness;
2. To increase the use of the learning on the job by HRD interventions through job enrichment and job-analysis;
3. To improve the quantity and quality of service HRD provides to the various organisations;
4. To evaluate the quality of HRD resource persons;
5. To make decisions about the learning in the organisation and to find new ways to create learning opportunities within the organisations. Evaluation of HRD is not an end in itself: rather evaluation processes—such as need analysis, performance measures of learning and measures of usage on the job—are more effectively used as tools within the total plan for HRD quality.[11] The system of evaluation and follow up should be carried out by an independent expert body for impartial and objective assessment.[12] Evaluation can provide useful information serving several purposes:

1. Justify budget over HRD activities.
2. Justify specific gains to the learners in terms of improved job behaviour and find out the extent to which HRD objectives are being achieved.
3. Justify specific gains in terms of improved work,

process, bottomline performance and business results.

4. To suggest measures to remove organisational ailments and create healthy work culture.

Evaluation changes from a complicated elusive generality into clear and achievable goals when the following logical steps are adopted:

Step 1. **Reaction**—How well the conferees and trainees have liked the HRD progamme?

Step 2. **Learning**—What principles, facts and techniques were internalised?

Step 3. **Behaviour**—What change in job behaviour resulted from the programme?

Step 4. **Results**—What were the tangible results of the programme in terms of cost reduction and quality enhancement.[13]

Human Resource Development in India has not received required attention, particularly in the rural sector where abundant manpower is available. A very objective evaluation of macro-level HRD of India reveals that there is a need to initiate measures for upgradation of knowledge, skills, creativity, education, health, nutrition, employment, empowerment and rights of people. Human resources cover both quantitative and qualitative aspects. Human resource development should focus on the development of personality besides developing skills and knowledge."Personality is the seed that can only develop by slow stages throughout life... for in every adult there lurks a child—an eternal child, something that is always becoming, is never completed, and calls for unceasing care, attention and education (compare this with the child ego state of transactional analysis).....The developing personality obeys no caprice, no command, no insight but brute necessity, it needs the motivating force of inner or outer fatalities."[14] HRD both at macro and micro levels must facilitate development of human personality to the maximum extent possible. How far in India are we succeeding in this field?

Nearly all HRD departments evaluate the programmes, with a view to improve the design and delivery of learning by the following four types of measurements.

1. Performance measures of skills, knowledge and attitudes;
2. Profile of the characteristics of the learners;
3. Analysis of the design and delivery; and
4. On the job measures of usage and retentions."[15]

There is an urgent need to carry out empirical studies about HRD climate in various organisations and units. An empirical study of HRD climate in B.H.E.L. has been carried out by P.Murali Krishna and P. Subbarao.[16] More such studies need to be carried out by researchers. The Evaluation process consists of following main steps: 1. Identifying areas for development. 2. Decision on strategies and methods of evaluation. 3. Tabulation, analysis and interpretation of evaluation. 4. Recommendation for further modifications. 5. Means of evaluation are observations, ratings, surveys, and interviews. 6. Evaluation of HRD managers, HRD strategies and HRD outcomes. Time-frames are needed for performance measurements. For purpose of evaluation, learning outcomes can be classified as motor skills, intellectual skills, verbal information and cognitive strategies.[17] Generally performance measurements can be objective measures (true/false, multiple choice, etc., attitudinal rating scales and demonstration of performance like projects, rating scales, simulated work tasks etc. HRD managers express mainly the following three concerns about implementing performance measures:

1. Concerns about being judged.
2. Time lost during performance measures.
3. Treatment of students as adults being judged.

Peter Drucker has asserted that few factors are as important to the performance of the organisation as measurement. He has lamented that measurement is the weakest area in management today. Edward Deming taught statistical techniques of evaluation. Various thinkers still differ about exact connotation of evaluation of HRD. Evaluating HRD is described variously as "a part of the personnel function, a programme with distinct objectives and time boundaries, a system and an O.D. intervention. However an evaluator has to be clear about "what", "how" and "why" of evaluation of HRD. HRD to be effective should be long-term, consistent and supported with continuous development programmes.[18] HRD professionals generally find three type of problems in implementing evaluation, namely, costs of evaluation, consequences of negative results and evaluation opening a Pandora's box. A large number of personnel are required for carrying out evaluation; interaction with HRD's customers, constructing and validating measurement tools, administering the evaluation and implementing decision based on the results of the evaluation. Proper evaluation requires valid performance measurement tools.

Cost Evaluation and Cost/benefit Analysis

The Government of India has invested Rs. 1,72,438 crore by the end of March,1996. Restructuring this sector is need of the hour as it is spread in twenty-one sectors of the economy accounting for seventy-eight per cent of investment.[19] HRD needs to be evaluated from the perspective of cost benefit analysis.The total cost of evaluation is usually estimated to be between five to nine per cent of the cost of total HRD budget. There are about 166 Central Government Public Sector Enterprises producing goods, seventy-four rendering services at the total investment of Rs. 1,62,322 crore. While 120 public enterprises made a profit of Rs. 9,722 crores,117 enterprises suffered a loss of Rs. 4,435. The net profit in 1993-94 to capital employed was just 2.78 per cent. There are nearly 1000 state public enterprises with a total investment of Rs. 38,283 crore incurring a total loss of Rs. 863 crore. Only HRD and good management can help make a turn around. The most significant cost of evaluation is personnel, which constitutes about seventy-five per cent of the total expenditure incurred on evaluation. An evaluation is a very costly affair and generally the total cost is usually about five to nine per cent of the cost of HRD event. The following factors generally influence the level of costs of evaluation.

1. Previous evaluation experience of the HRD staff.
2. Number of purposes for the evaluation.
3. Length of organisation's experience with HRD evaluation.
4. Number of participants involved.
5. Size and complexity of the organisation.
6. Number of stake holders/customers.
7. Number of data items to be completed; scored and analyzed.
8. Degree of automation of scoring and data input.
9. Number of evaluators required and duration of work.
10. Costs associated with development of evaluation tools.
11. Costs associated with construction reports by the HRD consultants and facilitators.

For HRD professionals, HRD is a double-edged sword since it is the only way to get the data needed to increase HRD's effectiveness and at the same time it can cause concern for HRD professionals if inadequate HRD needs assessment has been done. Evaluation requires people with time to dig out the facts, with sophisticated measuring device and the courage to admit that the last programme was a bit of bomb.[20] In HRD, evaluation is not a glamorous HRD activity since sifting through training records, interviewing organisational HRD beneficiaries, playing with the mean, median and mode and talking with HRD facilitators is hard work and largely a dull activity. Evaluation of management development reveals that management development programmes differ in the quality, quantity, duration and areas of main focus. After examining eighty-four studies from 1950-1970, researchers found no evidence that participation in training and development was related to success as a manager.[21] Campbell summarizes personal beliefs of what is known about evaluation of management development programmes in the following words:"We know that management development can change managers towards more employee-centred attitudes. We know that laboratory education probably can change behaviour in the work role but the nature and implications of these changes are unclear....We know almost nothing about what makes orientation, sales or team training effective."[22] A number of studies reached the conclusions about the limited effectiveness of management development on performance.[23] About the performance appraisal rating, Martelli concluded that supervisory training did not have a significant influence on performance as judged by performance appraisal ratings.About evaluation, a report of forty-five fortune 500 companies of USA showed that although 100 per cent of the organisations used some form of participation reaction form, only thirty per cent used measures of learning and only fifteen per cent used measures of behaviour.[24] The challenge to HRD professionals is to create new ways to help managers develop ways that bring learning and worker closer together than treating HRD as a separate and independent event. In management development programmes, HRD professionals are successful in developing verbal information, intellectual skills or attitudes. However they have been less successful at both producing and measuring results when the learning outcome is development. HRD evaluators need to create new formats that integrate learning and work. Evaluation indicates that development occurs when managers take action in real work situations and their thinking is challenged by the results of their actions or by their peers. Most HRD departments keep records of which employees attend each learning event and transfer that information to personnel record. Such records reflect attendance and not necessarily learning.There are the following six conditions for reporting participant's learning :

1. Measurement tools have been validated.
2. Management has specified minimum competence in terms of skills, knowledge and attitudes (SKA).
3. Participants have been informed that competence will be measured.

4. Alternative ways to meet minimum competency have been established.
5. Pre-requisites are enforced.
6. Records specify that participants have met or have not met competence, not their relative scores.[25]

Employees can gain skills, knowledge and attitudes (SKA) from other sources such as attending universities, attending distance learning programmes, external workshops, conferences or they may read books, journals etc. on their own. Learning in organisations can take place by the following additional events:

1. Coaching by the participant's mentors or managers.
2. Learning from other colleagues at the work sites.
3. Tutoring of individual participants at their work sites by the HRD staff.
4. Providing self-paced learning packages by a professional HRD group.
5. Allowing attendance in outside organisation conferences, workshops and seminars.

There are many ways to determine costs of learning. Head and Buchanan (1981) proposed five categories: student cost, instructional costs, facilities costs, administrative costs and instructional development costs.[26] Learning costs generally include participants salaries, travel expenses, instructor salary, instructor travel, infrastructure, facilities costs (classrooms), materials (participants materials, instruments). Equipment (computers, overheads, video), registration and record keeping costs, and other miscellaneous overhead training costs. Performance demonstrations are employed at the end of a learning event to determine or measure both intellectual or motor skills. As part of evaluation, interviews can be used to find out the extent to which skills, knowledge and attitudes (SKA) are being used on the job as well as to identify the constraints participant face in implementing their learning. Questionnaires and surveys are useful evaluation tools when information is needed from a number of trainees.Anonymity is considered necessary and numerical data are preferred from the target population.Validity measures the degree to which the evaluation gets the true and full correct picture of HRD learning event—Validity depends on the following three questions:

"1. Did the data collection tool measure what is intended to measure?

2. Was the data collection process appropriate?

3. Was the data analysis process appropriate."[27] Reaction evaluation is the most commonly preferred method by the HRD professionals. Learning evaluation is simply an attempt to assess the amount and quality of human resource development that has taken place during a particular training session. Behaviour evaluation and results evaluations are more complicated areas for HRD professionals.

HRD Profile and HRD Systems Evaluation

Udai Pareek has propounded the HRD systems, which are concerned with developing commitment and integration of the individual employees with the organisation.HRD systems should respond to the needs and aspirations of individuals, and teams in terms of their growth (competency), advancement and recognition, socialisation, getting necessary facilities and gains and sharing power in the organisation.Appraisal systems, career systems, training systems, work systems, cultural systems and self-renewal systems need to be evaluated in terms of main focus and main concerns. Udai Pareek while making an evaluative statement on current HRD practices has observed: "While HRD has made some progress, more qualitative changes are needed, in the current decade."[28] HRD systems should focus on the six human units in terms of commitment and integration, humanisation, competence, values, power and organisational learning.Participation is emerging as another vexing aspect of HRD. HRD systems such as appraisal systems, career systems, training systems, work systems, cultural systems and self - renewal systems can be evaluated by internal or external evaluators. There is a need for periodical monitoring and evaluation of HRD systems. The HRD profile and HRD climate can be evaluated with the help of instruments. Dr. T.V. Rao has prepared a checklist of activities the HRD department can undertake to achieve HRD goals and one can map HRD practice profile by assessing the effectiveness with which these roles are performed. HRD practice profile can be completed by all the staff in the HRD department and line managers and the data may be used to prepare action plans.[29] HRD practice profile has enumerated ninety-four HRD activity tasks under the following nine main headings:

1. HRD philosophy and liaison with top management;
2. Creating Development motivations in line managers;
3. Strengthening HRD climate through HRD systems;
4. Directing HRD effort to goals and strategies of the organisation;
5. Monitoring HRD implementation;
6. Inspiring unions and associations;
7. Human Process Research;
8. Influencing personnel policies;
9. Miscellaneous.

However, Dr. T.V. Rao has not included evaluation of HRD systems as one of the tasks of the HRD department. XAVIER Labour Relations Institute, Jamshedpur, Centre for Human Resource Development has developed an instrument for carrying out HRD climate survey consisting of thirty-eight statements to be replied in 5-point scale answers.[30] This thirty-eight item HRD climate survey developed by T.V. Rao and E. Abraham —at the XLRI centre for HRD is an instrument that is widely used to survey the HRD climate. These thirty-eight items assess OCTAPAC (Openness, Confrontation, Trust, Autonomy, Proaction, Authenticity and Collaboration) culture and implementation of HRD mechanisms.The questionnaire could be administered and HRD/climate profile can be drawn.

Table 1

A Matrix View of Evaluation of HRD Systems

EVALUATION AND REASSESSMENT OF HRD SYSTEMS

Human Units		Appraisal Systems	Career Systems	Training Systems	Work Systems	Cultural Systems	Self-Renewal Systems	Futuristic Skills
1.	Person	Performance Analysis Potential Appraisal	Career Dev Career Planning	Identify Training Needs	Role Efficacy	Rewards Acculturation	Involvement	1. Futuristic thinking 2. System's thinking
2.	Role	Dev. of KPA's Developing Critical Attributes	Job Rotation	Task Analysis	Job Enrichment		Stress Management	3. Inter-displinary skills/integration skills
3.	Dyad	Performance Review Coaching Feedback HRD	Mentoring	Training in Performance	Communication			4. Planning change 5. Entrepreneurship
4.	Team	Appraisals Work Counsel Team Team Appraisal Team Coaching		Identification of Training Needs Developing Curricula	Autonomus Work Groups		Team Building Team Maintenance	6. Continued learning 7. Research in human areas.
5.	Interteam	Common Procedures of Appraisal Parity of Appraisal			Productivity Quality of Work	Communication	Collaboration	8. Knowledge management

6.	Organisation	Linkage of Appraisal with Goals and Values	Succession Planning		Quality of Work Life	Climate Rituals Celebrations	HRD Research Organisational Learning

HRD PROFILE AND ROLES

HRD Climate AND VALUES SYSTEMS

EVALUATION, MONITORING AND FEEDBACK Through internal Evaluation systems, outside researchers and tasks forces.

Fig. 2 : Nadler's Critical Events Model

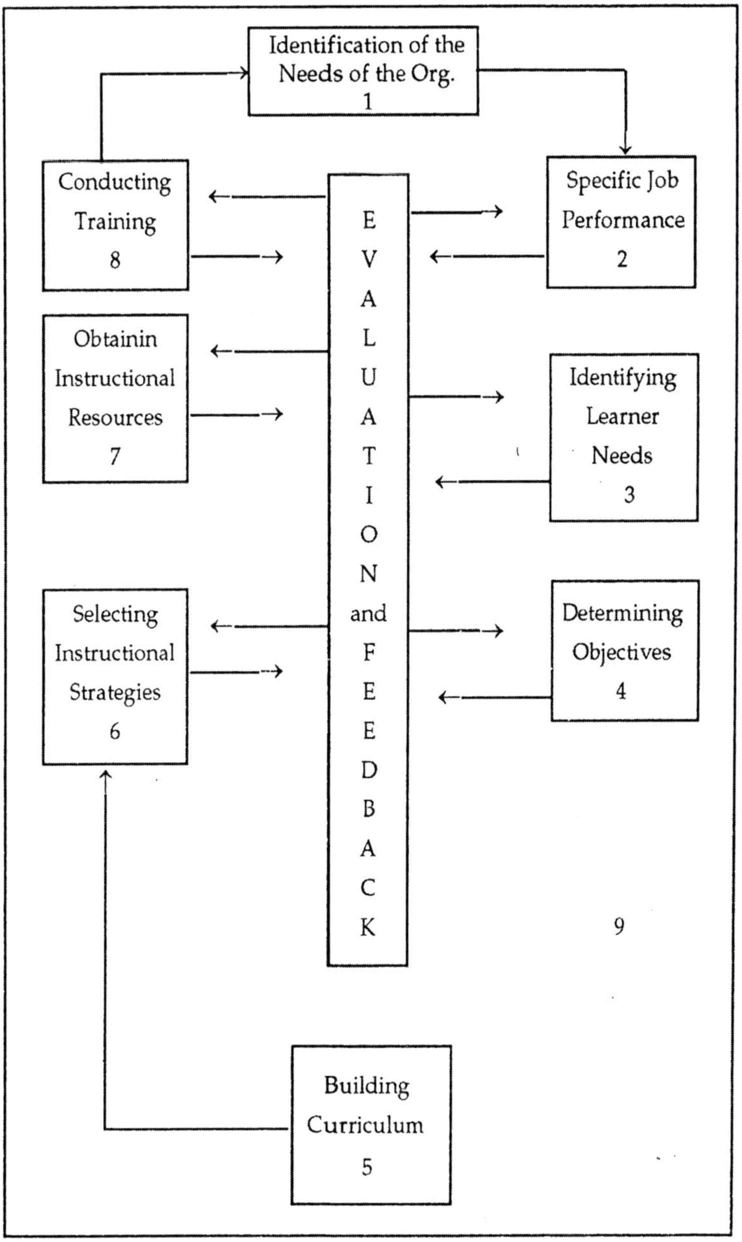

The scores may range from 0 to 156 when the scores of all the thirty-eight items are added to get a composite score. Scores above 114 indicate a good HRD climate: scores closer to 150 indicate an excellent climate (which is rare). Scores below seventy-six indicate that there is considerable scope for improvement. Annual surveys for HRD climate could be conducted and profiles maintained. HRD Systems Evaluation can be depicted as given in Table 1.

Nadlers Programme of Evaluation of Critical Events Model

Nadler (1982) has suggested evaluation feedback for the dynamic equilibrium to various components of HRD. The interrelationships among various components of the model are as given in figure 2 below:[31]

Nadler is concerned with three activities, namely, Training, Education and Development, which are designed to produce behavioural change. According to Nadler, "HRD is concerned with focussing on learning experiences provided by organisations to achieve the goals of the organisations." In Nadler's frame-work Training is focussed on the present job, Education on the future job and Development is concerned with prodiving learning experiences to employees so that they may be ready to move in new directions that organisational changes may require. "The times utilization for development is some time in future. Indeed, the manager must be prepared for the eventuality that the learning may never be used, though it might become relevant on a present or future job."Evaluations and feedback will help in improving human resources development through a series of organised activities designed to produce behavioral change.[32]

HRD Evaluation as a Multi-dimensional Dynamic Exercise

Evaluation of HRD is a multi-dimensional, pre-planned, well-organised continuous exercise, which needs to be carried out by expert professionals. The evaluation process can be shown in the figure 3 given below :

Fig. 3. Figure Indicating Techniques of Evaluation of HRD

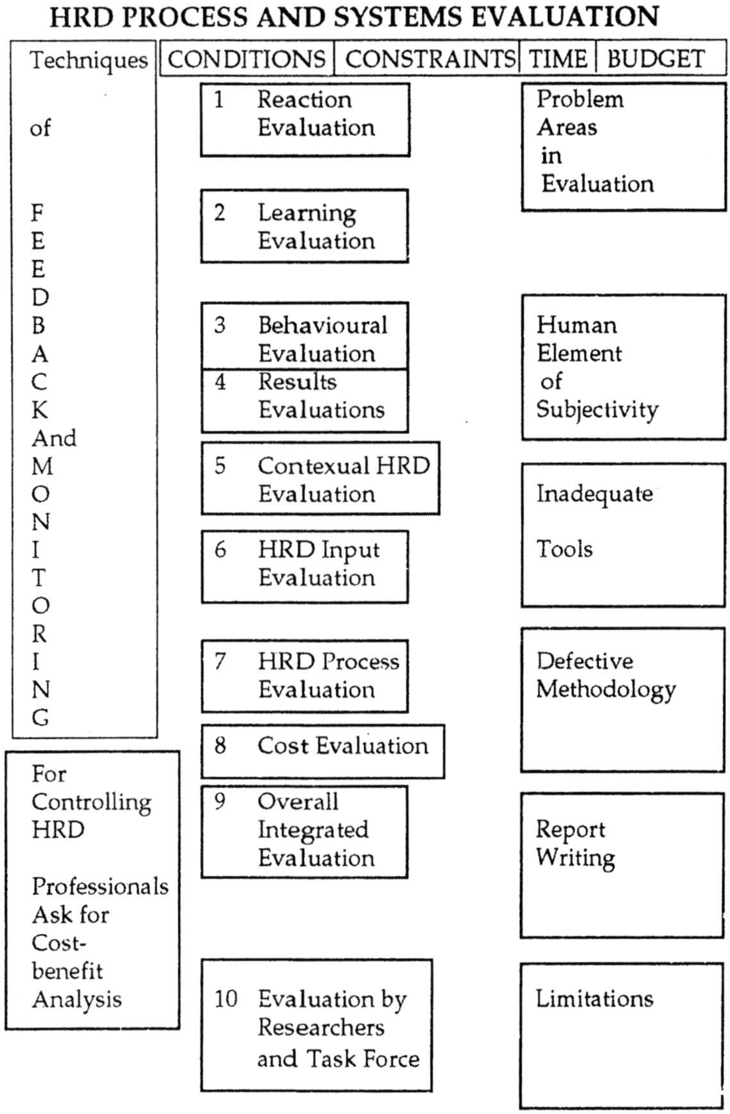

Reaction Evaluation

To evaluate effectively, HRD managers can obtain reactions and feelings of people who participate in HRD programmes. Generally reactions are tabulated and quantified. Virmani and Seth (1985) have suggested a Proforma in which the respondents are asked to:

"1. Mention the major contributions of the programme to their personal learning:

2. Mention the extent to which the objectives of programme are related to their objectives and how far each objective has been realized through the course.

3. Rate the content/inputs on a five point scale—(Excellent/very good/good/fair/poor) on three dimensions, namely, contents of inputs, relevance and applicability, and clarity of exposition.

4. Rate the exercises, case studies, group discussions etc. in terms of learning from the session, relevance and process of conducting on a five-point scale.

5. Comment on extremely useful sessions, sessions needing improvements, elimination of sessions and inclusion of sessions.

6. Comment on the time allocation to different topics, reading material, library facilities, social activities etc.

7. Comment on the training methodology adopted in the course etc."[33]

Reaction evaluations can give indications whether the programmes have been interesting, useful and educative or not. Reaction Evaluation denotes impressions, viewpoints, perceptions and learner's reaction to the HRD programme generally invited after the completion of a programme. Favourable reactions to a programme do not assure learning.

Learning Evaluation

Learning evaluation is simply an attempt to assess the amount and quality of learning which has taken place in the trainees in terms of knowledge, skills and experience.[34] Four important dimensions of learning are:

1. **Level**—To what level of performance or proficiency can a behaviour be learned?
2. **Rate**—How fast can a given level of proficiency to be achieved?
3. **Retention**—How well or for how long does the learned behaviour remain in the subject's behaviour repertoire at a given level of proficiency?
4. **Generalisation**—To what degree—can the learned behaviour be appropriately applied to other, similar behaviours.[35]

Evaluation in terms of learning is much more difficult than evaluation in terms of reactions. Donald L. Kirkpatrick has given following guide-posts for measuring the amount of learning that takes place:

1. The learning of each conferee should be measured so that quantitative results can be determined.
2. A before and after' approach should be used so that any learning can be related to the programme.
3. As far as possible, the learning should be measured on an objective basis.
4. Where possible, a control group (not receiving the training) should be used to compare with the experimental group, which receives the training.
5. Where possible, the evaluation results should be analyzed statistically so that learning can be proved in correlation or level of confidence."[36] Pen or Pencil tests, oral teste, classroom performance, multiple choice tests, role-plays and job instruction training can be useful evaluation methods of training. Assignments, short answers and completion answer—matching tests can be some of the other measurements of learning.[37]

Behavioural Evaluation

HRD should make all possible efforts to strengthen the ethical, moral and spiritual base of human resource. The HRD must bring human resources in time, with the requirements, the needs and the psychology of the people.Demographic factors are strategically important in human resource development because of their interrelationship with employment, education skill and capability development, health and nutrition and the status and role of women. Human Resource Development planners should recognise that individuals value education, health and other human resource investments as important elements in the quality of their life. Government should improve human resource development programmes in the fields of education, employment, food, nutrition, housing and health and welfare service.[38] HRD, although a creative and challenging process, can be at times frustrating, beset with anxiety and turmoil at the national, sectoral and individual levels. Robert Katz stated that if a person is going to change his job-behaviour, five basic requirements must exist:

1. He must want to improve.
2. He must recognise his own weaknesses.
3. He must work in a permissive climate.
4. He must have some help from someone who is interested and skilled.
5. He must have an opportunity to try out new ideas. There is a clear transition between learning and changes in behaviour on the job."[39] A number of scholars have attempted to make evaluation of the job behaviour.

People learn new behaviour through one or more of the four learning processes—classical conditioning, operant conditioning, observational learning and cognitive learning.

1. *The Classical Learning*—The work of the famous Russian physiologist Ivan Pavlov demonstrated the classical conditioning process with the help of a dog and a piece of meat. Thorndike called this the "Law of Exercise"

which states that behaviour can be learned by repetitive association between a stimulus and a response (S-R association).

2. *Operant Conditioning*—Operant conditioning, basically a product of Skinnerian psychology, explains that individuals emit responses that are rewarded and do not emit responses that are either not rewarded or are punished "Of the several responses made to the same situations, those which are accompanied or closely followed by satisfaction.....will be more likely to recur, those which are accompanied or closely followed by discomfort will be less likely to occur.[40] Positive reinforcement, negative reinforcement, extinction and punishment are four types of reinforcement strategies to influence the behaviour of employees.[41]

3. *Observational Learning*—Observational learning occurs as a result of watching the behaviour of another person and appraising the consequences of that behaviour. Observational learning plays a crucial role in altering behaviour in organisations.

4. *Cognitive learning*—Here the main focus is on knowing how events and objects are related to each other. Most of the learning that takes place in the classroom is cognitive learning. Learning theories provide a basis for changing behaviors but the relevance of the material to the explaining and predicting of organisational behavior is marginal.[42] Any observable change in behaviour is *prima facie* evidence that learning has taken place. There are some thinkers who believe that behaviour modification disregards employee's perceptions, beliefs and expectations and is an exercise in oversimplification. Fleishman has developed a study design and a battery of research instruments for measuring the effectiveness of training in terms of behaviour.[43] One of the most comprehensive research studies that has been done to evaluate the effectiveness of a training programme in terms of on the job behaviour was made at the Croton

Ville advance management course on the General Electric Company, generally called "Observed Changes Enquiry."[44] In this extensive research, Sorensen used experimental as well as control group and used four different approaches to measure observed changes. These included the man himself, his subordinates, his peers and his superiors. For on the job - behavior changes, this Sorensen study is generally most widely used.

Evaluations of Results

The objectives of most HRD programmes can be stated in terms of results such as: reduced turnover, improved efficiency, reduction in grievance, increase in quality and quantity of production or improved morale.[45] At present our research techniques are not adequate to separate "the role of other variables" and make it very difficult that can be attributed directly to the specific HRD intervention.Results evaluation denotes the impact of specific HRD on the job and organisational performance and to quantity benefits of a particular programme to the organisations in financial or physical terms. The most important aspect in result evaluation is the selection and determination of suitable performance indicators and measures. Performance measures must elicit unbiased and retrievable information with the help of before and after evaluation system. Very broadly the results an organisation looks for can be stated simply in terms of higher profits—the bottom line. Human Resource Development can contribute to a favourable bottom line by reducing employee turnover, reducing workmen's compensation costs, reducing the number of grievances that must be arbitrated, reducing the amount of scrap, reducing inventory shortage, improving management decison-making and a host of other factors that mean higher profits or lower costs of operation to an organisation.[46]

Contextual Evaluations

A contextual level evalution has to be conducted to assess whether the specified HRD objectives are relevant to the organisational objectives. HRD mechanisms such as quality circles, task forces, job-rotation, performance planning, career planning, are required to respond to the objectives, needs and aspirations of the individuals in terms of their professional growth and self fulfilment in the context of organisation's mission and goals.HRD mechanisms have to play a pivotal role in improving productivity and competitiveness of the organisations.[47] The context of the human resource development has to shift from corporate organisations to entire nation. There will be enormous challenges for HRD in order to help India attain economic, social and spiritual vision for 21st century.[48] To be contextual and relevant, HRD must be evolutionary in approach and characterise "search" in its spirit and performance to keep pace with the newly emerging challenges of globalisation, liberalisation, competitive market and highly complex and sensitive human resources. HRD must exhibit the ability to honour a human being, trust in human capabilities, capacity for relationships of reciprocity with others. HRD must keep itself aware of the contextual evaluation in terms of raising competencies in the employee, strengthening discipline system, earning union partnership and deepening worker involvement in quality production, cost reduction and higher productivity. Contextual evaluation refers to the obtaining and using information about current operational context, about organisational deficiencies, new challenges and individual difficulties and how far HRD can help in providing correct contextual analysis and feedback. Various contextual factors of the organisations— its culture and tradition, technology, level of existing skills available, support for the function, availability of outside help need periodical evaluation.HRD evaluation in terms of operational context is needed to prepare future human resource to take up emerging contextual challenges from the forefront and successfully overcoming them. Contextual evaluation must bring out the discrepancies and performance gaps between present HRD practices and changing challenges of external and internal environment of the organisation. Periodic review of progress made in developing human resources can be useful in rectifying mistakes, if any. The task forces appointed to implement HRD should review the progress once a year. Progress could be assessed using questionnaires to survey the perceptions of the line managers.[49] For strengthening HRD, short-term and long-term needs of the organisations in the context of the organisations, history, plans, mission and challenges have to be worked out and proper HRD linkages should be identified for implementation of the required HRD strategy. For analysing future organisational challenges, services of external consultants can also be utilized. The main thrust from sixth five-year plan onwards has been on harnessing the country's abundant human resources, especially the weaker sections and improving their capabilities with equity. The HRD strategy should have been such as to release the latent power of socially and economically weaker population groups, so that they may make an increasing contribution to the socio-economic development of the country.[50] Evaluation of macro-HRD approaches of rural sectors reveals that there is growing class consciousness and widespread unrest among agricultural labour which calls for suitable structure and processes of HRD for rural upliftment. In any developing country, Human Resource Development (HRD) is the key to development in all sectors of the economy, more particularly rural sector, where majority of the people are very poor, illiterate, and lack the necessary knowledge, skills, initiative, etc. for economic growth.[51]

HRD Input Evaluation

Input evaluation refers to the various efforts made by HRD department as inputs in terms of manpower, man-hours, various HRD processes and whether these resources are being put to optimum use. "Whenever an HRD mechanism subsystem is introduced to ensure employee development and climate creation, its implementation needs to be carefully monitored and evaluated until the system gets stabilized."[52] Such monitoring may involve designing instruments like survey questionnaires, collecting feedback, organising review workshops, constituting task forces, conducting orientation programmes etc. Conducting human process research and renewal exercise periodically are very good efforts to keep diagnosing the learning environment, vitality and dynamism of the organisation and taking corrective action once proper input evaluation has been done.

HRD inputs in the form of mechanisms like performance appraisal, counselling, organisation development, and potential appraisal, job - enrichments etc. need to be evaluated from time to time by surveys and in-house research projects. HRD department should monitor effectively the implementations of various HRD sub-systems and mechanism, by regular input evaluation. There are few HRD questions regarding courses on HRD such as:

1. Do you know in depth—what actually is taught in these programmes and courses? Do you know how these are taught?
2. Does this kind of education prepare entry-level executives who hold promises to emerge as world -class HRD professionals within a short time of practical experience in the world of work?
3. If the above scene continues, will the profession really be relevant?[53] These issues are most relevant as a part of discussion on HRD input evaluation.

HRD Process Evaluation

Each HRD process needs to be adequately evaluated from different perspectives. HRD change processes are involvement, industrial relations, manpower planning, incentives, communications, team building, training and development.[54] Performance appraisal, potential appraisal and development, feedback and performance coaching, career planning, training, organisational development or research and systems development, rewards, employee welfare and quality of work life and human resources information are the various HRD processes which need to be periodically evaluated for their effectiveness and further improvement.

Overall Integrated HRD Evaluation

HRD of middle level and first level supervisors has not been given adequate attention.The first line supervisors and the middle level supervisors are generally considered as the weaker links in Indian management. The real nature of the jobs of supervisory levels is still unrecognized since they generally deal with inconsistent signals and changing messages. Most senior managers see their jobs as providing direction, ideas, information and delegation. To some extent, that is what they should do, but most senior managers ignore another part of their job—to provide an environment that unleashes the supervisor and removes the obstacles in his way.[55] For scientific evaluation systems approach should be used as a tool to gain insightful appreciation of the HRD problems and dividing the HRD on functional basis without having a big complete picture of the HRD can be self-defeating. At the macro- level, human resource development of the nation has emerged as a major challenge. HRD specialists have to work out strategies for training man-power resources in health sector, industrial sector and rural sector. An integral HRD evaluation is needed to analyse how much integration of various development programmes of the agriculture, industry and tertiary sectors has taken place and what are the major areas of shortcomings. Expenditure on HRD in relation to total GNP (Gross National Product) has to be checked. Braindrain is a macro-level challenge to HRD professionals in India. At the macro-level in the global context, UNDP has drawn following conclusions:

1. Economic growth does not automatically improve people's lives either at inter-national level or national level.
2. Underdeveloped and developing countries need massive investment in human capital and technological development to compete on equal footing with advanced and rich countries.
3. Global markets do not operate freely and persons with same capabilities are discriminated for various national, religious and other considerations.
4. Human resource accounting is the process of identifying and measuring data about human resources and communicating this information to the interested parties.[56]

The female work participation in India in the tertiary,

corporate and industrial sectors is not upto the desired level because of illiteracy of women folk in India. Percentage of women workers and their work participation rates are given below:

TABLE WOMEN PARTICIPATION

(Percentage Total Workers)

	1951	*1961*	*1971*	*1981*
Female workers				
out of total workers	28.96	31.52	17.32	19.97
Male/ Female work	Male	Male	Male	Male
participation rate	54.05	57.10	52.55	60.70
(workers as	Female	Female	Female	Female
percentage to	23.30	27.96	12.13	14.44
total population)				
National work				
participation rate				
of women	39.11	42.98	32.97	33.14

HRD for women as a human resource would mean helping women employees to realise their full potential for future jobs and preparing them by sharpening their technical, professional and knowledge capabilities to the fullest extent possible.At micro level various types of evaluation need to be integrated for an integral evaluation. HRD is not given its due place in India because of the misconception that we have the third largest scientific manpower in the work and we have surplus qualified workforce. The tragedy is that the right man with the right job knowledge, skill and attitude is rarely placed at the right place. We must constantly evaluate our HRD practices and match them with the best of the HRD practices prevailing abroad. HRD practices need constant evaluation by qualified, unbiased team of objective evaluators. The HRD managers of the future shall have to face problems like increasing size of workforce, changing psycho-social system, technological advances, computerised information system, mobility of professional personnel, changes in legal environment and management of human relations. The problems of HRD evaluations will also be effected by the new trends mentioned above.

Evaluation of HRD by Researchers

HRD can be evaluated either by internal HRD staff or by an outside HRD researcher or research team. Committees can be constituted by the organisation for internal HRD evaluation. Sometimes an external agency can be hired to carry out HRD evaluation. Sometimes internal and external researcher can jointly carry out evaluation. Individual researchers can also carry out evaluation of HRD of various organisations. Macro - level HRD evaluations are generally very vague because macro pictures of HRD at national level are quite disturbing. Developing human resources is a daunting task for which active collaboration between the state and organisations is needed. The states foster HRD through collaborative networking with organisations.The role of state can be analysed through three factor—Harbinger, Booster and Extension. These factors create the infrastructure necessary of HRD.[57]

Problem Areas and Challenges to Evaluation

No doubt, evaluation has to be regarded as an integral part of HRD systems, but generally evaluations are considered symptoms of some kind of uneasiness and discomfort by the HRD managers. There is a lack of unified theory of evaluation, which has universal acceptance and can be made a guidepost for evaluation system. Even to the best of HRD experts, evaluation evokes anxiety and uneasiness.In evaluation process one can notice the avoidance symptoms since it is perceived generally as a painful process that exposes many HRD created traps.At times there are attempts to cover HRD programme failures or errors by avoiding any objective appraisals and many times vindication replaces verification. This is generally termed as whitewash efforts at evaluation. Sometimes evaluations are eye-wash efforts when an unsatisfactory HRD programme is justified by deliberately selecting those aspects of HRD that look good on the surface. In evaluation process sometimes rituals replace research and an attempt is made to give a semblance of objectivity and professionalism to a report which carries out pleasant remarks of the learners given at the time of their departure after the programme. In some cases evaluations work as submarines when politics replaces service and attempts are made to torpedo or destroy a programme regardless of its effectiveness or quality. Evaluation systems of HRD are yet to be scientifically validated and accepted by the professionals universally. Evaluations are expected to provide guidelines for future improvement or measure the effectiveness of the HRD programmes but in many cases due to limitations of human nature and other factors, evaluation objectives are not achieved. Various pitfalls of evaluation can be lack of objectivity, evaluation errors, improper interpretation of data and inappropriate use of results. In effective evaluation of Human Resource Development at the micro level, there are mainly following difficulties:

1. Vague nature of HRD (Training) objectives.
2. Conflict over whether the objective of HRD is to bring about individual change or organisational change.
3. Difficulties is specifying the period in which HRD (Training) objectives may be accomplished.
4. Difficulties in selecting a good yardstick to measure whether or not the objectives are accomplished in full measure.[58]

In evaluation of HRD, there are possibilities of human errors like misinterpretations, inadvertent errors, lack of technique, conscious errors, halo effect, prejudice or subjective interpretation. Evaluation of HRD can be inappropriate due to inadequate tools and measuring techniques, defective methodology or limitations in report writing. HRD evaluation has to focus on target groups, and selection of appropriate HRD interventions. The HRD interventions at the macro-level call for structural links like inter-ministry and inter-organisation groups. At the micro -level problems such as service rules, financial rules and performance appraisal, appropriate linkages need to be strengthened. The HRD could open up the windows of HRD professionalisation for the younger members who are receptive to new ideas.[59] HRD programmes need to build up a well - qualified and competent workforce, which is physically healthy and strong, emotionally rich and sound, intellectually alert and capable of dealing with various future challenges with confidence. Human Resource Development has to take care of ethical and spiritual development of the individuals with an overall development of their personality and value system. HRD should try to bring about a transformational change in Indian management by emphasising values of *Dharma*, duties and ethical orientation. A"shared philosophy" and "family feeling"cannot be imposed artificially to create Japanese—style organisation which is typified by (ancient) India's own "export—quality culture (*Dharma*).[60] The present day materialistic self-centred mindset of our HRD professionals springs from three factors:

1. Cultural rootlessness and surficial drifting.
2. Absence of a sound philosophical foundation.
3. Not being conscious of India's mission of providing an alternative model of human development.[61] Our Indian *shastras* and religious scriptures repeatedly assert that the truth of human existence lies in realizing the self whose character is *purpatva* (wholeness), *amrit* (eternal) and *anand* (bless). Human development therefore should focus on self-realization, *Nishkam Karma*, ethical principles of good conduct and disciplined *sadhana* for the inner world of our deepest subjective layer-*nihitam guhyam* (lodged in the hearts care). HRD should teach character, values and vision and marriage of *Dharma-Sadhana* with *Karma-Sadhana* coupled with ethical and moral uprightness.[62] HRD in India should include teaching and training in Vedantic wisdom which can help managers in resolving the modern problems of (a) crisis of character, (b) crisis of leadership, (c) crisis of focussing, (d) crisis of bureaucracy, (e) crisis of motivation and (f) crisis of vision.[63] Continuous and scientific evaluation of such Vedantic teachings should also be carried out by an expert body of HRD experts. Indian HRD

efforts should focus on Vedic wisdom and Vedic technologies of consciousness as suggested by Maharishi Mahesh Yogi which are bound to bring transformational impact on mental health, physical health and business health.[64]

Concluding Remarks

Task analysis, Contextual analysis, Activity analysis, Competency analysis, Discrepancy analysis and Performance analysis are some of the major problem areas of HRD evaluation task. HRD professionals and facilitators must undertake serious research in these areas. Evaluation of HRD at both macro and micro-levels has to be carried out periodically by expert evaluators. Analysis should be carried out only after developing an understanding of the particular organisational context involved.[65] For effective evaluation, periodical auditing of human resource development is most essential because it will focus clearly on (a) how well the HRD plans have been made out suiting to organisational mission and objectives; (b) how well these HRD plans have been translated into action and practice; (c) how much HRD efforts have produced tangible and intangible results and (d) how well HRD climate has been built in the organisation. All HRD systems have to be evaluated separately and their total impact has also to be evaluated. HRD systems are to be seen as an integrated package (HRD as a total system), for evaluating their overall impact on the organisation. HRD systems need systematic monitoring to review the progress preferably annually and re-appraisal every three years. If evaluated properly and needed improvements carried out, integrated HRD systems can contribute significantly to positive cultural changes, increased productivity and excellence in organisation. It would be relevant to quote the famous words of Albert Einstein "It is not enough to teach a man a speciality, Through it, he may become a kind of useful machine, but not a harmoniously developed personality. It is essential that the students acquire and understanding and a lively feeling for values. He must acquire a vivid sense of the beautiful and of the morally good. Otherwise, he, with his specialized knowledge more closely resembles a trained dog than a harmoniously developed person. He must aim to understand the motives of human beings, their illusions, and their sufferings in order to acquire a proper relationship to individual fellowmen and to the community.[66] Swami Ranganathananda has further elaborated the ultimate goals of the HRD by emphasising on the harmonious and equilaterally coordinated use of the three power thus:

1. *Bahu-bala* (strength of hand and muscle, including machine power);
2. *Mano-bala* (strength of mind and intellect); and
3. *Yoga-bala* (energy of spirituality and ethical morality) to meet the challenges of modern age. These three *balas* when developed through various HRD mechanisms, can bring about a total human transformation which can help us to achieve dedication, efficiency, work-commitment and excellence in all fields.

REFERENCES

1. Dayal Ishwar, *HRD in Indian Organisations: Some Approaches Towards Effectiveness through HRD Conference Papers,* National HRD Networks, Jamshedpur, 1989 pp. 236-46.
2. Warr P.B., *Evaluating Management Training—Personnel* Vol. 2, No. 2, 1969, pp. 26-29, 36.
3. Hamblin, A.C., *Evaluations and Control of Training.* McGraw Hill Book Co., U.K. 1974, pp. 1-10.
4. Belasco J.A. and Trice H.M., *The Assessment of Change in Training and Therapy,* McGraw Hill Book Company, New York, 1969.
5. Ethan M. Raisel, *The Mc Kinsey Way,* Mc Graw Hill, 1999, p. 16.
6. Lawrence J. Peter *The Peter Principle,* Morrow, New York, 1969.
7. For details about various skills consult - Robers L. Katz, Skills of an Effective Administrator. *Harvard Business Review - September - October,* 1974, pp. 90-101.
8. For similar views see Ranjita Das, *Evaluations of Training in Human Resource Development in a Changing Environment,* Edited by Dr. S. Ravi Shankar and others, Dhruv and Deep Books, Bombay, 1988, p. 199.

9. William R. Tracey, *Managing Training and Development Systems*, Taraporevala Publishing Industries, American Management Associations, Indian Reprint 1980, p. 401.

10. Dr. Krishna Mohan Mathur, *Administration of Police Training in India*, Gyan Publishing House, New Delhi, 1987, p. 185.

11. Nancy M. Dixon, *Evaluations, A Tool for Improving HRD Quality*, S. Chand and Company Ltd., New Delhi, 1985, p. 9.

12. For similar views see K.M. Mathur, *Problems of Police in a Democratic Society*, RBSA Publishers, Jaipur,1987, p. 148.

13. Dr. Donald L. Kirk Patrick, *Evaluation of Training* in Training and Development Handbook, American Society for Training and Development, Edited by Rober L. Craig and L.R. Bittel, McGraw Hill Book Company, New York,1967, p. 88.

14. Carl Jung, *The Development of Personality—in Facilitating Development*: Readings - Rolf P. Lynton and Udai Pareek (Eds.), New Delhi, Sage Publications, 1992, pp. 66-67.

15. Nancy M. Dixon, *Evaluations A Tools for Improving HRD Quality*, S. Chand and Company Ltd., New Delhi, 1985, p. 9.

16. For futher details consult, P. Murali Krishna and P. Subba Rao - *Organisational and HRD climate in B.H.E.L.*—An Empirical study -Indian Journal of Public Administration, Vol. XLIII No. 2 April June, 1997, pp. 209-16.

17. Gagney R.M. and Briggs L.J. (1979), *Principles of Instructional Design*, New York, Holf Rinehart and Winston.

18. *Evaluating Human Resource Development*, Edited by Udai Pareek, HRD Research Foundation, Jaipur, 1997.

19. Venkata Swamy, G., *Training and Development in Public Enterprises in India*, Indian Publishers and Distributors, Delhi, 1988.

20. Calvin P.Otta and Rollin O Glaser, *The Management of Training - A Handbook for Training and Development, Personnel, Addison* Wesley Publishing Company, 1970, p. 153.

21. Compbell J. Dunnette M. Lawer E, and Weick K. (1970)—*Managerial Behavior, Performance and Effectiveness*, McGraw Hill, New York.

22. Campbell R.W. (1971), *Personnel Training and Development*—Animal Review of Psychology, 22, pp. 565-602.

23. Clement R.W. (1981) *Testing the Hierarchy Theory of Training Evaluation Public, Personnel Management*, Journal II (2) pp. 176-84 Miles W.R. and Biggs W.D. (1979). "Common, Recurring Avoid-

able Errors in Management Development", *Training and Development Journal*, p. 33 (2) 32-35.

24. *Bracenburg D.C. and Schultz E. (1968 April)*, "The Status of Training An Update"—Presentation at the National Society of Performance and Instruction Conference, Washington D.C.

25. Nancy M. Dixon—*Evaluations—A Tools for Improving* HRD *Quality*, 1985, p. 149.

26. Head G.E. and Buchannan C. (1981) "Cost-Benefit Analysis of Training—A Foundations for Change", *SPP Journal*, 20 (10) pp. 25-27.

27. Nancy M. Dixon—*Evaluations - Tool for Improving HRD Quality*, p. 223.

28. Udai Pareek, *Challenges for HRD in the Nineties—"Managing the Transition—The HRD Response.* Edited by Udai Pareek, Rupande Padaki and PR Nair, Tata McGraw Hill Publishing, New Delhi, 1992. p. 4.

29. For HRD Practice Profile see Dr. T.V. Rao, *The HRD Missionary - The Role and Functions of HRD Managers and Departments*, Oxford and IBP Publishing Co. (P) Ltd., New Delhi, 1990 National HRD Network, 1990.

30. For details consult Exercise 2—*HRD Climate Survey* —given in T.V. Rao - HRD Missionary, pp. 60-63.

31. Nadler, Leonard—*Corporate Human Resource Development A Management Tool*, ASTD Van Nostrand Reinhold Co. U.S.A. 1980, 1982, Also Leonard Nadler - *The Handbook of HRD*, John Wiley - U.S.A., 1984.

32. Nadler Leonard, - *The Handbook of HRD*, John Wiley - U.S.A., 1984 and also see Nadler, Leonard *Developing Human Resource* ASTD V Gulf Publishing Company, Texas, USA, 1970.

33. Vir, B.R. and Seth Premilla, *Evaluating Management Training and Developing*, Vision Books, 1985.

34. Dr. Krishna Mohan Mathur, *Administration of Police Training in India*, Gyan Publishing House, New Delhi, 1987, p. 241.

35. John D. Folley, Jr., *The Learning Process in Training and Development Handbook*, A STD - Edited by Robert L Craig and Lester R. Bittel, Mc Graw Hill Company, New York, 1967, p. 37.

36. Donald L. Kirk Patrick, "Evaluation of Training"—In *Training and Development Handbook—A STD*—Edited by Craig and Bittel, p. 96.

37. David A. Payne, *The Specifications and Measurements of Learning*

Outcomes, Walthmam Mass, Blaisdell Publishing Company, 1966, pp. 40-45.

38. Fourth Asian and Pacific Population Conference held at Bali (Indonesia), on August, 19-27, 1992- *Indian Journal of Public Administration,* July-Sept. 1992, p. 251.
39. Robert Katz, *Human Relations Skills can be Sharpened. Harvard Business Review,* July-August, 1956.
40. Edward Thorndika, *Animal Intelligence,* The Mac Millan Company, New York, 1911, p. 244.
41. Robert A. Baron, *Behavior in Organisation,* Allyn and Baco Inc, New York, 1983, pp. 66-67.
42. Stephen P. Robbins, *Organisational Behavior,* Prentice Hall Inc. NJ, 1979, p. 148.
43. Fleishman E.A, E.F. Harris, and H.E. Buntt, *Leadership and Supervison in Industry,* Personnel Research Board, Ohion State University, Columbus, Ohion, 1955, p. 110.
44. Soresen Olaav, *The Observed Changes Enquiry—Manager Development Consulting Service,* General Electric Company, Crotonville, NY, May 15, 1958.
45. Donald L.Kirk Patrick, *Evaluation of Training—A STD,* Edited by Craig and Bittel, 1967, p. 106.
46. Calvin P. Otto and Rollin O Glaser, *The Management of Training —A Handbook for Training and Development Personnel*—ADDISON Wesley Publishing Company, 1970, p. 165.
47. Krishna S. (1990), "HRD Issues, Opportunities—Top Management's Views" in MRR Nair and T.V. Rao—*Excellence through Human Resource Development,* Tata McGraw Hill, New Delhi pp. 16-24.
48. For comprehensive treatment see Athreya M.B. (1996). *HRD for India Vision for the 21st century* in D.P. Sinha and others (Ed), Aligning Human Resource Processes—Challenges of Development, TATA McGraw Hill, New Delhi, pp. 19-31.
49. T.V. Rao, "Planning for Human Resource Development" in *Human Resource Development,* Strategic Approaches and Experiences- Edited by B.L. Mathur, Arihant Publications, Jaipur, 1989.
50. Mohd Fazal, "Key - note Address on Human Resource Development" in Uddesh Kohil and Vinayshil Gautam (Eds.), *Human Resource Development and the Planning Process in India,* New Delhi, Vikas Publishing House, 1993, pp. VI -IX.

51. C.H. Bala Ramulu, "Human Resource Development and Liberalisation Policy: A study of Rural Employment Programmes in India" *India, Journal of Public Administration*, Vol. XLII No. 3 July-September, 1966, p. 462.

52. T.V. Rao, *HRD Missionary.*

53. Prof. C. Balaji, Editorial *HRD News letter*, Vol. 14 No. 4. October-December, 1998, p. 1.

54. MRR Nair and T.V. Rao (Ed), *Excellence Through Human Resource Development*, Tata McGraw Hill, New Delhi, 1990.

55. Kapoor, Gitika—*Collaborative Advantage Framework, Vision* 2(2), July-December,1998, pp. 13-28, Administrative change 25 (1) July- Dec. 1997, pp. 55-61.

56. Report of the Committee on Human Resource Accounting. The Accounting Review- Supplement of Vol. 481973.The American Accounting Association Committee.

57. Belssco J.A. and Trice H.M., *The Assessment of Change in Training and Therapy*, McGraw Hill Book Company, New York, 1969.

58. N.P. Rao, *New Technologies, Production Systems and Human* Resource *Development* Vol. 2, Anmol Publications, New Delhi, 1993, p. 295.

59. Om Prakash, "Can Indian Management Transform the Japanese Way?"—in *Management of Transformation* (ed.) by Anjila Saxena and Harsh Dwivedi, National Publishing House, Jaipur,1996, p. 24.

60. S.K. Chakraborty, *Ethics in Management - Vedantic Perspective*, Oxford University Press, Delhi, 1996, p. 117.

61. For similar views see J.B.P. Sinha, *Work Culture in the Indian Context*, Sage Publications, New Delhi, 1990, pp. 207-8.

62. Krishna Mohan Mathur, "Vedantic Wisdom and Contemporary Management" *Indian Journal of Public Administration*, Vol. XIV No. 1, January-March,1999, p. 8.

63. For further details and further elaboration see Dr. Ian Brown, *US Leadership Deficiencies - Lessons for India*—Indian Management, Vol. 38 No. 7, July, 1999, p. 52.

64. Udai Pareek, "Task Analysis for Human Resource Development", Published in 1998 *Annual Developing Human Resources*, San Diego - University Associated, 1988.

65. Einstein, Alberts, *New York Times*, 1932.

9

Implementation of Human Resource Development

Implementation of HRD is a process of interaction between setting of HRD goals and actions geared to achieve them. Implementation of HRD implies converting of HRD goals, objectives and strategies into action by proper use of various management processes of organising, staffing, administering, directing, controlling and evaluation. The policy implementation can be regarded as an action-oriented process of converting HRD policies into action. Organisational structure is one of the principal determinants in successfully implementing various HRD policy decisions and intervention strategies. Confidence building, mutual trust, communication as well as putting rewards and incentives in place in order to avert resistance are some of the behavioural aspects of implementation of HRD. HRD can be implemented within a given organisational framework. Human resource availability, time frame, financial resources and commitment are other important variables for effective implementation. Avoidance of conflicts, enlisting of cooperation and compliance as a fundamental condition is prerequisite of HRD implementation. Effective communication and control are necessary for HRD implementation. Lack of ability to change behaviour of people, lack of managerial knowledge and support from people can create implementation gaps. Also lack of coordination, conflict of interest, lack of communication and funds can create implementation gaps in HRD. Implementation of HRD is an integral part of HRD evaluation and HRD maintenance and upkeep. Policy implementation is an integral part of the interwoven stages of policy making rather than a single isolated act. These interwoven stages are shown as follows:

Stages of Policy Formulation and Implementation

Policy Formulation
Policy Implementation Task Force
Policy Evaluation, Assessment and Implementation Feedback
Policy Succession, Termination and Maintenance Feedback
Implementation Gaps and Revision of Policy Formulations and its Further Implementation

Behavioural approach is very cardinal in influencing policy implementation. To separate a policy design from implementation is fatal.

Human Resource Development (HRD) can be defined in different ways and Lim Teek Ghee (1986), Lorraine Corner (1991) and Bacchus (1992) have given different approaches. According to Lim Teek Ghee, HRD should refer not only to aspects of physical well-being of people such as life expectancy, infant mortality, rates of morbidity and levels of nutrition but also to socio-cultural aspects, including education and employment, social cohesion and stability, political expression, cultural diversity and even ecological harmony. In fact the only dimension of intrinsic value in development is the human dimension in its totality.[1] Lorraine Corner finds use of HRD in three senses; the first adopts a supply orientation and uses the phrase HRD as a synonym for manpower planning and development. The second approach emphasizes "quality of life" in the context of contribution of human capital to economic growth and as an output of development. In his approach HRD is defined as social development particularly at the social and the individual level. The third approach integrates the first two approaches and seeks a complementarity between economic and social development.[2] According to Bacchus (1992), HRD encompasses all those activities which would lay the foundation for a fuller and more productive utilisation of the total human resources (both actual and potential) of a country and thus the ultimate goal of human resources development in any country is and should be, to improve the quality of life of all its people.[3] In the Harare Declaration of 1991, human resource development (HRD) has been recognised as central to the promotion of sustainable development and reduction of poverty. The working group on HRD set up in 1992 under the chairmanship of Dr. Sam Pitroda, prepared its report, entitled "Foundation for the Future." It identified the following five key strategies for effective HRD:

1. A well-managed and professional government;
2. Partnership with non-governmental organisations (NGOs) and private sector;
3. Priority for women;
4. Mobilisation of resources; and
5. Use of technology.

Human resource development aims at certain universal goals, which all efforts should aim to achieve. At the individual level these goals may include developing capabilities for ensuring a happy, prosperous and healthy living. At the organisational level, the goal of HRD is normally to have motivated and competent employees to ensure higher levels of productivity, profitability and growth of the organisation. At the national level, HRD aims at ensuring that people in the country live longer, happily, free from disease and hunger; have sufficient skill base to learn their own livelihood and well-being; have a sense of belongingness and pride through participation in determining their own destinies and ultimately help for income-generation and upgradations of quality of life in the family, organisation and the nation. In India the first experiment of human resource development was initiated in 1952 as the Community Development Programme (CDP). The National Extension Service Programme (NESP) was launched in 1953, which encouraged popular participation of villagers in formulating integrated rural development programmes. On the recommendation of a special taskforce known as Balwantrai Mehta Committee, these programmes were later merged to become part of the *Panchayat Raj* Programme launched in 1959. It was started with fifty-five pilot projects each covering a population of two lakhs. The resource crunch did not permit the government to implement the programme to other development blocks. Implementation of HRD needs commitment of resource, will to implement and adequate human resource to translate policies into action plans.

For achieving HRD goals at the national level, the strategic process interventions include: using the NGOs; decentralisation, mobilisation of resources, coordination and professionalisation of executive. Human resource development should be seen both as means and an end in itself. Competencies may include knowledge, skills, attitudes and values and these competencies may deal with any field: agriculture, industry, science, technology, management, politics, public administration and other such fields. The capabilities may be developed in individuals, groups, and communities. Developing people is the essence of any HRD effort and it is an important goal of all other development activities (plans, policies, programmes, and establishment of new structures, mechanisms). HRD also holds the key for economic development by enabling it to become more productive. HRD strategies have to focus on alleviation of poverty existing at present by appropriate investment in education and health services and the creation of more employment by involving people through participation, empowerment, better access and opportunity. There is the synergistic value of the HRD concept in increasing understanding of the linkages that exist between literacy, basic education, health, nutrition, sanitation, environment, population growth, technology, role and status of women, unemployment, and the quality of human resources indicated by the composition of their knowledge, attitude, skill base and other capabilities. According to T.V. Rao, strategic human resource development involves the development of those sectors of human activity and those human resources which are considered as strategically important to that country at a given point at time.[4] At the national level, national governments have a critical role to play in designing and implementing such strategies. The World Development Report, 1991 observed: "Many studies document the high returns on investment in education." The revolution of information technology, liberalisation and globalisation of economy, have brought a new emphasis on HRD. One of the imperatives of the new environment is to have a skilled and educated workforce which can understand and cope with the requirements of I T and other technologies in the manufacturing and service sector.[5] Therefore state has to make heavy investment in education and vocational training. HRD will also cut across boundaries of culture, geography and language and will have greater emphasis on learning. India has to aim at improving the situation of employment, poverty, illiteracy, build infrastructure and provide basic health care to the people in the 21st century. Organisational learning, building core competencies in the government, building creativity at all levels are some of the dimensions that need effective implementation at the macro level. Any HRD strategy must emphasise on the need for productivity, quality, efficiency, effectiveness and skill development of government officers and workers to achieve the professed objective of public service and welfare of the community in the present day context of globalisation and liberalisation. Data on health, nutrition, water and sanitation, medical care, employment and income, poverty, education all indicate poor state of implementation of HRD at macro-level in India. Low sensitivity to people's needs and problems, low concern for goals, authoritative states-quo-orientation are reasons for ineffective implementation of various HRD programmes. Lack of political and bureaucratic support, inadequate time for implementation, lack of financial and human resource commitment are some of the key elements which account for defective or inadequate implementation of programmes.

Inhibiting Factors in Implementing HRD at Macro Level

Implementation faces problems at each stage of execution and action. Red tapism, financial constraints due to budgetary controls, lack of training and development practices and prevailing "government culture" where a positive feedback is hardly given to an employee, are some of the factors impeding implementation of HRD programmes in proper perspective.[6] The budgetary constraints which apparently come in the way of implementation of HRD may be taken as a challenge to the creative skills of the public administrators. A continuous exercise/how best financial resources could be utilized may help in achieving the objective of HRD. Faulty perception of training and low priority to training hinders the organisational effectiveness of the many government organisations. Implementation of HRD would encourage administrative entrepreneurship and initiate action for a suitable HRD culture. Tools and implements are needed to execute HRD along with dedicated staff.

Rural Employment Programmes and Implications for HRD Systems

HRD is essential in view of the decreased motivational levels and counterproductive behaviours. Restructuring of the administrative machinery of the government has several HRD implications and may involve creation of more enabling HRD system such as; (a) work and career system, including performance appraisal, career planning and career paths; (b) development systems including training, job rotation and team building and (c) culture system including reward and communication. In India, rural sector is in need of HRD. There is a need to initiate measures for upgradation of knowledge, skills, creativity, interpersonal relations, team building, leadership, motivation, training, education, health, nutrition, employment, empowerment and rights of people of rural areas in India.[7] In India, the development of human resources has not received required attention particularly in the case of rural sector where abundant manpower is available, where people are very poor, illiterate and lack the necessary skills, knowledge and initiatives for economic growth. Only from the Sixth Five. Year Plan onwards, efforts were made for proper utilisation of rural human resources. The rural employment opportunities have been created through the following programmes:

1. Rural Works Programme (RWP in 1961);
2. Crash Scheme for Rural Employment Projects (CSRE in 1971);
3. The Pilot Intensive Rural Employment Projects (PIRE in 1972);
4. Food for Work Programme (FWP in 1977);
5. National Rural Employment Programme (NREP in 1980);
6. Rural Landless Employment Guarantee Programme (RLEGP in 1983);
7. Jawahar Rozgar Yojana (JRY in 1989);
8. Employment Assured Scheme (EAS in 1992).

The greatest tragedy with regard to our country's human resource is not only neglect of its development but also wastage through unemployment, underemployment, persistence of poverty, ill-health, malnutrition and undernourishment. Education at all levels including technical and professional, medicare and sanitation, agricultural extension services and use of mass media to bring about attitudinal change and to inculcate appropriate psychological propensities are all ingredients of the human resource development process. Through proper planning and effective implementation it is necessary to ensure human resource development as an integral part of the rural development and economic planning.

The evaluation studies on the implementation of these programmes both at macro and micro level have identified the following reasons for poor implementation and unsatisfactory performance.[8]

(1) Lack of manpower planning; (2) Undertaking unproductive works; (3) Selection of schemes without proper examination; (4) Lack of supervision—both technical and

administrative; (5) Erratic distribution of food grains; (6) Supply of poor quality of food grains; (7) Undertaking the works on political consideration and on adhoc basis; (8) Undertaking expenditure oriented programmes; (9) Lack of serious efforts to provide continuous employment to the beneficiaries; (10) Undertaking the new schemes near the residence of rich farmers; (11) Frequent changes in the guidelines; (12) Undertaking schemes which are useful to the industrial class and absentee landlords leaving the tenants as labourers; (13) Lack of provision for the maintenance of assets; (14) Delay in undertaking the schemes and consequent non-completion of works; (15) Payment of low wages to the beneficiaries; (16) Employing the labourers from outside the village concerned; (17) Lack of committed administrative officers; (18) Corruption, wastage of money and resources; (19) Emergence of regional political parties interested in politicising the schemes and (20) Lack of effective political will. Above factors have collectively rendered the rural employment programmes ineffective. The organisational factors and problems of delivery system have further limited the effective implementation of rural employment programmes.[9] Other problems of implementation have been haphazard implementation and feudalisation of its processes, gross violation of provisions, lack of planning in construction and absence of minimum facilities. The rural employment strategy in India has four basic ingredients; (1) to utilise human resources more effectively and efficiently and create gainful employment for the rural poor; (2) to maintain the highest feasible rate of growth; (3) to make the pattern of production more labour intensive; and (4) to regulate technological change to ensure adequate rate of growth of employment.[10] Lack of manpower planning, lack of facilities at the work place, misutilisation of funds, violations of regulations and rules in executing the schemes are some of the problems of implementing various HRD programmes.

Socio Cultural Factors in Implementation of HRD Programmes

Since human resource development may not yield short-term results, government should formulate both short-term and long-term policies. In translating policy into practice, the Government should attend to socio-cultural factors surrounding implementation and involve the implementers in the process.[11] Human Resource Development programmes are largely change programmes. By taking the examples of female literacy campaigns and out of reach primary education for the poor, Mathur (1992) cites evidence about the cultural constraints for educating girls and the socio-economic constraints for the poor to send their children to schools. Similarly for health and nutritional programmes, the greatest obstacles are beliefs about and attitudes towards disease and drug and food taboos. Mathur (1992) has suggested following useful guidelines for policy-makers and implementation of human resource development programmes in view of the socio-cultural factors :[12]

"1. Begin with a study of the socio-cultural context.
2. Introduce programmes in terms of the needs of people.
3. Combine the new with the old.
4. Respect indigenous knowledge systems.
5. Use influential village leaders.
6. Study previous experiences with development programmes in the region.
7 Consult the people involved.
8. Communicate development messages in such forms that make an impact.
9. Ensure that the development workers have qualities required to facilitate development in the region.
10. Use local community organisations.
11. Plan the change step by step, thoroughly and carefully.
12. Anticipate the consequences of changes and innovations.
13. Introduce programmes that require behaviour changes more patiently.
14. Coordinate the efforts of various means working on development.

15. Ensure that new facilities remain in use."

Implementation of HRD requires commitment and political will. Failures of the most governments in the past have been in the implementation of HRD programmes. Mobilisation of resources is the responsibility of the government. It is important to recognise the potential of non-government organisations, private sector and communities. India is a case of "support led security" and state action is important to secure "entitlements of education, health care and food security, without waiting for income per head to rise to high level through general economic growth.[12a] While examining HRD policy implementation in the public sector the existence of an implementation gap between policy formulation and implementation is clearly noticeable. The top down approach is also responsible for implementation gaps.

According to the personal experience of the author, implementation of HRD systems can be broadly categorized into the following seven stages:

Stage 1. Identification of HRD needs and formulation of HRD plans, sub-systems and mechanisms.

Stage 2. Identification of HRD philosophy, HRD objectives and plans within the organisation's framework.

Stage 3. Selecting and Development of appropriate HRD strategies for interventions.

Stage 4. Selecting and staffing HRD implementation task-force.

Stage 5. Briefing and directing HRD task-force and identifying HRD beneficiaries.

Stage 6. Implementing gradually various HRD sub-systems and establishing linkages with other already implemented systems.

Stage 7. Getting effective feedback, monitoring and auditing of HRD and making mid-way corrections after identifying implementation gaps.

HRD Central to the Decentralisation Process and Panchayati Raj

Although on December 22, 1992 the Lok Sabha passed the 73rd amendment to the Indian Constitution to provide a constitutional base to local governments, yet only twenty-one of the Indian states have legislated their *Panchayati Raj* Acts, defining devolution of power to the *Panchayats* in their regions. Implementation of the various provisions as conceptualised in the 73rd amendment like the political empowerment of women, is likely to achieve only very limited results, given the feudal and patriarchal structure of the Indian society and its various bureaucratic institutions. There is a direct correlation between local participation in decision-making in the *Panchayati* institutions and the proper implementation of the anti-poverty targets.[13] In India, growing awareness and concern has been expressed about the "implementation gap"—the difference betwen policies and their implementation. There are many intervening variables that contribute to the implementation gap; lack of research and relevant knowledge about the development processes and consequently absence of appropriate policies and strategies leading to development; shortage of managers and administrators for developmental tasks; no new institutional forms which could be related more appropriately to development projects and other intervening variables linked with social and political forces.[14] Implementation suffers because numerous problems crop up during implementation requiring decisions, mobilisation of funds and lack of a collaborative culture in bureaucracy and decision-makers. The case of implementation of 73rd Constitutional Amendment can be treated as a case study. In the past *Panchayati Raj* institutions have been handicapped by various shortcomings, the most crucial being the lack of capabilities of people associated with the *panchayats*. The recent field studies indicate categorically that participatory process at *Gram Panchayat* level is hampered by a number of factors such as lack of awareness among people at the grass root levels, lack of capabilities in elected members at *Panchayat* level, poor women's participation and interference by family members, especially of the husband of the elected women members. The poor attendance, lack of visible people's participation and narrow agenda of discussion in the *Gram Sabha* present a poor account of the functioning of *Panchayats* at the grass root levels. According to Amartya Sen, the lack of capabilities deprives a person of the freedom to take advantage of opportunities and it is education that can open for a person a whole range of opportunities and will facilitate him to participate in the development process at the grass root levels. HRD has an important role to play here. What is needed is greater understanding of the system and its objectives, and education and awareness building programmes among practitioners from villages who would vote, participate and watch the development process to those who would have to operate it at every level and in every position. It is a very challenging HRD task. For ensuring that every person at village level participates positively and constructively in the development process and is not swayed away by vested interests, a well-conceived capacity building HRD programme assumes great significance. If *Panchayati Raj* system has to succeed in India, HRD programmes must be implemented at the grass root levels with commitment and dedication. People's empowerment can be assured only after strategic human resource development has been achieved. It involves a constant dialogue and feedback mechanism between policy makers and those upon whom implementation depends. Internal rivalries and conflicting objectives, financial constraints and political pressures from vested interest groups are always to be reckoned with.

The Role of Government and HRD Priorities and Policies

According to Gunnar Myrdal, there are eight ingredients of HRD namely :

(I) Food and Nutrition;

(II) Clothing;

(III) Housing and sanitation;

(IV) Health facilities;

(V) Education;

(VI) Information media;

(VII) Energy consumption; and

(VIII) Transport.[14a]

In developing societies government have a very important role to play in human resource development. Myrdal in his celebrated work *Asian Drama* (1968) rightly observes, "Development does not start with goods, it starts with people, with education, organisation and discipline, without these three, all resources remain latent, untapped potential." Implementation of HRD is possible only through guidance, support and involvement of the government at all levels in India.

Human Resource Development policies and priorities give rise to a complex set of strategic issues and choices to be addressed by the Central Government and State Governments in India. J.S.T. Quah (1993) has drawn the following inferences from his analysis of human resources development in four Asian counters (Japan, Singapore, South Korea and Taiwan):

"1. Government support is the most important pre-condition for economic development.

2. Corruption is a barrier to efficient HRD commitment. To minimise corruption is another common factor among successful countries. All HRD efforts will be futile without a clean civil service.

3. Investments in education and training have played a key role and governments have invested heavily in developing people through education and training.

4. Comprehensive reforms are needed in public personnel management in the direction of attracting, retaining, developing and utilizing competent employees."[15]

Government has an important role to play in the establishment of a long-term HRD policy to guide development of human resources of the country. Four necessary initial steps in formulating human resource development policies and plans can be as under:

First, a detailed human resource development profile of the

country should be formulated to cover life expectancy and health, education and communication, income patterns, female-male disparities.

Secondly, human resource development goals should be formulated.

Thirdly, budget allocation to various goals, sectors, activities, and programmes on the basis of the priorities should be decided, and

Fourthly, strategies of implementation should be decided upon. The responsibility for human resource development policy formulation and planning is very complex because HRD interventions are of multi-sectoral nature. According to T.V. Rao, in order to achieve HRD goals, the government should perform the following roles:

1. Policy Formulation (articulation of policies and their dissemination).
2. Translating policies into plans and programmes.
3. Mobilising resources required for implementing programmes (including finance, private sector, NGOs, community leaders and their communities).
4. Establishing and/or strengthening the institutional structure and other infrastructures and frameworks required for implementation.
5. Implementing the programmes.
6. Continuous collection of information to monitor the implementation including mid-course corrections and evaluation.
7. Experimentation in select areas.
8. Review of experiences and reformulation of policies on the basis of review.[16]

The role of the government is to improve the efficiency and effectiveness of existing institutions and organisations, which are responsible for HRD of the country. Government must also strengthen institutional structures, mobilise and facilitate the use of other resources like NGOs, communities and private sector to supplement the HRD efforts of the nation. In India there have been many efforts in various HRD areas. A whole lot of programmes—ranging from Community Development and National Extension Service, *Panchayati Raj*, IAAP, IADP to special programmes for weaker sections, like the small farmers, Marginal farmers and Agricultural Labourers Development Programmes, Drought Prone Area Programme, Dedesertification Programme, Community Area Development Programme, Tribal Development Programme, Hill Area Development Programme, Minimum Needs Programme, IRDP, Integrated Child Development Programme, NREP, Rural Landless Employment Guarantee Programme, TRYSEM, JRY etc. have been implemented to achieve integrated development to human resources, removal of poverty and employment generation. All the above HRD programmes have been formulated by the government. However the greatest concern today lies in the area of implementation. Where we fumble, however, is in implementing them.[17]

Implementation of HRD in Corporate Sector

Interaction with the top management, rapid rotation through different functions and departments, continuous dialogue with the assigned mentors, presentation on projects undertaken and feedback sessions at regular intervals are some of the basic steps in implementing HRD programmes in organisations such as Hindustan Lever, Philips, Asian Paints, Citibank and Standard Chartered. Nowadays implementation of HRD provides beneficiaries with multi-functional, multi-industry and multi-locational experiences on a continuous basis. In corporate sector HRD implementation has become necessary to improve employee motivation and organisational effectiveness in terms of productivity, quality control and cost control. Only when the chief executives and top management have high level commitment to HRD, implementation of HRD gets its proper attention. The Role of Chief Executive in HRD include the following; (a) identifying a corporate philosophy on HRD; (b) developing an HRD oriented leadership to create and maintain HRD climate; (c) identifying HRD needs of the organisation;

(d) preparing an action plan for implementing HRD; (e) staffing the HRD department with competent people; (f) getting the appraisal system examined and initiating OD (Org. Dev.) exercises; (g) formulating a training and development policy; (h) allocating separate financial resources for HRD; (i) ensuring proper HRD evaluation; (j) encouraging HRD managers to share their experience and develop professionally; and (k) developing incremental changes in human resource competencies, skills, values and attitudes. In implementation and promotion of HRD systems, labour unions have a very important role to play. According to Anil K. Khandelwal, seven different roles the unions can play in HRD include :- (a) initiating HRD by taking up HRD role; (b) communicating with workers; (c) counselling them; (d) organising education and training activities; (e) welfare; (f) starting family and vocational guidance services; and (g) research on workers. In many public and private sector organisations HRD implementation got proper attention only after crises situations developed or cracks started appearing. It was only in the early 1980s that a large number of private sector organisations started implementing HRD as a systemic intervention for organisational dynamism and vitality. In some organisations HRD taskforce was made responsible for implementation of HRD. The implementation of HRD is generally performed by the HRD departments and their main tasks should be as under:

1. Work out an action-plan to implement HRD designs, sub-systems and HR philosophy.
2. Keep inspiring the employees to have a constant desire for learning and development.
3. Execute various training programmes, workshops and HRD interventions.
4. Maintain a learning climate.
5. Keep top management constantly informed about various HRD implementation problems and get their commitment openly and consistently.
6. Constantly design new methods and systems for

executing HRD plans and strengthen the HRD climate.

7. Mobilise all available resources for executing and implementing HRD plans.
8. Conduct HRD related research and human process research.
9. Monitor effectively the implementation of various HRD sub-systems and mechanisms.
10. Mobilise available financial resources and other infrastructure for effectively executing various HRD interventions and mechanisms.
11. Keep constant links with other departments for various types of support and assistance.
12. Ensure effective academic planning with the support of HRD faculty staff.
13. Maintain effective links between teaching, research and consulting and maintain high level of professionalism.
14. Ensure constant faculty evaluation and develop the staff for effectively implementing various HRD mechanisms.
15. Ensure effective decision-making process whenever needed during implementation of HRD interventions and sub-systems.
16. Implementation of HRD needs teamwork and effective collaboration at all stages.
17. Interpersonal relations become very important in implementing HRD policies and programmes.
18. Implementation of HRD demands self-discipline and "self-regulation" among the executing staff.
19. HRD staff must find out "implementation gaps" from time to time and carry out mid-term corrections to bridge the implementation gaps.
20. HRD staff must assist the top level management in preparing future HRD blue prints and keep up their

tasks of organising, direction, coordinating and motivating working in implementation of HRD.

According to Dr. M.B. Athreya, there is a need for inculcation of six basic skills to ensure effective implementation of HRD system, once a positive organisational climate has been established. These are the skills of; (I) goal setting; (II) appraisal, (III) counselling, (IV) reviewing, (V) learning and (VI) self-development. Athreya's integrated HRD system's model includes linkages with corporate planning, and a derived manpower forecast. The ultimate aim of HRD is full participation of the individual in job and life (both social and political).

Implementation of HRD is a definite move towards an integrated approach of human resources management. In Bharat Heavy Electricals Limited (BHEL) training convention was organised in May, 1982 to give a new thrust to training and development efforts. Human Resource Mobilisation workshop was also organised to implement HRD effectively by working out action plans. For proper implementation of HRD it is necessary to develop HRD professionals and involve line managers actively in HRD. Implementation of HRD can be broadly depicted through the given matrix below.

Implementation of HRD in the corporate sector depends on the following main factors.

(A) Mobilisation of resources;

(B) Mobilisations of top management support and patronage;

(C) Mobilisation of manpower including HRD staff;

(D) Motivation of HRD;

(E) Formation of implementation taskforce and assigning specific duties and responsibilities to them.

(F) Mobilisation of Infrastucture, equipment, training aids and HRD support structure (Workshops);

(G) Monitoring;

(H) HRD Audit;

Matrix Showing Implementation of HRD in Corporate Sector

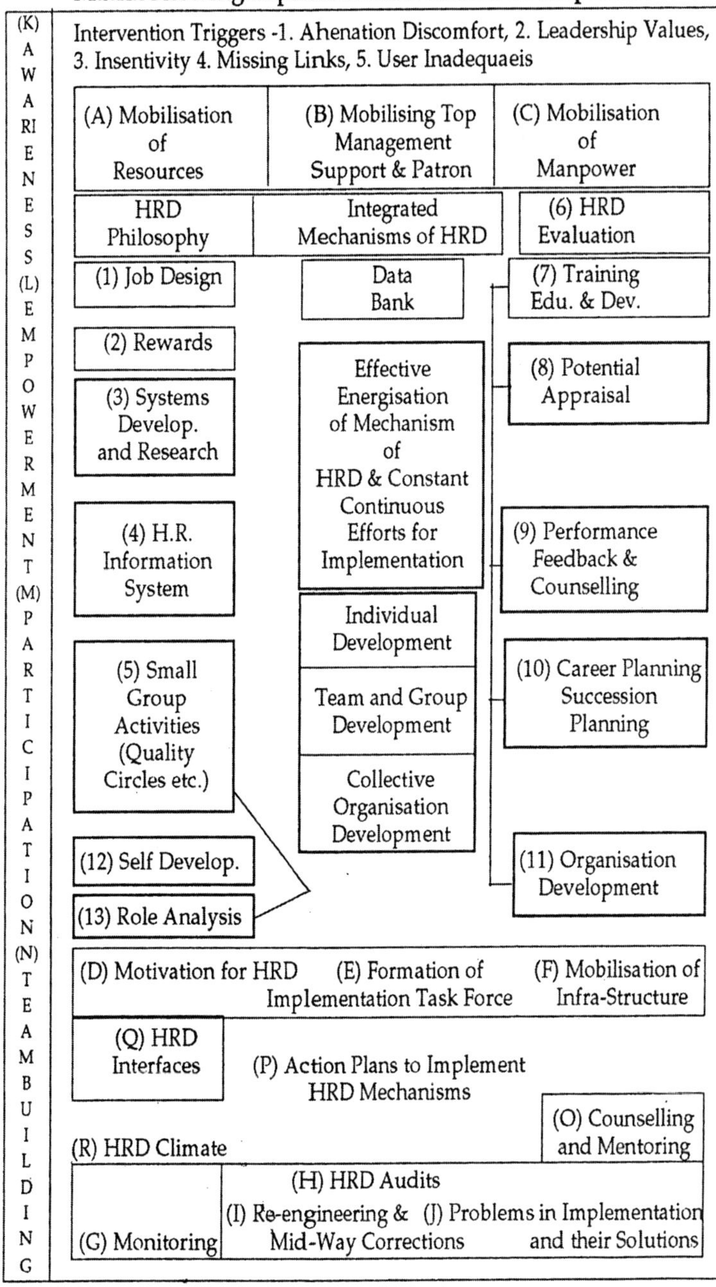

(I) Reengineering of HRD interventions and mid-way corrections;

(J) Problems in HRD implementation and their solutions;

(K) Awareness about HRD programmes and support from the beneficiaries;

(L) Empowerment to the HRD directing staff for effective intervention;

(M) Participation and support from line managers and other members of the various departments;

(N) Team building and group cohesion particularly among the HRD staff;

(O) Counselling and mentoring;

(P) HRD climate in the organisation;

(Q) HRD interface with unions, and other departments.

Implementation of HRD is not a one man's job, it is a teamwork of a large number of HRD trainers and line managers who execute, implement and monitor various instruments and interventions. All these implementors need high level of commitment, professional knowledge and skill and necessary supporting infrastructure. In implementing HRD instruments, cooperation, interest and active participation of all beneficiaries is also needed. An organisational climate that supports the HRD culture needs to be created in the organisation. Evaluation and effective feedback of HRD implementation at periodical intervals in constant basis is needed. During the last three decades Indian corporate organisations have been developing explicit strategies and systems for facilitating and maximum utilisation of human resources. In the larger organisations, HRD interventions are triggered due to alienation discomfort, leadership values, insensitivity, missing links and use inadequacies.[18] When there is more resistance to transfers, rotations and rising degree of careerism with self-interest, when due to large size of the organisational structure, multiple levels of hierarchy, strong unions and perceived external interference leads to varying degree of alienation, this perceived alienation can be the primary trigger of HRD. With the change of top level leadership, when need for renewal, turn-around and growth are felt as the urgent priorities for action, the recognition to involve, develop and utilize human resources is realised by leader, they can trigger HRD interventions as happened in SAIL in 1985. When certain organisations fail to give full benefits of various HRD sub-systems due to utter insensitivity and top leadership does not get required support, cooperation and commitment from the middle level, a series of interventions in the form of workshops on strategic planning, organisational development, team building and leadership to enhance sensitivity to human issues can trigger building up of an HRD climate in the organisation. When some organisations have not developed a comprehensive HRD system, incorporating other sub-systems, like career planning, and succession planning through rotations and transfers, the missing links at times trigger HRD interventions when crisis situations develop and leadership wants to build up morale in the organisation. HRD interventions are triggered when top level management and middle level executives are not able to make full and integrated use of HRD. HRD surveys can easily identify the user inadequacies and can trigger HRD interventions. Effective HRD implementation can bring organisational effectiveness through;

(a) better role-person match;

(b) inter-role and inter-personal skills;

(c) inter-group collaboration;

(d) improved behavioural skills; and

(e) high morale and motivation of the employees.

Implementation of various HRD programmes for different categories of the workers, supervisors and managers can be carried out through internal resources, external resources or through cooperative joint efforts of internal and external resources. Effective communication and involvement of people however most vital.

Implementation of HRD is not a one-time shot, it has to be a continuous on-going organisational activity. Now in HRD the emphasis has shifted from "maximisation of performance" and compensation towards "employee potential awareness creation and "employee potential realization". The focus of implementation is on enhancing employee involvement in internalizing organisational objectives through vibrant HRD interventions in order to release the springs of dynamism and creativity of both individuals, as well as work groups. The approach of implementations of HRD should be to develop an organisational culture to develop team work, positive inter-personal relations, and effective communication at all levels and collaboration among all employees. Before doing effective implementation, the first step is to carry out the diagnosis of the health of the organisation by HRD experts and behavioural scientists. Initiating and implementing HRD have been mostly reactive steps for most organisations in our country when everything else seemed to fail or crisis situations emerge in the organisations at many fronts. There are bound to be new challenges for the knowledge workers in the 21st century. "The new demands according to Peter F. Drucker, projected on the knowledge workers are: Who am I ? What are my strengths ? How do I work? Where do I belong ? What is my contribution ? What is my relationship responsibility ?"[18] We have to understand the implication of these issues and have to implement HRD strategies-in a more meaningful manner. The spiritual, ethical and moral dimensions of HRD have to be made not only a part of training syllabus but need to be given due emphasis and practical shapes.

Implementation of HRD is a serious challenge to HRD staff. Some of the difficulties generally faced by the HRD staff at various stages while implementing the HRD systems have been:

1. Complicated HRD integrated system;
2. Time consuming;
3. Too many routings;
4. Delays due to number of persons reporting being too many;

5. Becoming a number game;
6. Becoming ritualistic;
7. Low leadership commitment."[19]

There are mainly six contextual factors which influence the implementation of HRD: (1) state of technology, (2) attitude of managerial segment, (3) employee attitude towards HRD, (4) union leaders attitude towards HRD, (5) organisational focus and (6) environment context of globalisation and liberalisation.

The size of the organisation and its geographical spread are often great hindrance in implementing HRD. The cultural and educational backgrounds of the people have a strong bearing on their belief and support of HRD efforts. Interventions and mechanisms in the HRD area which have a "nurturant" or "mothering" orientation can often be counter-productive in certain situations. HRD implementation is a dynamic organisational process, which needs effective leadership support, dedicated HRD staff and a healthy HRD climate in the organisation.

Concluding Remarks

The task of drawing up comprehensive HRD plans in the developing countries is beset with a number of paradoxical difficulties and problems.[20] It is difficult to get dedicated and trained human resource administrators in developing countries. There is generally inadequate infrastructure for providing and implementing HRD systems. There is a lack of adequate monitoring arrangements to get feedback on HRD programmes. The scientific evaluations of various HRD programmes are not possible due to various in-built problems of evaluation and validation. However, there is an urgent need to implement various HRD programmes. The HRD programmes have to be suitably strengthened, developed and organised in the field of public administration. To implement HRD in the rural sector, the important recommendations can be as follows:

1. The first need is to develop the educational and vocational institutions in the country particularly in the rural areas.

2. The weaker sections of the society, particularly the SC and ST community people and lower income groups should be the target groups for HRD.
3. The non-government organisations and voluntary agencies should be invited and motivated to join in the HRD programme implementation.
4. The mass media and the extension services can play a positive role in moulding the attitude and outlook of the people towards education and vocational training.
5. The policies and programmes of HRD can be implemented by seeking cooperation of village *panchayats* and various social organisations.

There is an urgent need to formulate a clear-cut and far sighted national policy on HRD in administration.[21] A realistic and long-term HRD plan appears to be the most important prerequisite for attaining a self-sustained, self-accelerating economy and for implementing the general developmental five year plans. It is essential to undertake HRD action plans, which promote positive attitudes. The HRD action plan should aim at development of individuals as well as development of the whole cluster of administrators as a team committed to high ideals of efficiency, democracy, development and social justice. The HRD can be easily compared to the growth and development of the human resources personnel of a big orchestra. Symphonic music of the orchestra has to be so integrated in the performance that while it should be possible to hear it and appreciate it individually, in the total ensemble of the group of instruments and while each instrument maintains its separate identity, it also adds richness, melody and meaning in the performance of the entire orchestra on the whole.[22] The implementation of HRD is a stupendous and most challenging task but like nurturing a big orchestra group, it can help in creating happiness and lot of inner satisfaction to the persons involved.

REFERENCES

1. Ghee. L.T. (1986), *Policies and Priorities in Human Resource Development in Asia and the Pacific*, Bangkok-UNESCAP.
2. Corner L. (1991), *Human Resource Development Strategies; Regional Survey for Asia and the Pacific*, Report HRD g 41, London; Common Wealth Secretariat.
3. Bacchus, M.K. (1992), *Human Resource Development Definition, Importance and Strategies*, London, Common Wealth Secretariat.
4. T.V. Rao., *Human Resource Development; Experiences, Intervention and Strategies*, Sage Publications, New Delhi, 1996., p. 52.
5. Arun Monoppa and Mahrukh Engineer, *Liberalisation and Human Resource Management* Challenges for the Corporations of Tomorrow, New Delhi, 1999.
6. Bharati Sharma, Perspective on HRD Measures for Effective Governance, *The Indian Journal of Public Administration*, July-September, 1998, Vol. XLIV No. 3, pp. 501-502.
7. For similar views see Sartaz Aziz, *Rural Development, Some Essential Pre-requisities*, International Labour Review, Geneva, May-June, 1984, pp. 277- 85.
8. For details see Ch. Bala Ramalu, *International Organisation and Rural Employment Programs in India, Emerging Trends*, New Delhi, Ajantha Book International, 1996.
9. Suresh D Tendulkar and L.R. Jain, Economic Relations and Poverty. Economic and Political Weekly, Vol. XXX No. 23, June 10, 1995.
10. Ch. Bala Ramalu, "Human Resource Development and Liberalisation Policy; A Study of Rural Employment Programs in India—The Indian Journal of Public Administration, July-September, 1996, Vol. XLII No. 3, p. 465.
11. T.V. Rao, *Human Resource Development; Experiences, Intervention Strategies*, Sage Publications, New Delhi, 1996, p. 372.
12. Mathur H.M. (1992), Socio-Cultural Factors in Implementing Human Resource Development Programs." Paper prepared for the Regional Meeting of the National Focal Points for HRD, UNESCAP Meeting of the National focal Points for HRD, MANILA.

12a. Jean Dreze and Amartya Sened, *Hunger and Public Action*, Oxford, Clarendon Press, 1989, p. 26.

13. Reeta Chowdhari Tremblay, "Growth with Justice Understand-

ing Poverty" in C. Steven La Rue (Ed.). *The Indian Handbook Prospects onto the 21st century,* Chicago Fitzroy Dcarborn Publishers, 1997, p. 99.

14. Kamla Chowdhry, "Bureaucracy and Development" in S.C. Dube (Ed.). *Public Services and Social Responsibilities,* New Delhi.

14a. Gunnar Myrdal, *Asian Drama,* Penguin, 1968, p. 21.

15. Quah J.S.T. (1993), *Human Resource Development in Four Asian Countries : Some Lessons for the Commonwealth Countries,* London Commonwealth Secretariat.

16. T.V. Rao, *Human Resource Development; Experiences, Intervention Strategies,* Sage Publications, New Delhi, 1996. p. 361.

17. Atal Behari Vajpayee, "Indian Administration Today—Remedying its Weaknesses" Lecture at IIPA, New Delhi, March 29, 1999- *Indian Journal of Public Administration,* January-March, 1999 Vol. XLV No. 1, p. 4.

18. For similar views and further elucidation consult M.B. Athreya— "Integrated HRD systems-Intervention Strategies" in T.V. Rao & others (Eds.). *"Alternative Approaches and Strategies of Human Resource Development,* Rawat Publication, Jaipur, 1989, pp. 374-85.

18a. Peter F. Drucker, *Management Challenges for the 21st Century,* Distributed by Viva Books Pvt. Ltd., New Delhi.

19. C.M. Srivastava "HRD in Larsen and Turbo Limited" paper presented at National HRD Network.

20. Dr. Krishna Mohan Mathur, *Concerns and Constraints in Administration,* RBSA Publishers, Jaipur, 1991, p. 67.

21. Dr. Krishna Mohan Mathur, *Human Resource Development in Administration,* 23 p. A Vol. XXXIII No. 2. April-June, 1987.

10

Human Resources Development for Indian Police

"Indian Police" is an umbrella term, which denotes not only state police forces of India but also various Central Police Organisations (CPOs) like CRPF, BSF, ITBP, CBI, RPF, Intelligence Bureau, CISF and other law enforcing agencies.[1] Roughly speaking approximately 14.5 lakh state police personnel and 5 lakh 60 thousand personnel of central police organisations constitute Indian police. It has more than two hundred training centres including police academies and recruit training centres. At district and range level also police personnel are given various training and orientation programmes. SVP National Police Academy, Hyderabad is the premier training institution for training senior police leaders of Indian police. Bureau of Police Research and Development is the coordinating authority for training of senior level police officers.[2] Police organisations have human resources as their greatest assets and driving force in attaining and performing its various assigned functions and responsibilities. Research studies reveal that the biggest challenge confronting police organisations today is to make optimum utilization of human resources and to keep its qualitative and quantitative character at the desired level of effective use. Police personnel in India require HRD for improving their job performance by developing the key competencies in terms of knowledge, habits, skills, techniques, attitudes, habits and value-system. Police organisations will have to prepare both long-term and short-term plans for human resources development for coping with fast changing environments and newly emerging challenges.[3] Human resource development means (1) a series of planned and organised activities, (2) conducted by professional experts within a specified time and (3) designed to produce behavioural change.[4] Human Resource Development system includes performance appraisal, potential appraisal, employee feedback and counselling, assessment of training needs of various categories of employees, designing and using special interventions, organisational diagnosis, organisational development, evaluation of various interventions, and increasing the motivation of the people for optimum effectiveness of the organisation.[5] Human Resource Development is a very difficult, challenging and uncertain process because "growth is always from within.[6] HRD programmes in many countries have gained momentum because economists like T.W. Schultz, Simon Kuznets and others have tried to enthrone man as a productive source of production. At the macro-level, HRD strategy includes population control, employment generation, planned urbanisation, improvement in industrial relations, restructuring educational system, international cooperation for health measures and empowerment of the human resources. Robert Owen, Andrew Ure, F.W. Taylor, Oliver Sheldon, Elton Mayo, Roethlis Berger, Gardener, Hikert, Whyle etc. have made useful pioneering experiments for developing human resources by their unique emphasis on worker's productivity. Human resource development can bring about job-enrichment with better planning and allround development of human personality. Human resource development is largely synonymous with training but it has following dimensions :

1. Intellectual—knowledge development and knowledge generation.
2. Physical—health, vigour and stamina development.
3. Aesthetic—appreciation of beauty of form, sound and

thought.

4. Moral—ethical and moral values.
5. Professional—vocational and economic.
6. Spiritual—development of spiritual and religious faculties.
7. Social—social aspects of human life.
8. Psychological—mental and psychological aspects.

Human resources development is multi-dimensional intervention strategy with the overall following objectives, namely—

1. Preventive strategy by arresting both organisational and individual obsolescence.
2. Curative strategy by bridging pro-active inadequacies of knowledge and professional skills.
3. Adaptive strategy by making proper adjustments with socio-politico-technological and environmental changes.
4. Promotive strategy by developing new outlook and attitudes for achieving excellence and maintaining total quality improvements.
5. Transformative by bringing out a new HRD culture and organisational climate and making a total man with new octapace values and cultural attributes.

All above mentioned dimensions must receive adequate attention of police organisations. Human resources development policy both at macro and micro level and human resource planning should be focussed directly on these objectives. According to Dr. Udai Pareek the twelve dimensions of any organisational climate are as follows : (i) Orientation, (ii) Interpersonal relations, (iii) Supervision, (iv) Problem management; (b) Management of mistakes, (vi) Conflict management, (vii) Communication, (viii) Decision-making, (ix) Trust, (x) Management of rewards, (xi) Risk taking and (xii) Innovation and change. Police organisations in India must build up a healthy organisational climate which is conducive for development of human resources of the organisation. The organisations climate has the following six motives :[7]

1. Achievement—concern for excellence and achievement of goals;
2. Expert Influence—emphasis on expertise;
3. Extension—concern for relevance to others;
4. Control—concern for personal power;
5. Dependency—dependence on seniors;
6. Affiliations.

All the above motives are quite relevant for police organisations with special reference to their roles. Indian police must develop a new organisational climate which should be relevant to roles and long-term goals of the organisations.

An Integrated HRD Matrix

HRD is a multi-dimension dynamic process with various sub-systems and processes. An integrated HRD matrix developed by the present author is given in figure-A at the end of chapter. To be put along side the para above. HRD system starts with the realisation of dis-equilibrium in the human resource system. It is motivated by a need for increased effectiveness of the organisation felt by the top management. The key result areas are to be properly identified for any HRD system. Development of human resources can be brought about at Individual, Group and Organisational levels. HRD evaluation of present system can assist in planning future strategies. HRD subsystems need to be integrated at various levels of organisation.[8] In all central and state police organisations, all the above given elements of HRD exist in some form or the other but their integration for HRD purposes has not been done at satisfactory levels. For senior police officers of Indian Police Service, there is adequate career planning and succession planning along with all other elements of HRD but for subordinate ranks, the position differs from state to state and organisation to organisation. During the last decade, computerisation has enabled various police organisations to streamline their various HRD elements

Figure-A
An Integrated HRD System Matrix

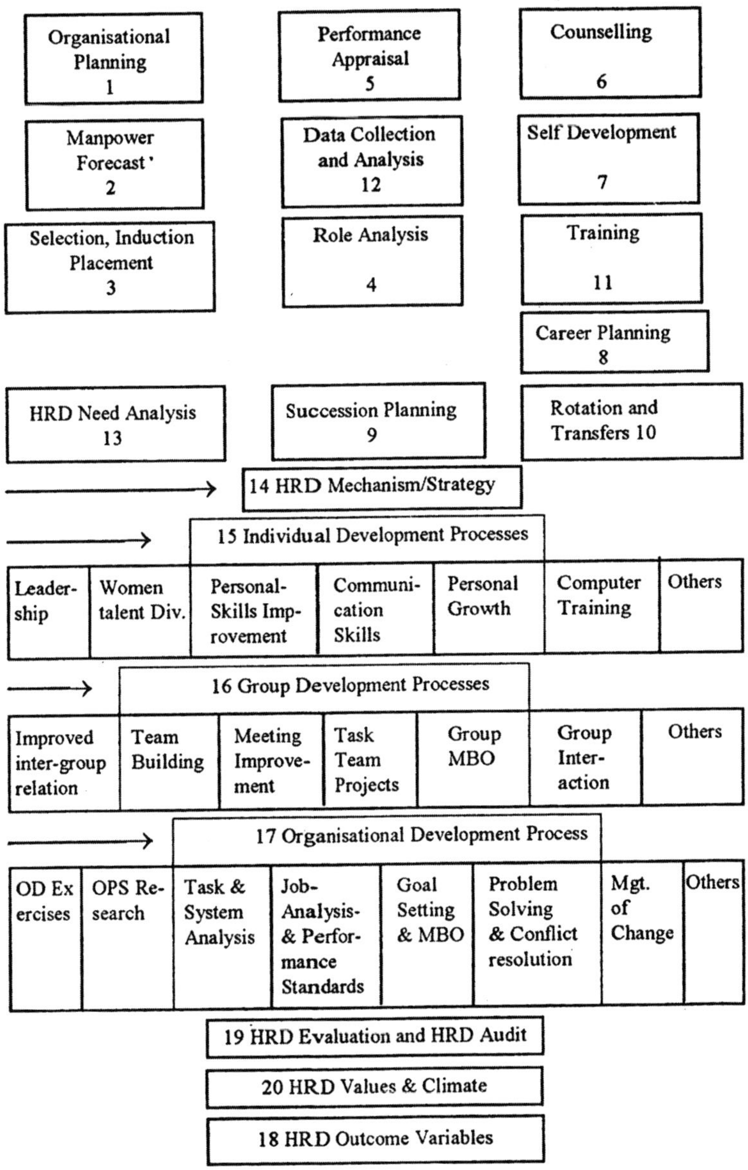

but comprehensive integration is still far from satisfactory.

Human Resource Development (HRD) is a dynamic approach to pro-actively deal with issues related to individual employees and teams, and organisations and a movement to develop organisational capability to manage change and challenges.[9] For evolving a holistic HRD programme for Indian police, SWOT analysis "(Strength, Weakness, Opportunities, Threats") of the police is to be carried out in terms of :

(a) Philosophy and Style
(b) Systems and Procedures, Socialisation System
(c) Morale and Career Planning
(d) Leadership and Motivation
(e) Performance Standard and Performance
(f) Organisational Climate and Culture
(g) Public Expectations and Community Support
(h) State of Technology and Contextual Factors
(i) Police Image and Role Expectations

The goals of HRD in police organisations can be briefly summarised as under :

1. To develop pride in police work;
2. To develop commitment and joy (ecstasy) in police work;
3. To provide total quality police service to the public in a democratic society;
4. To develop synergy (collaboration and support to build strong dyads, teams and inter-teams) with a view to achieve police mission;
5. To develop human sensitivities towards weaker sections of society and human rights;
6. To control and contain crimes, illegal activities and anti-national subversive operations by pro-active preventive police operations;
7. To develop and nurture a healthy organisational climate of trust, impartiality and mutual help.

8. To develop competencies required by police professionals into the following main areas :
   (a) Interpersonal competencies and human relation capabilities;
   (b) Competencies in terms of knowledge, attitudes, skills, techniques and habits, relating to police work;
   (c) Competencies to deal with the individual in the context of the role and the organisation;
   (d) Personal competencies to act as change agent and culture-builder.

It is necessary that police organisations should promote organisational learning. Pareek (1988) defined organisational learning as the process by which an organisation acquires, retains and uses inputs for its development, and the process results in an enhanced capacity for continued self-learning and renewal." Indian police should utilize and adopt the following mechanisms of organisational learning :

1. Experimentation and flexibility;
2. Mutuality and teamwork;
3. Contingency and incremental planning;
4. Specialisation and expertise;
5. Competency building.

Organisational planning, counselling, career planning and self development programmes have not been given adequate importance in India police organisations. HRD interventions for subordinate officers and lower ranks of the police in most police organisations have not been properly carried out. Central Police Organisations have carried out HRD interventions in case of subordinate and lower ranks in a more sincere manner than the state police organisations. However, Tamil Nadu, Kerala, Karnataka and Andhra Pradesh state police have much improved HRD systems than other state police organisations. Like other organisations HRD in police depends upon leadership. Motivation is an important area of HRD for police organisations in India. Today Indian police is facing many challenges and serious crises due to its various internal organisational maladies and it needs a very heavy dose of organisational learning and holistic human resource development. Indian police, in general, is subjected to many dysfunctions, such as poor image, undue militarisation, psychological morbidity, police brutalities, illegalities and violations of human rights by the police. In order to build up a communication, co-ordination, motivation, job satisfaction, close supervision, opportunity for creativity, and HRD interventions are needed in Indian police organisations.

Contextual Factors Influencing Implementation of HRD— While HRD has gained an over-riding emphasis in private sector and corporate world due to globalisation, liberalisation and keen competition, its perception in government hardly goes beyond training. In actual life many factors influence implementation of HRD for Police as given in the figure below :

Fig. 2. Showing Contextual Factors

Indian police have to prepare its human resources keeping in view the following factors :

1. State of Technology and Chellenges before Police— Criminalisation of politics and politicisation of criminals, economic liberalization policy, increasing caste consciousness and awareness in the plural society, growing cult of explosives and low intensity conflicts, new modes of economic offences and judicial activism, increase in computer crimes, sophistication of criminal activities by use of latest scientific techniques, increasing mobility of criminals due to better transportation facilities—all above factors demand a new type of Indian police to deal with these new trends and challenges.

2. Managerial Approach Towards Police Personnel— Police personnel need better treatment by their leaders and managers. There is need for proper career planning of police personnel with due consideration of their potential and actual performance. Performance appraisal needs to be carried out in a more holistic manner to develop human resources to the fullest extent. Career development strategies must track down high potential performers and enhance their various competencies. Empathy, genuine concern and more humanistic approach is needed towards police personnel.

3. Attitude of Police Personnel—HRD in the police organisations, must be used as a systematic process by which police personnel are continuously helped in a planned way.

(a) To acquire better capabilities in terms of knowledge, attitudes, values and skills required to perform their various tasks and functions associated with their present and future expected roles in secular, democratic plural society;

(b) To develop and nurture their general enabling capacities as individual, so that they are able to discover and utilize their own inner potential for their own and organisational development purposes.

(c) To develop and sustain an organisational culture where superior-subordinate relationships, teamwork and collaboration among different sub-units are strong and contribute to the organisational health, dynamism and pride of employees in their police work[10] HRD can bring about a change in the attitude of police personnel towards sound police professionalism.

4. Organisational Culture and HRD Climate—There is need for a healthy HRD climate in police organisations which can be characterised as consisting of the following:

(i) Openness and freedom to express ones ideas and opinions; (ii) Collaborative attitude or team spirit; (iii) Trust; (iv) Authenticity or correlation between words and actions; (v) Pro-action or encouraging some degree of initiative and risk taking by employees; (vi) Autonomy or certain degree of freedom for each individual and (vii) An interest in confronting issues and solving them rather than hiding them.[11] Such climate is most essential in police organisations to meet the complex challenges of the 21st century. Police leaders have a vital role to play in nurturing and building such organisational culture and climate.

5. Organisational Focus and Community Expectations—Indian police has gradually evolved high level of organisational focus and each police organisation must keep its focus on the organisational mission and goals. While state police should focus on crime control and maintenance of law and order, BSF should concentrate on border security, Central Reserve Police Force should specialise in internal security tasks and Intelligence agencies must concentrate on collection and dissemination of intelligence. Each police organisation must focus its HRD efforts to achieve organisational goals. Community expectations must be fulfilled by Indian police organisations.

Challenges for HRD in the Future

The major HRD challenges of Indian police are to develop a human environment, preserve human dignity and show concern to retain the workforce. HRD functions in Indian police must work in a decentralised environment and must constantly strive for Kaizen (continuous improvement).[12] Udai Pareek defines HRD as encompassing six human units, namely, individual, the role he plays, the dyadic relationship, the team processes, inter team processes, and at the organisational level. I find a lot of relevence in analysing HRD processes for the police against the backdrop of the six cited units.

1. The Individual Employee—During the last 25 years, the quest for self-actualization, is getting more and more attention. According to Maslow, the highest level need of a human being is "self-actualization" which is a state of "being" and demanding spiritual management to fulfil spiritual needs. In police organisations training and development must commence from the time of induction of new entrants to police service. Each central and state police organisations have their training centres for conducting basic pre-induction training of police personnel. There is a general impression that police training institutions in India are concentrating more on basic training programme, rather than on refresher training courses for various ranks. A study of twenty-five training institutions carried out by the author has revealed that sixty per cent of the police training institution in the country do not have adequate accommodation for trainees and even bare minimum physical facilities are not available in more than seventy per cent of the police institutions of the country.[13] HRD facilitators must focus their efforts in nurturing the human capabilities and potential talents of all the police personnel and in enhancing human element in police work. Police persons must be sensitised to the human rights issues in India.

2. The Role—Police role in a democratic society remains a matter of great controversy. The glamorous exterior of a police job overshadows the challenges encountered in role enactment which are often life threatening and endanger the personnel in uniform, not only while on duty but even otherwise.[14] Indian Police has not yet defined its role so far in the context of democratic system of governance and social control. Police role can be broadly categorised under following headings :

1. Police as a law-enforcing agency,
2. Police as the strong arm of the executive government,

3. Police as the protector of human rights and liberties of citizens,
4. Police with a role in political development of the country,
5. Police as social service agents of social change,
6. Police as guardians of secular, plural and secular society.

Human Resource Development must prepare the Indian police for its various responsibilities by carrying out various HRD intervention strategies.

3. Dyadic Relationships—Earlier the superior police leadership was given training in controlling the subordinates and to control them by authoritative styles of leadership. With the change of politico-social environment, police needs better quality of cooperation and collaboration between seniors and subordinates. The compulsions of a democratic system, the rising expectations of the weaker section of society and the emergence of a new liberal economy throw new challenges to the dyadic relationships in the police. Human Resource Development has a crucial role to play in preparing police organisations for the delicate dyadic relationships with focus on motivation and job-enrichment. The educated police constables and sub-inspectors of today do not see their leaders as anything different from them in competence, skills or even knowledge and demand a very different types of interaction from their seniors. Political interference, corruption and frequent transfers do not allow a healthy dyadic relationship between them.

4. Team Development—Demand for a better teamwork in police organisations originate from the need of a well-structured, trained and motivated police force to deal with militant groups, insurgents, armed rebellions and organised criminal groups. While state police force still works in singles as traffic policemen, team work is expected in areas where people have to deal with organised criminals and militant insurgent groups. Even for dispersing a violent demonstrating mob, a good police teamwork is expected. HRD professionals have a crucial role to play in building teamwork and team spirit among police personnel particularly in the armed branches of the Indian police. Even for an organisation like C.B.I., there is a need for high quality of teamwork for working out organised economic crimes having international and national ramifications.

5. Inter-team Collaboration—Between different central police organisations and the state police, there is a greater need today for inter-team collaborations. While on internal security duties, CRPF, BSF, ITBP, and state police organisations have to work in very close coordination and cooperation. HRD persons have a very critical role to play in bridging linkages between different organisation and even units of the same organisations. In police organisations, there is a need to enhance mutual understanding, trust and synergy. Different organisations need not be competitive, with cut-throat competition spirit, since they are all expected to secure and work for a common national goal and mission. Since internal security and protection of society from criminals are the broad goals of all police organisations, a higher level of coordination and cooperation is needed by Indian police.

6. Organisational Level Intervention—Organisational culture and capabilities, values and beliefs determine how people will be managed, motivated and inspired.[15] Each central police organisation/state police will have to identify its goals and missions for the twenty-first century and thereby identify the development needs of the people in the organisation.[16] Organisational level intervention will be needed as suggested in figure 'A'. In the present day context various police organisations have to continuously rejuvenate themselves and prepare to face the ever growing demands and challenges of the future. Such an organisational restructuring and renewal is largely possible through successful implementation of HRD processes. Indian police needs a lot of organisational level interventions for encouraging continuous upgradations of skills, habits, knowledge and attitudes of its personnel in view of the changing scenario. Indian police must continuously carry out organisational level interventions to create a spirit of social service in its personnel and build up a responsible, committed empowered frontline. It should help the police personnel to improve their ability to :

(i) Be more sensitive to other human beings and respect human rights;

(ii) Listen to, respond and counsel subordinates;

(iii) Maintain physical, moral and psychological fitness;

(iv) Ensure high level of discipline and self-control;

(v) Maintain cordial relations with the community;'

(vi) Generate enthusiasm, pride and creativity in work groups.

Need for Core Values

Success of HRD implementation in police in turn will depend on certain core values. Udai Pareek and T.V. Rao (1991) define such values as openness, confrontation, trust, authenticity, pro-activity, autonomy, collaboration and experimentation (OCTAPACE).[17]

1. **Openness**—Extent of willingness to share and receive changes in the offing like technology. Police organisations are to a very extent considered closed organisations and there is hardly any openness in their working. The democratic demands of the society are now gradually expecting more openness in police organisations. Media is becoming more and more powerful nowadays and is regularly exposing false "police-encounters" and "disappearances." National Human Rights Commission and other Human Rights outfits will not allow police to carry out their out-dated techniques of interrogation and investigation. In *Kishore Singh vs State of Rajasthan, AIR,* 1981, S.C. 1597, the Supreme Court showed its deep concern regarding police atrocities and expected more openness in police functioning.

2. **Confrontation**—Willingness to face problems and solve rather than avoiding. Police concern with potentially riotous incidents is not basically for riot control only but preventing such occurrences and of minimising the internal strife.[18]

Confrontation management techniques and strategies must be constantly upgraded and practised by the Indian police. Principles of police accountability, use of minimum force, objectivity and functional responsiveness need to be strictly followed by Indian police in their various operations and duties.

3. **Trust**—Extent of faith in each other. In police organisations where many orders by senior officers on the spot are issued verbally in most cases, trust is one of the most crucial factor of organisational culture. Trust has to be earned, needs boundaries and learning. It is the processes of trust-building which can help police organisations to perform their functions well. The most historic success of police organisation against the terrorists of Punjab was built on trust between police officials and informants and public trust between different operating police agencies and people of the community.

4. **Authenticity**—Saying what one means and meaning what one says—Indian police has to develop authenticity so that others may trust them and they may operate with public confidence and support. It is generally seen that while top police hierarchy continues the extravagant expenses on new cars, air conditioners, they talk of austerity and reduction of general expenses. While police leaders generally treat subordinates at various levels without human dignity, they talk of HRD and human values in seminars and lectures. The gap between talks and practices need to be narrowed down.

5. **Autonomy**—Degree of freedom with respect to others freedom—This implies autonomy as a major source of work satisfaction, and flexible working time. Police top hierarchy does not allow autonomy and freedom to their subordinates. On the other hand subordinates and lower ranks of police personnel are expected to work much more than eight hours a day, months after months. These things need change and there is need for autonomy at all ranks. Government should give police autonomy and freedom from political interference.

6. **Pro-activity**—Thinking and preparing oneself ahead—In police organisations in India there is generally no proactive thinking preparation. Police organisations in India need to be

more forward-looking and should carry out strategic planning and management. Why can not Indian police change Police Act of 1861 and why National Police Commission Report recommendations be implemented at least at the organisational levels? Police in India must carry out long-term strategic and pro-active planning.

7. **Collaboration**—Extent of cohesiveness and synergy—Indian police must develop better team work and synergy in their efforts to control and contain crimes. Today senior police leaders do not, on the whole, allow a more collaborative style of working. They should encourage collaboration through collective training and value teamwork. Central police organisations have been exhibiting a culture of collaboration while in many state police organisations it is missing or very meagre. HRD can initiate a total transformation of an organisation by bringing about:

(a) A change in "mind-set".

(b) A feeling of team-work and collaboration at all levels.

(c) A cultural change involving people by job enlargement.

(d) A feeling of pride and commitment to the organisation.

HRD in Indian police can improve its present image and can transform the organisation completely by adopting above values.

The main distinguishing feature of Indian HRD work is that HRD concepts and systems are anchored in "OCTAPACE" values[19].

8. **Experimentation**—To take risk and innovate—Indian police must encourage new ideas and suggestions for continuous improvement in the organisation. Some central and state police organisations have experimented with new ideas with great success. Delhi police have carried out many experiments to enlist public support in community policing. Tamil Nadu police, Kerala police and Karnataka police have also made many new experiments with varying degrees of success.

Above mentioned values need to be developed as a part of

HRD in various organisations, success of HRD in police organisations can be achieved only by generating above mentioned values.

Indian Police have Inadequacy of HRD Managers

Due to various reasons HRD department has not been very popular area of posting in police organisations in most of the states. Most of the HRD managers in state police organisations have no desire to develop their HRD skills and consider posting to HRD department as a punishment posting. Frequent transfers, loss of social status, lack of powers and social interaction are some of the reasons for inadequacy of skilled HRD managers in state police organisations. Central police organisations have a relatively better position and do build up HRD skills in their managers such as learning and self-development, feedback, counselling and subordinate development, appraisal, role clarification and objectivity in review and moderation. In police organisation training is the most popular HRD sub-system for obtaining good results. Police organisations have, historically, strengths in three sub-systems of HRD, namely—

(a) Selection, induction and placement

(b) Training

(c) Appraisal including potential appraisal

Since police organisations have a very large number of people to be developed, Indian police must develop HRD managers who should be able to perform the following important roles :

1. Human systems development with planning role.
2. HRD culture building with linking role.
3. Competence building and educating role.
4. Motivational development.
5. Organisational diagnosis and intervention planning with consulting role.
6. Change agency with ability for creating synergy in the organisation so that teams work effectively for

organisational goals.

7. Achieving equity and justice ensuring that police personnel who work for the organisation are rewarded according to their contributions through a well-conceived reward system.
8. Role models as HRD facilitators and managers. HRD professionals of Indian police have to build up HRD culture with emphasis on the following philosophy:

(a) Police persons are valuable resource i.e. there is a need to invest time and effort in their development.

(b) Police persons are human beings with values and culture and there is need to develop human values.

(c) Human resources include various human processes and units such as roles, team, inter-team and the whole organisation.

From the very beginning, Indian police expected superior and subordinate police officers to shoulder responsibilities for development of their subordinates through system of performance appraisal, reward system, empowerment and constant counselling. But probably Indian police have not been able to develop a proper HRD culture. Lack of support from top level in police is one of the important factors that prevented human resource development of police personnel to the desired extent on the right lines.

Role of Top Level Police Hierarchy in HRD

Directors General of Police and Inspectors General of Police of CPOs and state police forces have a very important role in HRD. Top level police hierarchy have following important roles:

1. Provide a proper HRD philosophy for the organisation.
2. Develop supervisory style and leadership which should be in congruence with the HRD and HRM Philosophy.
3. Ensure proper need analysis of HRD and prepare suitable HRD Action-Plan.

4. Post competent, qualified and motivated people in HRD departments and ensure their proper development.
5. Restructure the performance appraisal systems to make it a tool of HRD.
6. Prepare proper strategic HRD plans for the organisation and ensure its effective implementation.
7. Provide suitable monetary provisions for HRD department to carryout HRD plans.
8. Provide full infrastructure required to effectively implement HRD policies and programmes.
9. Develop and maintain an HRD culture in the organisation and the HRD taskforce.
10. Promote professionalism of HRD specialists by encouraging HRD managers to share their experiences with others by reviewing periodically the progress of implementing HRD.
11. Consider HRD both as staff and line function and ensure continuity in HRD processes and mechanism at various organisational levels.
12. They have to exhibit their faith and commitment to HRD by setting personal examples and act as HRD "Institutional builders".

They should themselves attend HRD orientation programmes given to the HRD managers. The level of commitment of police chiefs for HRD has been varying in the past from person to person and organisation to organisation. Central police organisations particularly Border Security Force, CBI, CRPF, ITBP and Intelligence Bureau have been lucky at times to get police chiefs who were persons with good vision and commitment to HRD. Among the state police organisations, Andhra Pradesh, Tamil Nadu, Uttar Pradesh and Rajasthan have some of the police chiefs who exhibited their commitment and concern for HRD. Studies conducted by the author indicate that there has been great inadequacy of HRD managers in

Indian police. Regular conferences on HRD and training are regular features of a number of police organisations. Police chiefs must demonstrate a development style of leadership with attempts to constantly educate the police subordinates and involve a belief in developing the competencies of his subordinates in the organisation.[21] Police chiefs must realise that training is only one of the sub-systems of the HRD systems and HRD interventions for police constables and other lower ranks are most critical for the overall improvement of the efficiency, competence and image of the police force.

Need of HRD for Constabulary and Subordinate Officers—Actually policing is done by constabulary and subordinate officer in police organisations and HRD for them is a process by which policeman are helped in a planned and continuous way to :

1. Develop confidence, initiative and discipline.
2. Develop physical, intellectual, psychological, social and cultural aspects of personality.
3. Develop occupational and professional competencies, capabilities and skills.
4. Develop higher level of achievement, motivation and cultural aspect of individual's personality.
5. Develop teamwork and inter-team collaboration.
6. Development of collaboration personality of policeman and an HRD culture.
7. Develop better communication skills.

This particular aspect of HRD has so far remained neglected in most of the police organisations. Studies by the author have revealed that HRD for police constabulary and subordinate officers is really a most collosal and challenging task in view of their large number and non-availability due to round the clock duties and pressure of work. However, very commendable efforts have been made by most of the police organisations by providing regular training in Human Rights orientation for constables and subordinate officers.

Personal Experience as HRD Manager

My journey as HRD professional started when I joined a postgraduate college as lecturer in economics. It continued during my long thirty-four years of police-service in a central police organisation and now as a full time HRD professional. This long journey has been full of challenges, thrills, frustration and self-actualisation. The author got a very unique opportunity of practising HRD in various premier training institutions during different phases of his career. It is an attempt to share the experience of HRD processes for institutionalising values and systems. As Assistant Principal of Central Training College, CRP, Neemuch, it was my valuable experience and then as Vice-Principal of a newly created Recruit Trainning Centre, CRP at Barwaha. Later I had the opportunity of serving Internal Security Academy as Assistant Director, then Deputy Director and ultimately as Director and head of the premier national institution of the country which provided specialisation to all the senior level police officers from the rank of Deputy S.P. to Additional Director General and District Magistrates. In between I also got the opportunity of commanding central training college (Telecommunication) CRP, Neemuch for a brief spell of six months. The process of culture building and OD was based on a process of identifying, articulating, communicating, understanding and getting the involvement of the colleagues to the mission, vision, values and culture of the organisation. Indian police, I firmly believe, must develop OCTAPACE values (openness, confrontation, trust, authenticity, proaction, autonomy, collaboration and experimenting) in various police organisations through HRD interventions. In my humble way I tried my best to develop these values as Deputy Director and later as Director of a national level training academy which trained officers of central police organisations and state police forces. How far I succeeded in my venture is for future research scholars to evaluate and assess. As HRD professional I always stressed the appraising and developing managerial performance of the participants and tried to impress need for objective, fair and correct performance appraisals.[22] With senior level command management course, HRD philosophy and concepts were discussed and all possible perspectives of HRD were given to the participants.[23] For Top management level, HRD concepts must be clear and this role in development of HRD should be stressed. Evaluation of HRD needs constant objective endeavours in all organisations case studies, training monographics and articles were prepared for various programmes. There is great inadequacy of attention on human resource development in Indian police. There is great need to initiate measures for upgradation of knowledge, skills, attitudes and habits and also requirement for development of creativity, interpersonal relations, team building, leadership, motivation and empowerment of lower and middle ranks of Indian police. As head of a national level HRD institution of police, I always emphasised in depth HRD audit of various aspects of HRD such as manpower planning, selection and recruitment. Induction system, performance appraisal, potential appraisal, career and succession planning, employee morale, organisational development, training and development, participative mechanisms and exit interviews, need to be carried out periodically by the specialists for achieving organisational excellence.[25] Unless periodical HRD audits are carried out, Indian police organisations can not come upto the expectations of the people and the government. Human Resource Development, like "broad-spectrum antibiotic" has multi-coverage and acts like travelling salesman's cure-all-etxir. HRD includes performance appraisal, potential appraisal, employee feedback and counselling. Assessment of training needs of various categories of employees, designing and using special interventions, organisational diagnosis, organisational development, evaluation of various intervention are critical for optimum effectiveness of the organisation.[26] As HRD professional some of the following issues emerged in the mind :

(i) Do we know in depth what is actually taught in various police training programmes ?

(ii) Does this kind of education prepare policemen to emerge as qualified police professional ?

(iii) Have the proper standards of training been set up by the national level institutions ?

(iv) What are the various HRD instruments and techniques which need to be introduced in Indian police organisations ?

It is continuous on going process and needs to be carried out by experienced HRD professionals with the help of top level hierarchy of the Indian police. HRD mechanisms must cater to the growing challenges and newly emerging needs of the Indian police organisation. During the last two decades due to various external and internal factors, certain attitudinal changes are clearly visible in the new generation of police officers, in terms of:

(a) emergence of highly educated and enlightened police leadership.

(b) more cohesive team efforts by the subordinate officers and others.

(c) greater identification and pride in the organisation.

(d) an urge to excel and improve over police performance.

(e) better discipline and sensitivity to human rights and demands of plural society.

(f) creative problem solving abilities among police officers at junior and middle levels.

(g) higher levels of motivation and trust in new generation of policemen.

(h) greater awareness of management techniques and concepts.

(i) greater awareness of new political, social and economic environment.

Evaluation of HRD—Evaluation of HRD in India has remained a patently neglected area. HRD evaluation should be carried out in Indian police with the following objectives:

(1) to improve the design or delivery of learning events; (2) to increase the learning on the job; and (3) to make correct decisions about HRD in the organisations. A qualified evaluation team should periodically carry out HRD audit and evalu-

ation of various police organisations in India. An objective evaluation of course objectives, participants, material, instructor's material and media should be carried out along with research on HRD climate. HRD systems and process in Indian police organisations need to be constantly evaluated.

HRD managers express the following concerns about implementing evaluation:

1. Cost of evaluation.
2. Consequences of negative results and
3. Evaluation will open a Pandora's box.[27]

Evaluation of HRD has to give a wide coverage in terms of various facets and approaches and must focus on training, organisational change, empowerment and stress.[28] It is crucial that scientific and comprehensive evaluation of HRD in Indian police is carried out based on KirkPatrick's four levels:[29]

Level 1—Reactions of employees-measured by post-programme surveys.

Level 2—Level of employee learning and development-measured by pre-test and post-test results.

Level 3—Changes in behaviour of employees-measured by their actual daily efficiency rating, based on daily work output.

Level 4—Results in productivity.

The following four types of measures can be used in Indian police to improve the design and delivery of learning events :

1. Performance measures of skills, knowledge, attitudes and techniques required for various police organisations.
2. Analysis and evaluation of HRD mechanism and systems used as the designs and delivery.
3. Learning outcomes in terms of skills, attitude and cognitive strategies.
4. Evaluation of infrastructure and HRD inputs and HRD efforts to prepare the HRD professionals in the organisations.

S.V.P. National Police Academy, Hyderabed has started some measures to carry out HRD of senior level police officers. Top Management Courses and Training Management Courses are steps in the right directions. Many central police organisations have also initiated some steps and must adopt latest HRD techniques, instruments and linkages for holistic development of police personal of the country.

Indian police must devise and develop a comprehensive HRD system to match the work elements, the new job environment, the relationship patterns, the social network, behavioural dynamics, HRD climate, future job requirements and the total HRD perspective by realigning the attitudes, broadening the outlook and developing the new value-system based on democracy, secularism, social justice and human approach to various police problems.[30] HRD is a continuous dynamic process of living organisations for achieving organisational goals and missions and keeping pressure upon the employees to strive for excellence and fulfilment of organisational mission. Indian police organisations must make all concentrated efforts in:

(i) knowledge generation through research, seminars, conferences and data-bank of HRD prevalent practices;

(ii) knowledge dissemination through management development programmes;

(iii) capacity building for organisational development through in-house training and other related services.

Institution-Building—As HRD professional it is important to give importance to institution building and development of HRD culture in the organisation. Figure B shows institution building model. Institution building is a strategic management and needs vision, patience, social networking and dynamic leadership Dr. S.M. Diea, Shri A.A. Ali and Dr. S. Subramanian can be counted as outstanding police officers who did institution building of S.V.P. National Police Academy, Hyderabad.

Figure B

Institution Building Model for Institutions Training

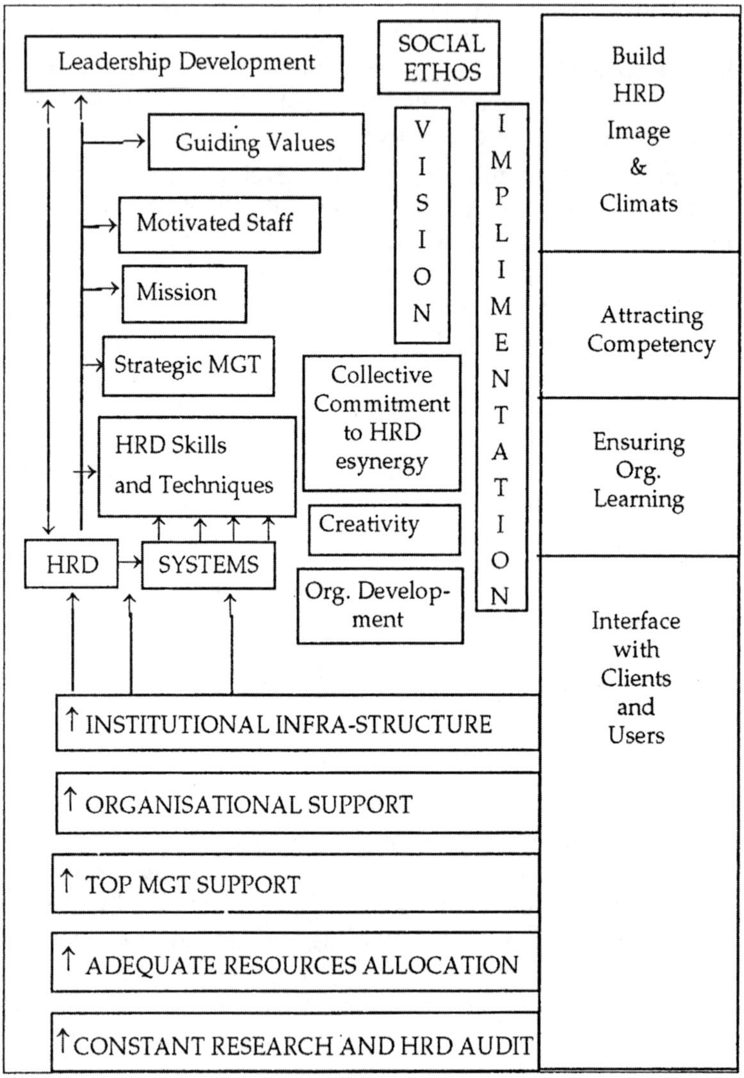

Prof Ishawar Dayal has done praise-worthy institution building at I.I. M. Lucknow as its Director. Institution building is a continuous long-term process and needs a transformational leadership with a professional commitment to HRD Institution building and needs a very dynamic and forward looking leader who can provide guiding values to the institutions and identify a forward looking mission of the institution. Motivated staff is one of the prime requirements of institution building. Highly qualified, committed and motivated staff alone can bring excellence in HRD in training institution. Institutional infrastructure in terms of buildings, hostels, classrooms, scientific laboratory, modernised office equipment, well lit, air-conditioned library, sports grounds, swimming pool, adequate parade and training grounds, lecture rooms, audio-visual aids, adequate transport, commnication facilities etc. are some of the basic infrastructures needed for a police training institution. Organisational support, top management support, adequate resource allocation and constant research and HRD audits are other aspects of institution building. Developing synergy for institution building requires special attention. Team building and organisational development have to be integrated parts of the institution-building. Institution-building, making HRD facilitators and development of competencies in trainees involve a long journey in human and organisational process and need to be planned with utmost care and professional commitment of the leaders.

HRD Vision for 2010 AD in Police

Indian police must develop a vision for 2010 AD. Indian police must focus on its improved image, efficiency, effectiveness and organisational learning. It must become a dynamic, pro-active organisation. Indian police should become a truly democratic people committed to the ideals of human rights, effective control of crimes and good police-community relations. The focus of HRD professional in Indian police should be on "Total Quality Service" to the Indian people by right conduct based on ethical and spiritual considerations. The HRD vision it for Indian police must be realised and achieved with the help of HRD professionals and cooperation of all training institutions of the police. The challenge is massive and Indian police leadership at various levels have heavy responsibilities for making positive contribution in this exciting human journey.

REFERENCES

1. Dr. Krishna Mohan Mathur,"*Fifty Years of Indian Police—A Reappraisal" Indian Journal of Public Administration Family,* March, 1998, Vol. XLIV No. 1, p. 59.

2. For greater details consult Dr. Krishna Mohan Mathur, *Administration of Police Training in India,* (1987), Gyan Publishing House, New Delhi.

3. Dr. Krishna Mohan Mathur, *Indian Police—Role and Challanges,* (1994) Gyan Publishing House, New Delhi p. 231. Also see H.R. Meena, "Human Resources Development in Police" *Indian Police Journal,* Vol. XLIV No. 12., July-Dec, 1997.

4. Leonard Nadler, *Developing Human Resources,* Austin Texas Concepts, (2nd ed.) 1979, p. 3.

5. K.M. Mathur, "Human Resources Development in Administration" *Indian Journal of Public Administration,* Vol. XXXIII No. 2 April-June, 1987, pp. 210, 241.

6. P.F. Drucker, *The Practice of Management,* (6th Printing 1973), p. 322.

7. Pareek, Udai, *Motivational Analysis of Organisations—Climate (MAOC).* The 1989 Annual, University Associates, San Diego, California, pp. 161-71.

8. Also consult M.B. Athreya, "Integrated HRD System—Intervention Strategies "in *Alternative Approaches and Strategic of Human Resource Development,* Edited by T.V. Rao & others,—Rawat Publications, Jaipur, 1989. p. 2.

9. Udai Pareek, "Challenges for HRD in the Nineties"—in *Managing Transition—The HRD Response, TATA* McGraw Hill Publishing Company Ltd, New Delhi, 1992, p. 4.

10. For proper introduction of HRD see T.V. Rao and others, *Alternative Approaches and Strategies of HRD,* 1989, Rawat Publication, Jaipur.

11. T.V. Rao "Role of Chief Executive in Human Resource Development" in *Alternative Approaches and Strategies of HRD,* Rawat Publications, Jaipur, 1989. p. 18. For similar views see Dayal, Ishwar *et al. Successful Applications of HRD—Case Studies in Indian Organisations,* New Delhi, New Concepts Publishers.

12. K.M. Mathur, *Problem of Police in a Democratic Society,* RBSA Publishers, Jaipur, 1987, p. 139-40.

13. K.M. Mathur, *Police in India—Problems and Perspectives, Gyan* Publishing House, New Delhi, 1991, p. 263.

14. K.M. Mathur, *Indian Police—Role and Challenges*, Gyan Publishing House, New Delhi, 1994, preface p. VII.

15. Dharni P. Sinha, *Human Resource Development—Global Changes and Strategies for 2000 A.D.*—Edited by Uddesh Kohli and Dharm p. Sinha, Allied Publishers Ltd., New Delhi, 1995, p. XXV.

16. K.M. Mathur, *Management of Internal Security and Related Issues*, Gyan Publishing House, New Delhi, 1995, p. 81.

17. Udai Pareek and Rao T.V., *Designing and Managing Human Resource Systems*, New Delhi, Oxford and IBH, 1992.

18. K.M. Mathur, *Internal Security Challenges and Police in a Developing Society*, RBSA Publishers, Jaipur, 1989, p. 55.

19. Udai Pareek, *Making Organisational Role Effective*, New Delhi. Tata Mc Graw Hills, 1993. Also see Udai Pareek "*HRD in India Prospects and Restrospect*" *The Indian Journal of Social Work*, Vol. LR No. 1 Oct. 1992, pp. 457-475.

20. Udai Pareek and T.V. Rao, *Designing and Managing Human Resources Systems*—New Delhi, Oxford and IBH, 1992.

21. For Similar views see T.V. Rao "Role of Chief Executives in Human Resources Development"—in *Alternative Approaches and Strategies of Human Resource Development* Edited by T.V. Rao & others, Rawat Publications, Jaipur, 1989.

22. For proper understanding of the subject, refer T.V. Rao—*Appraising and Developing Managerial Performance.* Academy of H.R.D.

23. For further details also consult—T.V. Rao, E Abraham and Baba Raj V. Nair (Ed)—*HRD Philosophies and Concepts : The Indian Perspective*, National HRD Network.

24. For further reference consult the book, *Administration of Police Training in India*, written by Dr. K.M. Mathur, Gyan Publishing House, New Delhi, 1987.

25. For further details see K.M. Mathur, *Crime, Human Rights and National Security*, Gyan Publishing House, New Delhi, 1996, pp. 295-97.

26. K.M. Mathur, *Concerns and Constraints in Administration*, RBSA Publishers, Jaipur, 1991, p. 41.

27. Nancy M. Dixon, *Evaluation : A Tool for Improving HRD quality*, S. Chand and Company Ltd., New Delhi, 1995.

28. Udai Pareek (Editor)—"Evaluating Human Resource Development" Jaipur, HRD Research Foundation—Proceedings of Convention held at Jaipur, 1997.

29. Kirkpatrick, D.A. (1983), *A Practical Guide for Supervisory Training and Development* (2nd ed.)—Reading M.A., Addison Wesley.

30. For similar views see K.M. Mathur, *Police in India—Problems and Perspectives*, Gyan Publishing House, New Delhi, 1991, p. 270.

Appendix-A

"Management Education in India—Post Liberalisation Threats and Opportunities"—A Retrospect

"Progress is impossible without Change and those who cannot change their mindsets cannot change anything."

—*George Bernard Shaw*

"Management education was nowhere near popular as it is today". It is true that we have borrowed management education from the U.S.A.

Management education in India which began during 1960s and expanded substantially during last four decades, has reached a stage, where its learning - teaching infrastructure is next only to U.S.A. in terms of numbers, scope, breadth and depth. There are more than 620 management institutions in India, catering to about 50,000 working executives per year including government servants who are availing benefits of distance education management programmes. About seventy - five institutions are in Delhi and around (in 100 km belt) and sixty of them in Delhi and fifty km belt around it. There are national level institutions like ALTTC, NIFM, Indian Oil Institute of Petroleum Management which are offering PGDBM or AICTE approved programmes. Some of the management institutions are mere business shops, without proper libraries, faculty and infra structure, exploiting students and giving them mere certificates/ degrees without much worth.

Management education in India is now the most sought - after discipline. Today most youngsters in urban areas consider it a dream come true if they are able to get entrance in some Indian Institute of Management. Since there is a great demand for "MBAs", institutes are sprouting all over the country. "Pricking the bubble of management as a discipline is "The Witch Doctors' Management snake oil" by John Michleth Wait and Adrian Woodbridge, who call the new discipline, brash, pushy and full of mumbo-jumbo. But the philosophy of the "Witch Doctors has turned out to be a giant money spinning machine. Still how long can the magic last?"[1]. Fresh graduates from management institutes get paid Rs. two lakh or more. CEOs salaries range from 18 to 70 Lakhs a year. So far as the jobs are concerned, the most wanted sign hangs over the M.B.As. Management education is the latest boom after liberalisation policy announcement by the Government of India. The initial period after liberalisation have seen a major salary increase for MBAs. "Managers value status and powers comparatively high in a patriarchal tradition." It is not theory which makes the world go round: it is skills. And this is where MBAs steps in."[2] However, one has to accept that whenever anything is on the ascendant, there are negative fallouts. It is in this context that management education in India must be analysed in the context of liberalisation in India when the second generation reforms are being considered to provide greater dose of liberalisation in India.

The process of globalisation and liberalisation in developing societies and the accompanying forces of market economy have given rise to questions of far reaching substantial and procedural importance.[3] July 24, 1991 has been a historic day in the annals of Indian economy because on that day the economic liberalisation was initiated by the Government of India, making a paradigmatic change with the introduction of a new model of development and industrial policy, by opening out economy. After liberalisation, the paradigm shift made inescapably imperative by the sweeping changes across the globe can come about only through the process of learning, through interaction and education.

Liberalisation and globalisation having indeed arrived on the wings of science and technology are here to stay. India unshackled and uncased from governments regulations and dogmatism has unprecedented opportunities before it, provided it can meet the challenges and threats that come with the new way of life. Management education in India today has the challenge and responsibility of preparing a new breed of creative and dynamic managers who have the courage, skills, stamina, resilience and foresight to take the bull by the horns. Liberalisation of Indian economy has thrown open the challenges of competitiveness in terms of globalisation of the products and costs, quality certification of 15,09,000, innovations, systems improvement, technological and machinery upgradation, efficiency, customer satisfaction, modernisation and competiton with international business world in providing quality products and services both in India and abroad. Liberalisation has brought back required focus on productivity, quality, efficiency, effectiveness, technology, speed, customer service and competitive edge over others.Management education in India, therefore, has to be restructured, reformed and revamped to face the challenges and threats of post - liberation period by giving proactive synergic push to its structure, methods, techniques and mission.

Management Education in India can be broadly classified as under:

1. Management Education by Indian Institutes of Management at Ahmedabad, Bangalore, Calcutta, Lucknow, Indore and Kozhikode.
2. Management Education by universities and colleges. BBA and MBA courses.
3. Management Education by Management Institutes run by Business houses. (Kirloskar Institute of Advanced Management Studies).
4. Management Education by Government Institutions,

Indian Institute of Public Administration, LBS, NAS Mussorie, SVP NPA, Hyderabad and other service academies to Government servants.

5. Management Education through distance learning programmes of distance learning open universities (IGNOU, New Delhi).
6. Foreign Universities offering management education in India through collaboration with other Institutes / Management Centres.
7. Departments / Public sector organisations conducting in-service courses, Institute of Public Enterprise Course on Management.

Management, after more than a century of development as a practice and as a discipline burst into public consciousness in the management boom that began in India after liberalisation of the economy. The time has come to take stock of present status and to enquire, in words of Peter Drucker." What are the new knowledge we need, the new challenges we face, the new tasks ahead, now that the management boom is over?[4] Liberalisation has price but it has to be paid if we have to reap the gains of liberalisation. Management education in India has to improve both qualitatively and quantitatively in the context of post - liberalisation second generation reforms in the economic system introduced by BJP led Government of Shri Atal Bihari Vajpayeeji. Management education has to provide a vital link to connect "Industrial Islands" with the corporate main land. Management education must take care of the core areas and ensure good quality education. Management education continues to remain oblivious of a well thought out and proactive quality vigilance and assurance mechanism. At present there is a wide gap between the output from business schools and intake by the industry. Alongside the arguably largest pool of scientific and technological manpower resource which is unemployed and unproductive. India may soon boast of a large reservoir of equally large pool of management professionals, produced by the ever increasing number of business schools and management facilities of various universities. At the moment the India

Business Management *Bazar* has more than 620 institutions of various sizes. The total intake for MBA and other such programmes is around 40,000, half of it is in three states, Maharashtra, Tamil Nadu, and Andhra Pradesh. There are no checks or regulations of management teaching and the ways of these institutions are mostly run by universities and private individuals. There is enormous degree of variation with the syallabi and standards. There are many issues which need analyses and research. Who should be blamed? What has led to such a scenario ? How can things be improved? How to stop this dangerous trend? How to ensure high quality management training with qualified staff to teach ? What to do with so many jobless MBAs who know very little about management practices? Is our education system to be blamed? Although there is quality management training at Indian Institutes of Management and some other forty institutes, there is much dilution of management education in many of the other management/ business institutes. Management education in India can be broadly classified in two streams. (1) The management stream with professional character and (2) The commerce stream with liberal character. Management education in India made its beginning with the Well - known Person Report (Carnegie Report of 1959) and Gordon and Howell Report (Ford Foundation Report of 1959) which underscored the need for developing strong theoretical foundation and practical orientation of current business needs. Today there are more than 620 institutes/ universities/ academies providing management education with varying levels of academic and theoretical inputs. Inadequate computer literacy, inadequate research base, heavy curricular input, information stuffing, superficial coverage of Indian business and international economic scenario, very limited contact with industry and business and half baked Indian case material are some of the common ills of Indian management education. Management education in India, barring a few notable exceptions, needs to be upgraded, and modernised and given practical orientation with proper interface with industry. Present management education in India, leaving some notable exceptions, is not found suitable for developing participatory management. Managers learn to mistrust trade unions, suspect workers, and try to acquire methods to control them. It is necessary to institute massive re - education and management training programmes should be redesigned to help managers acquire new perceptions, attitudes, motivation, skills and competencies to response effectively to the new economic environment and rising expectations of the work-force. *Business Today*, May 7 -21, 1998 has brought out a survey of Indian business/ management institutes and has tried to rank them on the basis of various considerations like applications per seat, annual library budget, average opening salary, proportion of Ph D. in faculty, number of students per instructor and course tuition fees. The top ten ranked, respectively are IIM, Ahmedabad, IIM Bangalore, IIM Calcutta, Xavier Labour Relations Institute, Jamshedpur, IIM , Lucknow, Faculty of Management Studies, Delhi, Jamnalal Bajaj Institute of M.S., Mumbai, Management Development Institute, Gurgaon, S.P. Jain Institute of Management and Research, Mumbai and Narsee Monjee Institute of M.S., Mumbai. From an esoteric discipline in the engineering studies driven 1970s, through a grudging admission to the pedagogical mainstream in the 1980s to its current status of the hottest post-graduate course in the post-liberation 1990s management education in India is becoming increasingly diluted and mismanaged. The mushroom growth of management education, has created many institutions without adequate infrastructure, untrained faculty and corporate experience, thus resulting in poor quality of product. The basic problems of management education in India are large number of students in proportions to teachers, poor and inadequate infrastructure, demotivated teachers and lack of adequate rapport between students, teachers and parents of students.

Liberalisation has brought about an environment, characterised by among others, 1. Decontrol and Delicensing, 2. Globalisation of competition, 3. Information explosion with communications revolution, 4. Internationalisation fluidity in geo-economic reality, 5. Quality concerns, 6. Denationalisation and Privatisation, 7. Newer skill generation and diversification due to technological invasion, 8. A new freedom from the past orthodox and straight-jacketed ideology and protective economic strategy. In a post liberalisation scenario, some characteristic parameters, worth noting in this emerging context are: - 1. Globalisation of human and material resources; 2. Total Quality Approach; 3. Upgradation of human resources by bridging the learning irrelevancies and obsolescence and narrowing the technological gap; 4. Interacting with the environment by developing the information system; and 5. Quality of life as the focus. According to Stephen H. Rhimesmith (1993) the core competencies required for global managers in the post-liberal economy can be summarised as follows:

1. Managing competitiveness by constantly scanning the environment for changes in market, socio-economic and political trends and global competition conditions.
2. Managing complexity by managing trade-offs of many competing interests as well as the inherent conflicts and contradictions of various global organisations.
3. Managing adaptability by developing a global culture with the values, beliefs, systems and norms of behaviour.
4. Managing teams within a multi-cultural sensitivity and demands cultural sensitivity and managerial skills to lead, supervise and manage people coming from a wide range of different nationalities.
5. Managing uncertainties to deal with constantly changing environment.
6. Managing learning on a continuous basis and building a learning organisation—Liberalisation requires administrators to put due emphasis on productivity, quality, effectiveness, efficiency, latest technology, skill development and customer satisfaction. In a liberal economy, globalisation throws the following main challenges:

1. Technology and machinery upgradation; 2. Attracting, maintaining and developing efficient, competent and trained professionals; 3. Competitiveness in terms of product and cost; 4. Surviving and maintaining growth with excellence.

CHALLENGES FACED BY ORGANISATIONS IN THE LIBERALISED ECONOMY

Liberalisation and globalisation are all means to achieve the following goods:

1. To achieve high rate of growth of national and per capita income.
2. To achieve full employment and development of human resources.
3. To achieve self-reliance and take off stage of the economy.
4. To reduce the number of people below poverty line and bring prosperity to the nation.
5. To become a world economic power.

Liberalisation has to deal with following challenges:

1. The excessive development of bureaucratic control as a shackle on growth.
2. Overstaffing in public sector enterprise leading to increase in cost of operations.
3. Low rate of return on investment in public sector.
4. Poor absence of incentive for better work.
5. Dilution of quality of management.
6. Public sectors incurring losses and burden on public exchequer.

Management Education has to find out solutions to above mentioned challenges. Main challenges of Liberalisation are as under:

1. Competitiveness in terms of the product and cost.
2. Export.
3. Quality and ISO 9000 certification.
4. Surviving in a liberalised environment.
5. Attracting and maintaining good and competent people.
6. Innovation.

7. Systems improvement.
8. Cost reduction.
9. Globalisation.
10. Maximising sales, productivity and growth.
11. Customer satisfaction and quality of service.
12. Maintaining growth and position in terms of market share or as market leader.
13. Reorganising to keep abreast of changes and creating viable plans to cope with changes.
14. Becoming more professional.
15. Indigenisation.
16. Technology and machinery upgradation.

Liberalisation in foreign investment policy marks exposition of Indian industry investment rate in India has risen in the past two decades. Our bureaucrats killed our industrial revolution by enfeebling private industry. Our entrepreneurs have been showing to innovate and respond to the more competitive economy after the liberalisation reforms in India. Management education has to bring awareness about these problems to our entrepreneurs and young people working in industry. India has to create industrial revolution and transform its industrial economy to an information economy.

Liberalisation has put focus on the following aspects of industry and management:

1. Productivity.
2. Quality.
3. Efficiency.
4. Effectiveness.
5. Technology.
6. Speed.
7. Customer and customer delight.

8. Skill development.
9. Computerisation programmes.
10. Improving vertical and horizontal communication.
11. Diversification.
12. Getting employees committed to organisational goals and mission.

Management education has to be revamped in view of the changed focus. Management education focuses the significant learning challenges.

Significant learning challenges in the liberal economy tasks for HRD professionals :

A. Pertaining to the learning environment

1. Coping with the market changes and competitiveness.
2. Coping with enhanced customer expectations.
3. Coping with changing government. policies.

B. Pertaining to internal environment

1. Implementing HRD.
2. Generating teamwork.
3. Technological upgradation.
4. Quality developing market orientation.
5. Improving productivity.

C. Pertaining to other challenges

1. Implementing computerisation programmes.
2. Generating and disseminating knowledge.
3. Budgeting and controlling.
4. Improving communication.
5. Diversification.
6. Getting employees committed.
7. Enhancing professionalism.

"Challenges and tasks before HRD professional in view of liberalisation and globalisation"

Stephen H. Rhinesmith in his book *A Manager's Guide to Globalisation* (1993) has summarised the competencies required for managers of tomorrow in the post-liberalisation period:

1. Managing competitiveness.
2. Managing complexity.
3. Managing adaptability.
4. Managing teams.
5. Managing uncertainty.
6. Managing learning.

In post-liberalisation era, corporate leaders have to develop and build competencies that enable them to:

1. Commit to a higher purpose mission,
2. Instil responsible leadership,
3. Encourage multi-disciplinary teaming,
4. Forge organic partnerships,
5. Promote knowledge networking,
6. Foster global search,
7. Embrace change.

(John Edwin Mroz and Ian Somerville - New competencies for New World) Above seven core competencies have to be developed through management education as an ongoing learning process.

Prof. Y.K. Bhushan has identified following abilities and characteristics for future managers in the context of liberalisation of economy.

1. The outbound skill:- It refers to the instinctive quality of looking out and ahead and keeping a tab on developments in the various regions of the world with global perspective.

2. Scanning skills with which they can see and seize business opportunities.
3. Ability to relate to diverse culture.
4. Capacity in relation to the swings in the environment through strategic thinking and scenario building skills.
5. Negotiation skills with other countries to drive hard bargains.
6. Analytical skills to identify the cost drivers and the factors responsible for high costs and low productivity for building up competition.
7. Obsession for quality and skills of total quality management.
8. Skills of skimming, study and reflections leading to autonomous learning "skills of learning to learn."
9. Linguistic skills in foreign languages.
10. People Management skills for team working and integration of ethnic diversity.
11. Information Management with computers so as to access data base for quick decision making.

The Post-Liberalisation Scenario: In the wake of liberalisation and globalisation of economic policies in India, the Indian business scenario is undergoing a dramatic metamorphosis. Investment opportunities have expanded, financing options have widened and above all, dependence on capital market has increased. The economic scenario is gradually becoming more competitive in view of multi-national entry and foreign capital inflow into the country. The global tide of corporate restructuring in now sweeping the Indian corporate world. Financial institutions in India are facing a severe cash - crunch.

Management education is needed not only for new MBA entrants but also for working managers and CEOs. It is also needed for senior IAS officers and secretaries of Central and State Governments working in Finance, Commerce,

International trade and industry ministries. Public sector managers also need reorientation and in-service courses to update their knowledge and competencies.

Liberalisation has resulted into the following phenomenon:

1. Privatisation of the economy and marketisation of public services and government functions;
2. Maximisation of profit for the private entrepreneurs;
3. Minimisation of taxes and a roll back for state activities;
4. Neglect of social security and social welfare measures for the vulnerable sections like women, children, indigent old, sick, disabled, backward or downtrodden;
5. False hope of the trickle down effects of the growth of economy on the masses which really does not take place in actual practice;
6. No statutory allocation of resources for human resource development.[5]

Impact of Liberalisation on Management Education: - In post liberalisation era, management education has become both a passport to better employment opportunities and as a means to deal with myriad problems facing the country. In 1993 the number of management institutions, recognised and approved by All India Council for Technical Education (AICTE) was just 150, this number shot to 450 by 1994.There has been very great growth of business schools and management institutes in India. There is lack of adequate infrastructure, inadequacy of resource and acute shortage of qualified and competent training staff in most of these institutions. In many management institutes the training staff is lacking in the will to teach due to malpractices of private management institutes. Evening Class Executive Development and three year management post-graduate courses have further diluted the quality of education.

Post-Liberalisation Threats, Challenges and Opportunities

1. Global Competition and Brand Equity

India's excellent companies have to focus on creating Brand Equity through customer ended quality and customer driven values. Infosys, BPL and Balrampur Chini (Sugar) are putting a premium on their credibility. In global markets, brand equity works as a strategic factor at three levels viz. product, firm and country.

Management education in India is facing the following main challenges post-liberalisation period.

2. Main Challenge

Development of interpersonal skills and familiarity with the use of infotech in business support systems should be given priority in management education. The present curriculum of MBA courses should be revised to increase interface with industry and more knowledge input needed in post-liberalisation period. Advancements in computer science and communication technology with innovations and entry of multi-nationals as a result of liberalisation need to be given due weightage in management education.

1. Lack of adequate resources.
2. Reliance on other Faculty (Guests).
3. Lack of Interactions among departments/industries/organisations.
4. Little interaction with industry.
5. No emphasis on resource and teacher development.
6. Pedagogical challenges—student participation.
7. The case study method—inadequacy.
8. Management Games—Inherent limitations.
9. Seminars—Speakers do not restrict to core knowledge and indulge in rhetoric talks.
10. Focus on globalisation, liberalisation

The process of liberalisation and globalisation have created enormous opportunities and understanding of the global environment has become imperative. Following are some points on global environments:

1. Employment opportunities in other countries.
2. Entrepreneurial opportunities in other underdeveloped countries.
3. Opportunities to experience cross-natural diversities of cultures and need to manage diverse culture-oriented people.
4. Opportunities for quality of work life—The ultimate aim of liberalisation should be to make quality of human life more comfortable, happy and self-actualising.
5. Opportunities for total quality management (TQM) and technological progress.
6. Can Indian Management education offer its Vedantic wisdom to the world ?
7. Liberalisation has opened a vast new horizon for management education.

Harnessing of human capital is key to our future. In the 21st century, a nation's status will be determined by the share of brands it commands and the share of brains it could utilise to get the competitive edge. Liberalised economy requires what I term three Es, "Education, Efficacy and Ethics." We cannot neglect our social sector (education and health). In the next ten years, corporate sector of India must develop a hundred brand names with a "made in India" label.

Problem Areas and Challenges to Management Education in Post-Liberalisation Era:

Liberalisation and globalisation will make workers suffer in the developing countries and inequalities will grow as can be seen from the details given below:-

1. In 1989, the top one per cent of Americans earned an average of $559795 (5 lakh 59 thousand 795 dollar) each, receiving as a group, more than all the bottom forty per cent.

2. In 1992, the top 1000 CEOs in America received on average, 157 times more salary than the average worker.
3. Forbes' top 400 richest people, had a net worth in 1993 of $ 328 billion, equal to the combined GNP of India, Bangladesh, Nepal and Sri Lanka.
4. Seventy per cent of the world trade is managed by 500 Corporations."[6]

How will a plural, democratic society tolerate a system in which top one per cent earn more, collectively than the bottom forty per cent ? Liberalisation and globalisation have many side-effects and unknown evil-consequences. Dick Bryan has clearly brought out compulsions of mass poverty bring out a case for interventions by the nation state although the real centre for economic power and decision-making now lies with the transnational corporations and not with nation states.[7] The citizens of a state are bound to demand economic relief from their own state when they face economic disaster caused by unemployment, underemployment and exploitation by the well-to-do persons. But the questions are: how can a state which withdraws from the productive sector of economy promote social welfare sector ? How can the democratic state of India abandon its agenda of economic development for achieving the goals of real social justice? Raja J. Chelliah has held that state should liberate the industrial economy and concentrate on irrigation, education, health, flood control, environment, railways, roads, and bridges, space, defence and power.[8] Dr. Man Mohan Singh's belated confession that the policy of placing excessive reliance on private investment was thoroughly mistaken, should produce serious introspection about liberalisation. Nation state must play a very active role in enforcing regulations regarding minimum wages, occupational health, foreign exchange laws, and law-making. Making India a world class knowledge society is the biggest challenge for the management education.

The two global trends have converged to India's advantage making one hope that India will finally take off. One is the liberal revolution of opening economy and the second is change from an industrial to an information economy. Liberalisation is dismantling controls and releasing the long suppressed energies of Indian entrepreneurs. They are changing the young Indians as a conceptual people. Knowledge are potentially plays to our advantage and our success in software and the internet is the first emerging evidence. In information technology, our core competence is invisible that could drive India's take-off and eventually transform our country.[9]

Challenges and Problems of Management Education

Some of the best twenty management institutions are really pride for India but that is not what is generally available to the common student. Management Education in India, on the whole, barring few notable exception of IIMS and other top 20 institutes suffers from the following weaknesses:

1. Institutional weakness, inadequacy of infrastructure.
2. Ideological hang-ups.
3. Inability to stand vested interests.
4. Poor governance.
5. Lack of accountability.
6. Lack of participation of students.
7. Lack of motivation and incentives for committed teachers.
8. Inadequate linkage with industry and others.
9. Lack of proper planning and poor implementation.
10. Lack of adequate evaluation of management programmes.
11. Centralisation of authority and financial powers.
12. Neglect of administrative arrangements related to training.
13. Inappropriate methods and techniques of management education.
14. Defective assessment system and either work overload or underload in some institutions.

15. Corruption and bureaucratic working system.
16. Inadequate inputs in management education.
17. Poor and unsatisfactory quality in input (students).
18. Lack of "model-syllabus". Curriculum has to constantly keep pace with demands of industry and the nation.
19. Faculty members and staff have to be qualified, experienced and professional.
20. The standard and quality of management education varies from institution to institution, from excellent to unsatisfactory quality of education.

Indian management education have to produce trained managers who would be globally sought after. What management education in India should teach to make them globally wanted? Some important subjects for syllabus are suggested below:

1. Self-development.
2. Human relations skills.
3. Environmental awareness.
4. Infotech and systems skills.
5. Specialisation in marketing.
6. Languages of the areas/countries.
7. International finance, communication and accounts.
8. Ethical and moral values.
9. Competitive spirit and orientation.
10. Quest for excellence.
11. The art and science of supervision and management.
12. Changing technology management.
13. International trade, international finance and international marketing.

Charles Handy in his book *The Hungry Spirit* has pointed out that management and traditional schools must think more imaginatively. "It is indeed a time for bold imaginations, for re-inventing what we understand by education." Modern day governments will have to play an active role in initiating actions to control the distortions of capitalism and inequalities of wealth and incomes through an imaginative tax structure. Nation cannot forget ethics and commitment to democracy, social justice for short-terms gains of a few business houses. Globalisation cannot provide sustainable development. Let us try to discover "Indian's" of Indian management education. Indian management education can achieve competitive edge over other countries of the world if we can properly project the rich treasure of management available in *Bhagwat Geeta* and Vedantic knowledge and other ancient Indian scriptures. "Vedantic knowledge and ethical education can be designed to produce balanced, pleasant, flexible and effective managers with the power of insight and courage to create and use ethically desirable means to sustain" organisations in an ambience of liberalism and democratic ethos."[10] To cope with changing times, organisations need trained managers who have core competencies to deal with present and future challenges. There is need for quality research in management field by Indian scholars. There is an urgent need for enhancement, upgradation and standardisation of management education in India.There is need for revamping management education which should include Indian values and new technologies. Management education must keep pace with the changing requirements of the industry and economy. Management faculty at the institutes should be encouraged to go in for consultancy with the industry so that they may bring in practical knowledge and feedback on the industry's requirements to the campus and share it with the management students. There is an urgent need for an overhaul of the management education in the country. Corporate houses and industry associations should come forward to "adopt" business schools to achieve two way movement of faculty and staff, preparation of life case studies, better summer placements and final absorption of trainees by the corporate world. There is a need for standardisation and mandatory revision of syllabi at definite intervals for different management institutes across the country.There is a need to upgrade the existing system of delivery of education. Management education should be mentored, and even guided by the industry and professional management trainers. Management education is a continuous ongoing learning to be reinforced by management development programmes and executive development programmes.

REFERENCES

1. Manju Mathew, "The Witch Doctors", *Saturday Times*, 20th Sept, 1997, New Delhi.
2. David J. Hickson and Derek S. Pugh, *Management World—The Impact of Societal Culture on Organisations Around the Globe."*
3. R.B. Jain and Hernz Bomgartz (eds), *Structural Adjustment, Public Policy and Bureaucracy in Developing Societies*, Har Anand Publication, New Delhi, 1994.
4. Peter Drucker, *Management, Tasks, Responsibilities, Practices*, Allied Publishers Ltd, Bombay, 1996, p. 2.
5. Noorjahan Bava, The Welfare State and Liberalisation in India" in Indian Journal of Public Administration II PANDLI, July-Sept. 1996 Vol. XLII No. 3, p. 346.
6. David Korten, *When Corporations Rule the World.*
7. Dick Bryan, *The Chase Across the Globe : International Accumulation and the Contradictions for Nation State*, Boulder, West View Press, San Francisco, 1995.
8. Raja J. Chelliah, *Towards Sustainable Growth—Essays in Fiscal and Financial Sector reforms in India Oxford*, University Press, Delhi, 1996-97.
9. Gurcharan Das, "Men and Ideas—Will we Now Take—off." *The Sunday Times of India*, November 14, 1999.
10. Krishna Mohan Mathur, "Vedantic Wisdom and Contemporary Management", Indian Journal of Public Administration IIPA, New Delhi—Vol. XLV January-March, 1999, No. 1, p. 10.

INDEX